DEAR FUTURE EXAM SUCCESS STORY

First of all, **THANK YOU** for purchasing Mometrix study materials!

Second, congratulations! You are one of the few determined test-takers who are committed to doing whatever it takes to excel on your exam. **You have come to the right place.** We developed these study materials with one goal in mind: to deliver you the information you need in a format that's concise and easy to use.

In addition to optimizing your guide for the content of the test, we've outlined our recommended steps for breaking down the preparation process into small, attainable goals so you can make sure you stay on track.

We've also analyzed the entire test-taking process, identifying the most common pitfalls and showing how you can overcome them and be ready for any curveball the test throws you.

Standardized testing is one of the biggest obstacles on your road to success, which only increases the importance of doing well in the high-pressure, high-stakes environment of test day. Your results on this test could have a significant impact on your future, and this guide provides the information and practical advice to help you achieve your full potential on test day.

Your success is our success

We would love to hear from you! If you would like to share the story of your exam success or if you have any questions or comments in regard to our products, please contact us at **800-673-8175** or **support@mometrix.com**.

Thanks again for your business and we wish you continued success!

Sincerely,
The Mometrix Test Preparation Team

I0892936

Need more help? Check out our flashcards at:
http://MometrixFlashcards.com/CEOE

Mometrix

TEST PREPARATION

OSAT®

Speech/Drama/Debate (116) Secrets Study Guide

TABLE OF CONTENTS

Introduction

Thank you for purchasing this resource! You have made the choice to prepare yourself for a test that could have a huge impact on your future, and this guide is designed to help you be fully ready for test day. Obviously, it's important to have a solid understanding of the test material, but you also need to be prepared for the unique environment and stressors of the test, so that you can perform to the best of your abilities.

For this purpose, the first section that appears in this guide is the **Secret Keys**. We've devoted countless hours to meticulously researching what works and what doesn't, and we've boiled down our findings to the five most impactful steps you can take to improve your performance on the test. We start at the beginning with study planning and move through the preparation process, all the way to the testing strategies that will help you get the most out of what you know when you're finally sitting in front of the test.

We recommend that you start preparing for your test as far in advance as possible. However, if you've bought this guide as a last-minute study resource and only have a few days before your test, we recommend that you skip over the first two Secret Keys since they address a long-term study plan.

If you struggle with **test anxiety**, we strongly encourage you to check out our recommendations for how you can overcome it. Test anxiety is a formidable foe, but it can be beaten, and we want to make sure you have the tools you need to defeat it.

Secret Key #1 – Plan Big, Study Small

There's a lot riding on your performance. If you want to ace this test, you're going to need to keep your skills sharp and the material fresh in your mind. You need a plan that lets you review everything you need to know while still fitting in your schedule. We'll break this strategy down into three categories.

Information Organization

Start with the information you already have: the official test outline. From this, you can make a complete list of all the concepts you need to cover before the test. Organize these concepts into groups that can be studied together, and create a list of any related vocabulary you need to learn so you can brush up on any difficult terms. You'll want to keep this vocabulary list handy once you actually start studying since you may need to add to it along the way.

Time Management

Once you have your set of study concepts, decide how to spread them out over the time you have left before the test. Break your study plan into small, clear goals so you have a manageable task for each day and know exactly what you're doing. Then just focus on one small step at a time. When you manage your time this way, you don't need to spend hours at a time studying. Studying a small block of content for a short period each day helps you retain information better and avoid stressing over how much you have left to do. You can relax knowing that you have a plan to cover everything in time. In order for this strategy to be effective though, you have to start studying early and stick to your schedule. Avoid the exhaustion and futility that comes from last-minute cramming!

Study Environment

The environment you study in has a big impact on your learning. Studying in a coffee shop, while probably more enjoyable, is not likely to be as fruitful as studying in a quiet room. It's important to keep distractions to a minimum. You're only planning to study for a short block of time, so make the most of it. Don't pause to check your phone or get up to find a snack. It's also important to **avoid multitasking**. Research has consistently shown that multitasking will make your studying dramatically less effective. Your study area should also be comfortable and well-lit so you don't have the distraction of straining your eyes or sitting on an uncomfortable chair.

The time of day you study is also important. You want to be rested and alert. Don't wait until just before bedtime. Study when you'll be most likely to comprehend and remember. Even better, if you know what time of day your test will be, set that time aside for study. That way your brain will be used to working on that subject at that specific time and you'll have a better chance of recalling information.

Finally, it can be helpful to team up with others who are studying for the same test. Your actual studying should be done in as isolated an environment as possible, but the work of organizing the information and setting up the study plan can be divided up. In between study sessions, you can discuss with your teammates the concepts that you're all studying and quiz each other on the details. Just be sure that your teammates are as serious about the test as you are. If you find that your study time is being replaced with social time, you might need to find a new team.

Secret Key #2 – Make Your Studying Count

You're devoting a lot of time and effort to preparing for this test, so you want to be absolutely certain it will pay off. This means doing more than just reading the content and hoping you can remember it on test day. It's important to make every minute of study count. There are two main areas you can focus on to make your studying count.

Retention

It doesn't matter how much time you study if you can't remember the material. You need to make sure you are retaining the concepts. To check your retention of the information you're learning, try recalling it at later times with minimal prompting. Try carrying around flashcards and glance at one or two from time to time or ask a friend who's also studying for the test to quiz you.

To enhance your retention, look for ways to put the information into practice so that you can apply it rather than simply recalling it. If you're using the information in practical ways, it will be much easier to remember. Similarly, it helps to solidify a concept in your mind if you're not only reading it to yourself but also explaining it to someone else. Ask a friend to let you teach them about a concept you're a little shaky on (or speak aloud to an imaginary audience if necessary). As you try to summarize, define, give examples, and answer your friend's questions, you'll understand the concepts better and they will stay with you longer. Finally, step back for a big picture view and ask yourself how each piece of information fits with the whole subject. When you link the different concepts together and see them working together as a whole, it's easier to remember the individual components.

Finally, practice showing your work on any multi-step problems, even if you're just studying. Writing out each step you take to solve a problem will help solidify the process in your mind, and you'll be more likely to remember it during the test.

Modality

Modality simply refers to the means or method by which you study. Choosing a study modality that fits your own individual learning style is crucial. No two people learn best in exactly the same way, so it's important to know your strengths and use them to your advantage.

For example, if you learn best by visualization, focus on visualizing a concept in your mind and draw an image or a diagram. Try color-coding your notes, illustrating them, or creating symbols that will trigger your mind to recall a learned concept. If you learn best by hearing or discussing information, find a study partner who learns the same way or read aloud to yourself. Think about how to put the information in your own words. Imagine that you are giving a lecture on the topic and record yourself so you can listen to it later.

For any learning style, flashcards can be helpful. Organize the information so you can take advantage of spare moments to review. Underline key words or phrases. Use different colors for different categories. Mnemonic devices (such as creating a short list in which every item starts with the same letter) can also help with retention. Find what works best for you and use it to store the information in your mind most effectively and easily.

Secret Key #3 – Practice the Right Way

Your success on test day depends not only on how many hours you put into preparing, but also on whether you prepared the right way. It's good to check along the way to see if your studying is paying off. One of the most effective ways to do this is by taking practice tests to evaluate your progress. Practice tests are useful because they show exactly where you need to improve. Every time you take a practice test, pay special attention to these three groups of questions:

- The questions you got wrong
- The questions you had to guess on, even if you guessed right
- The questions you found difficult or slow to work through

This will show you exactly what your weak areas are, and where you need to devote more study time. Ask yourself why each of these questions gave you trouble. Was it because you didn't understand the material? Was it because you didn't remember the vocabulary? Do you need more repetitions on this type of question to build speed and confidence? Dig into those questions and figure out how you can strengthen your weak areas as you go back to review the material.

Additionally, many practice tests have a section explaining the answer choices. It can be tempting to read the explanation and think that you now have a good understanding of the concept. However, an explanation likely only covers part of the question's broader context. Even if the explanation makes perfect sense, **go back and investigate** every concept related to the question until you're positive you have a thorough understanding.

As you go along, keep in mind that the practice test is just that: practice. Memorizing these questions and answers will not be very helpful on the actual test because it is unlikely to have any of the same exact questions. If you only know the right answers to the sample questions, you won't be prepared for the real thing. **Study the concepts** until you understand them fully, and then you'll be able to answer any question that shows up on the test.

It's important to wait on the practice tests until you're ready. If you take a test on your first day of study, you may be overwhelmed by the amount of material covered and how much you need to learn. Work up to it gradually.

On test day, you'll need to be prepared for answering questions, managing your time, and using the test-taking strategies you've learned. It's a lot to balance, like a mental marathon that will have a big impact on your future. Like training for a marathon, you'll need to start slowly and work your way up. When test day arrives, you'll be ready.

Start with the strategies you've read in the first two Secret Keys—plan your course and study in the way that works best for you. If you have time, consider using multiple study resources to get different approaches to the same concepts. It can be helpful to see difficult concepts from more than one angle. Then find a good source for practice tests. Many times, the test website will suggest potential study resources or provide sample tests.

Practice Test Strategy

If you're able to find at least three practice tests, we recommend this strategy:

Untimed and Open-Book Practice

Take the first test with no time constraints and with your notes and study guide handy. Take your time and focus on applying the strategies you've learned.

Timed and Open-Book Practice

Take the second practice test open-book as well, but set a timer and practice pacing yourself to finish in time.

Timed and Closed-Book Practice

Take any other practice tests as if it were test day. Set a timer and put away your study materials. Sit at a table or desk in a quiet room, imagine yourself at the testing center, and answer questions as quickly and accurately as possible.

Keep repeating timed and closed-book tests on a regular basis until you run out of practice tests or it's time for the actual test. Your mind will be ready for the schedule and stress of test day, and you'll be able to focus on recalling the material you've learned.

Secret Key #4 – Pace Yourself

Once you're fully prepared for the material on the test, your biggest challenge on test day will be managing your time. Just knowing that the clock is ticking can make you panic even if you have plenty of time left. Work on pacing yourself so you can build confidence against the time constraints of the exam. Pacing is a difficult skill to master, especially in a high-pressure environment, so **practice is vital**.

Set time expectations for your pace based on how much time is available. For example, if a section has 60 questions and the time limit is 30 minutes, you know you have to average 30 seconds or less per question in order to answer them all. Although 30 seconds is the hard limit, set 25 seconds per question as your goal, so you reserve extra time to spend on harder questions. When you budget extra time for the harder questions, you no longer have any reason to stress when those questions take longer to answer.

Don't let this time expectation distract you from working through the test at a calm, steady pace, but keep it in mind so you don't spend too much time on any one question. Recognize that taking extra time on one question you don't understand may keep you from answering two that you do understand later in the test. If your time limit for a question is up and you're still not sure of the answer, mark it and move on, and come back to it later if the time and the test format allow. If the testing format doesn't allow you to return to earlier questions, just make an educated guess; then put it out of your mind and move on.

On the easier questions, be careful not to rush. It may seem wise to hurry through them so you have more time for the challenging ones, but it's not worth missing one if you know the concept and just didn't take the time to read the question fully. Work efficiently but make sure you understand the question and have looked at all of the answer choices, since more than one may seem right at first.

Even if you're paying attention to the time, you may find yourself a little behind at some point. You should speed up to get back on track, but do so wisely. Don't panic; just take a few seconds less on each question until you're caught up. Don't guess without thinking, but do look through the answer choices and eliminate any you know are wrong. If you can get down to two choices, it is often worthwhile to guess from those. Once you've chosen an answer, move on and don't dwell on any that you skipped or had to hurry through. If a question was taking too long, chances are it was one of the harder ones, so you weren't as likely to get it right anyway.

On the other hand, if you find yourself getting ahead of schedule, it may be beneficial to slow down a little. The more quickly you work, the more likely you are to make a careless mistake that will affect your score. You've budgeted time for each question, so don't be afraid to spend that time. Practice an efficient but careful pace to get the most out of the time you have.

Secret Key #5 – Have a Plan for Guessing

When you're taking the test, you may find yourself stuck on a question. Some of the answer choices seem better than others, but you don't see the one answer choice that is obviously correct. What do you do?

The scenario described above is very common, yet most test takers have not effectively prepared for it. Developing and practicing a plan for guessing may be one of the single most effective uses of your time as you get ready for the exam.

In developing your plan for guessing, there are three questions to address:

- When should you start the guessing process?
- How should you narrow down the choices?
- Which answer should you choose?

When to Start the Guessing Process

Unless your plan for guessing is to select C every time (which, despite its merits, is not what we recommend), you need to leave yourself enough time to apply your answer elimination strategies. Since you have a limited amount of time for each question, that means that if you're going to give yourself the best shot at guessing correctly, you have to decide quickly whether or not you will guess.

Of course, the best-case scenario is that you don't have to guess at all, so first, see if you can answer the question based on your knowledge of the subject and basic reasoning skills. Focus on the key words in the question and try to jog your memory of related topics. Give yourself a chance to bring the knowledge to mind, but once you realize that you don't have (or you can't access) the knowledge you need to answer the question, it's time to start the guessing process.

It's almost always better to start the guessing process too early than too late. It only takes a few seconds to remember something and answer the question from knowledge. Carefully eliminating wrong answer choices takes longer. Plus, going through the process of eliminating answer choices can actually help jog your memory.

Summary: Start the guessing process as soon as you decide that you can't answer the question based on your knowledge.

How to Narrow Down the Choices

The next chapter in this book (**Test-Taking Strategies**) includes a wide range of strategies for how to approach questions and how to look for answer choices to eliminate. You will definitely want to read those carefully, practice them, and figure out which ones work best for you. Here though, we're going to address a mindset rather than a particular strategy.

Your odds of guessing an answer correctly depend on how many options you are choosing from.

Number of options left	5	4	3	2	1
Odds of guessing correctly	20%	25%	33%	50%	100%

You can see from this chart just how valuable it is to be able to eliminate incorrect answers and make an educated guess, but there are two things that many test takers do that cause them to miss out on the benefits of guessing:

- Accidentally eliminating the correct answer
- Selecting an answer based on an impression

We'll look at the first one here, and the second one in the next section.

To avoid accidentally eliminating the correct answer, we recommend a thought exercise called **the $5 challenge**. In this challenge, you only eliminate an answer choice from contention if you are willing to bet $5 on it being wrong. Why $5? Five dollars is a small but not insignificant amount of money. It's an amount you could afford to lose but wouldn't want to throw away. And while losing $5 once might not hurt too much, doing it twenty times will set you back $100. In the same way, each small decision you make—eliminating a choice here, guessing on a question there—won't by itself impact your score very much, but when you put them all together, they can make a big difference. By holding each answer choice elimination decision to a higher standard, you can reduce the risk of accidentally eliminating the correct answer.

The $5 challenge can also be applied in a positive sense: If you are willing to bet $5 that an answer choice *is* correct, go ahead and mark it as correct.

Summary: Only eliminate an answer choice if you are willing to bet $5 that it is wrong.

Which Answer to Choose

You're taking the test. You've run into a hard question and decided you'll have to guess. You've eliminated all the answer choices you're willing to bet $5 on. Now you have to pick an answer. Why do we even need to talk about this? Why can't you just pick whichever one you feel like when the time comes?

The answer to these questions is that if you don't come into the test with a plan, you'll rely on your impression to select an answer choice, and if you do that, you risk falling into a trap. The test writers know that everyone who takes their test will be guessing on some of the questions, so they intentionally write wrong answer choices to seem plausible. You still have to pick an answer though, and if the wrong answer choices are designed to look right, how can you ever be sure that you're not falling for their trap? The best solution we've found to this dilemma is to take the decision out of your hands entirely. Here is the process we recommend:

Once you've eliminated any choices that you are confident (willing to bet $5) are wrong, select the first remaining choice as your answer.

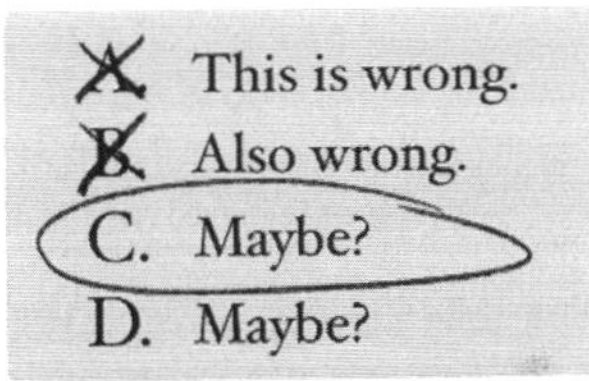

Whether you choose to select the first remaining choice, the second, or the last, the important thing is that you use some preselected standard. Using this approach guarantees that you will not be enticed into selecting an answer choice that looks right, because you are not basing your decision on how the answer choices look.

This is not meant to make you question your knowledge. Instead, it is to help you recognize the difference between your knowledge and your impressions. There's a huge difference between thinking an answer is right because of what you know, and thinking an answer is right because it looks or sounds like it should be right.

Summary: To ensure that your selection is appropriately random, make a predetermined selection from among all answer choices you have not eliminated.

Test-Taking Strategies

This section contains a list of test-taking strategies that you may find helpful as you work through the test. By taking what you know and applying logical thought, you can maximize your chances of answering any question correctly!

It is very important to realize that every question is different and every person is different: no single strategy will work on every question, and no single strategy will work for every person. That's why we've included all of them here, so you can try them out and determine which ones work best for different types of questions and which ones work best for you.

Question Strategies

✓ Read Carefully

Read the question and the answer choices carefully. Don't miss the question because you misread the terms. You have plenty of time to read each question thoroughly and make sure you understand what is being asked. Yet a happy medium must be attained, so don't waste too much time. You must read carefully and efficiently.

✓ Contextual Clues

Look for contextual clues. If the question includes a word you are not familiar with, look at the immediate context for some indication of what the word might mean. Contextual clues can often give you all the information you need to decipher the meaning of an unfamiliar word. Even if you can't determine the meaning, you may be able to narrow down the possibilities enough to make a solid guess at the answer to the question.

✓ Prefixes

If you're having trouble with a word in the question or answer choices, try dissecting it. Take advantage of every clue that the word might include. Prefixes can be a huge help. Usually, they allow you to determine a basic meaning. *Pre-* means before, *post-* means after, *pro-* is positive, *de-* is negative. From prefixes, you can get an idea of the general meaning of the word and try to put it into context.

✓ Hedge Words

Watch out for critical hedge words, such as *likely, may, can, often, almost, mostly, usually, generally, rarely,* and *sometimes.* Question writers insert these hedge phrases to cover every possibility. Often an answer choice will be wrong simply because it leaves no room for exception. Be on guard for answer choices that have definitive words such as *exactly* and *always.*

✓ Switchback Words

Stay alert for *switchbacks.* These are the words and phrases frequently used to alert you to shifts in thought. The most common switchback words are *but, although,* and *however.* Others include *nevertheless, on the other hand, even though, while, in spite of, despite,* and *regardless of.* Switchback words are important to catch because they can change the direction of the question or an answer choice.

✓ Face Value

When in doubt, use common sense. Accept the situation in the problem at face value. Don't read too much into it. These problems will not require you to make wild assumptions. If you have to go beyond creativity and warp time or space in order to have an answer choice fit the question, then you should move on and consider the other answer choices. These are normal problems rooted in reality. The applicable relationship or explanation may not be readily apparent, but it is there for you to figure out. Use your common sense to interpret anything that isn't clear.

Answer Choice Strategies

☑ Answer Selection

The most thorough way to pick an answer choice is to identify and eliminate wrong answers until only one is left, then confirm it is the correct answer. Sometimes an answer choice may immediately seem right, but be careful. The test writers will usually put more than one reasonable answer choice on each question, so take a second to read all of them and make sure that the other choices are not equally obvious. As long as you have time left, it is better to read every answer choice than to pick the first one that looks right without checking the others.

☑ Answer Choice Families

An answer choice family consists of two (in rare cases, three) answer choices that are very similar in construction and cannot all be true at the same time. If you see two answer choices that are direct opposites or parallels, one of them is usually the correct answer. For instance, if one answer choice says that quantity *x* increases and another either says that quantity *x* decreases (opposite) or says that quantity *y* increases (parallel), then those answer choices would fall into the same family. An answer choice that doesn't match the construction of the answer choice family is more likely to be incorrect. Most questions will not have answer choice families, but when they do appear, you should be prepared to recognize them.

☑ Eliminate Answers

Eliminate answer choices as soon as you realize they are wrong, but make sure you consider all possibilities. If you are eliminating answer choices and realize that the last one you are left with is also wrong, don't panic. Start over and consider each choice again. There may be something you missed the first time that you will realize on the second pass.

☑ Avoid Fact Traps

Don't be distracted by an answer choice that is factually true but doesn't answer the question. You are looking for the choice that answers the question. Stay focused on what the question is asking for so you don't accidentally pick an answer that is true but incorrect. Always go back to the question and make sure the answer choice you've selected actually answers the question and is not merely a true statement.

☑ Extreme Statements

In general, you should avoid answers that put forth extreme actions as standard practice or proclaim controversial ideas as established fact. An answer choice that states the "process should be used in certain situations, if..." is much more likely to be correct than one that states the "process should be discontinued completely." The first is a calm rational statement and doesn't even make a definitive, uncompromising stance, using a hedge word *if* to provide wiggle room, whereas the second choice is far more extreme.

☑ Benchmark

As you read through the answer choices and you come across one that seems to answer the question well, mentally select that answer choice. This is not your final answer, but it's the one that will help you evaluate the other answer choices. The one that you selected is your benchmark or standard for judging each of the other answer choices. Every other answer choice must be compared to your benchmark. That choice is correct until proven otherwise by another answer choice beating it. If you find a better answer, then that one becomes your new benchmark. Once you've decided that no other choice answers the question as well as your benchmark, you have your final answer.

✓ Predict the Answer

Before you even start looking at the answer choices, it is often best to try to predict the answer. When you come up with the answer on your own, it is easier to avoid distractions and traps because you will know exactly what to look for. The right answer choice is unlikely to be word-for-word what you came up with, but it should be a close match. Even if you are confident that you have the right answer, you should still take the time to read each option before moving on.

General Strategies

✓ Tough Questions

If you are stumped on a problem or it appears too hard or too difficult, don't waste time. Move on! Remember though, if you can quickly check for obviously incorrect answer choices, your chances of guessing correctly are greatly improved. Before you completely give up, at least try to knock out a couple of possible answers. Eliminate what you can and then guess at the remaining answer choices before moving on.

✓ Check Your Work

Since you will probably not know every term listed and the answer to every question, it is important that you get credit for the ones that you do know. Don't miss any questions through careless mistakes. If at all possible, try to take a second to look back over your answer selection and make sure you've selected the correct answer choice and haven't made a costly careless mistake (such as marking an answer choice that you didn't mean to mark). This quick double check should more than pay for itself in caught mistakes for the time it costs.

✓ Pace Yourself

It's easy to be overwhelmed when you're looking at a page full of questions; your mind is confused and full of random thoughts, and the clock is ticking down faster than you would like. Calm down and maintain the pace that you have set for yourself. Especially as you get down to the last few minutes of the test, don't let the small numbers on the clock make you panic. As long as you are on track by monitoring your pace, you are guaranteed to have time for each question.

✓ Don't Rush

It is very easy to make errors when you are in a hurry. Maintaining a fast pace in answering questions is pointless if it makes you miss questions that you would have gotten right otherwise. Test writers like to include distracting information and wrong answers that seem right. Taking a little extra time to avoid careless mistakes can make all the difference in your test score. Find a pace that allows you to be confident in the answers that you select.

✓ Keep Moving

Panicking will not help you pass the test, so do your best to stay calm and keep moving. Taking deep breaths and going through the answer elimination steps you practiced can help to break through a stress barrier and keep your pace.

Final Notes

The combination of a solid foundation of content knowledge and the confidence that comes from practicing your plan for applying that knowledge is the key to maximizing your performance on test day. As your foundation of content knowledge is built up and strengthened, you'll find that the strategies included in this chapter become more and more effective in helping you quickly sift through the distractions and traps of the test to isolate the correct answer.

Now that you're preparing to move forward into the test content chapters of this book, be sure to keep your goal in mind. As you read, think about how you will be able to apply this information on the test. If you've already seen sample questions for the test and you have an idea of the question format and style, try to come up with questions of your own that you can answer based on what you're reading. This will give you valuable practice applying your knowledge in the same ways you can expect to on test day.

Good luck and good studying!

Public Speaking and Debate

Communication Processes

Relationship Between Perception and Communication

Perception and communication are inextricably linked. Our ability to understand both verbal and nonverbal communication depends on our ability to accurately interpret the information we take in from the world. In a large part, our powers of perception are based on our experiences in the world. Over time, we develop **patterns** of perception and observation that structure and inform our interpretation and evaluation of what is communicated to us. There is no way to avoid this process of pattern formation and, indeed, we should be thankful that our brains are capable of assimilating the massive amounts of stimuli we are bombarded by every day. At the same time, it is important to take account of our own perceptual filters so we are clearly aware of where our prejudices lie.

Relationship Between Perception and Meaning

The ability to accurately perceive is closely related to the ability to derive accurate meaning from any communication. The **meanings** we ascribe to the communications of others are based on our perceptions. This means in part that how we interpret what anything means is based on our perception of verbal and nonverbal **communication cues**. Our impression of what another person is saying comes not only from their words but from their tone of voice and body language as well. Face-to-face conversation is perhaps the most effective form of communication because it provides both parties with the most information about one another. Thus, it is a better opportunity to correctly assess what is being conveyed. Generally, the more information one provides in any communication, the more accurate the reception of the message will be.

How Meaning is Encoded

When one person speaks to another, he or she is **encoding** the verbal message with supplemental nonverbal forms of communication. The precise "code" the speaker uses is the particular set of words, with their agreed-upon meaning, as well as syntax and grammar. To the degree that the speaker has a command of vocabulary and a strong sense of meaning, he or she will be able to construct a subtle and effective code. The process of encoding meaning is also influenced by individual bias, desire, and perception. People encode meaning differently based on the personal "agenda" they bring to any conversation. Two people speaking to one another should be able to increase the complexity and accuracy of their message encoding as the conversation progresses because they will be acquiring more and better information about one another's intentions, knowledge, and character.

Review Video: Phonics (Encoding and Decoding)
Visit mometrix.com/academy and enter code: 821361

How Meaning is Interpreted

When we listen to another person speak, we are attempting to decode their meaning through the filter of our own prejudices and perceptions. Speech communication theorists assert that listeners tend to emphasize the components of a message that are associated with their own pre-existing knowledge or interests. In particular, we all tend to emphasize the importance of aspects of a message that directly pertain to us. Starting out, we are more likely to make mistakes when interpreting what a speaker is saying. As we acquire more information and become more familiar with the other person's speaking style, however, we tend to make beneficial adjustments to our interpretation. The more time we spend with another person, the better able we are to correctly interpret the meanings of their communications.

Communication Appropriate to Cooperating on a Task

For people to cooperate effectively on a task, they all need good communication skills. This is especially true in the adult professional world. Without effective communication among those involved, success will be more difficult to achieve. Many people do not learn to work effectively with others until late childhood. For the most part, any job-related task is most easily accomplished when all parties know enough about the task-related tools, ideas, and skills to communicate effectively among themselves. In some cases, two individuals working together on a task may have unequal power, such as in the case of an employer and employee collaborating on a work-related project. Such unequal distribution of power also has a strong effect on communication.

Defensiveness as an Impediment to Communication

Defensiveness is a quality that can obstruct effective communication. When one of the parties in a conversation feels threatened, he or she is likely to become defensive and protective of his or her own ego. Such a person is likely to become preoccupied with his or her own interests and fail to seriously consider the content of the other person's message. Depending on past experience and temperament, individuals have varying degrees of natural defensiveness. Unfortunately, those with greater defenses may fail to obtain new information, thus making personal progress more difficult. This in turn can prevent them from hearing valuable future criticism. As this cycle continues, defensiveness can become more deeply entrenched. Stung by criticism, defensive people adopt a behavior style that is likely to lead to more criticism. Defensiveness must be challenged indirectly, as any direct challenges are likely to increase the self-protective instinct. The need to tailor one's words to avoid a defensive reaction in the listener takes more effort, reducing the chances of effective give-and-take.

Ulterior Motives as an Impediment to Communication

The phrase **ulterior motives** refers to intentions that are known only to one party but kept secret from the other. When one of the parties in a conversation has ulterior motives, it will be almost impossible for effective communication to take place. To a certain degree, everyone has ulterior motives in conversation, even when discussing the most banal and impersonal subjects. Each participant in the conversation essentially has his or her own personal interests at heart. However, the less forthright one is about his or her intentions in a conversation, the less likely he or she is to achieve solid understanding with the other person. Someone with a "hidden agenda" is likely to speak in a way that refers to these underlying intentions rather than to the more surface level intentions. When this is the case, the gap between stated and real intentions can lead to evasiveness and abstraction.

Importance of Feedback During Interpersonal Communication

Basically, **feedback** is the response that a communication message elicits from the receiver. For instance, if you are talking to a friend and that friend nods her head as you speak, she is giving you feedback that both of you understand to mean, "I agree with what you are saying", or "I understand." An entirely different message would be communicated if she started vigorously shaking her head from side to side. The amount and quality of the feedback in a conversation has a tremendous effect on the quality of the communication. As a conversation progresses, feedback allows each interlocutor to refine his or her message. This is another reason why face-to-face conversation is the format most conducive to effective interpersonal communication. In contrast, when we talk on the phone we cannot see the other person, and therefore cannot identify nonverbal forms of feedback that would allow us to refine our message appropriately.

Importance of Privacy for Effective Interpersonal Communication

In conversation, the general goal of both parties should be to create a positive environment in which **self-disclosure** is encouraged. Of course, there are limits to the amount of self-disclosure that is appropriate in any social interaction. There are certain thoughts and feelings that good manners and propriety keep us from expressing, even though they may influence our participation in a conversation. This need for privacy is universal. Most people have not only a desire to maintain personal privacy but also a desire to respect the privacy of others. There are certain things about other people that we simply do not want to know. What is perceived as a healthy balance between self-disclosure and privacy varies according to the relationship. For instance, a teenager will usually insist on a greater amount of privacy from his or her parents than from his or her peers. Part of the work of interpersonal communication is establishing the boundaries of self-disclosure.

How Holding Grudges Can Affect Interpersonal Communication

In some cases, interpersonal communication can be adversely affected by the **unspoken resentments** held by one party against the other. Anytime important information is known by one party but not the other, communication is impaired. When such information directly relates to the relationship between the two parties, a severe impairment may result. Furthermore, when an individual sits on important information and allows it to fester in his or her psyche, it may eventually emerge in a much more toxic and extreme form. Often, when an individual seems to overreact to a minor grievance, it is because he or she is consciously or unconsciously reacting to long-held grudges. For interpersonal communication to thrive conversation must be open and honest, and any important grievances must be made plain.

Basic Components of a Communication Event

Every communication event has four components: source, message, channel, and receiver. The **source** is the person who is speaking. The **message** consists of the words and the nonverbal forms of communication by which the desired information is conveyed. The **channel** refers to the communication venues used to deliver the message. For instance, if you encounter a friend and say "hello" while waving, you are using the channels of words and gestures. Finally, the **receiver** is the person or people receiving the message. For a communication event to be complete, it must include all four of these components. If there is no receiver, for example, we cannot say that a true communication event has taken place, since no information was transferred from one person to another. Similarly, if there is no message, there is nothing to communicate, and again no communication has occurred.

Process Model of Communication

Most speech communication theorists use what is called the **process model** of communication to diagram communication events. The four important components of a process model are speaker, message, channel, and receiver. These four elements will exist in any communication event, not just in a two-person conversation. For instance, consider typing an essay on a computer. During this act, all four components of the process model are represented: the speaker is the person typing, the message is the essay the speaker is typing, the channel is the keystrokes, and the receiver is the computer on which the essay is being typed. In a conversation, the interlocutors will alternate the roles of speaker and receiver. For the most part, though, speech communication theorists find the process model to be an easy way to organize their study of communication events.

Feedback is Treated by the Process Model of Interpersonal Communication

Communications are constantly being refined and adjusted based on feedback. The process model of communication takes this into account. Indeed, the very name of this organizational scheme indicates that communication is to be thought of as an ongoing process. The process model of communication breaks the **feedback process** into three components: actor, goal, and observer. The **actor** is the person communicating and the **goal** is the person or thing to which the actor is trying to communicate. During a conversation, the goal is another person or a group of people, whereas during written composition the goal could be your computer. As the actor is attempting to communicate to the goal, he or she also functions as an **observer**, taking in whatever feedback is offered and subsequently adjusting the communication. When you receive an error message on your computer, for instance, you are receiving feedback that will influence your choices of communication in the future. This is known as a **feedback loop**.

Codes Used in Interpersonal Communication

The formulations of words and gestures that we use to communicate with one another are known in speech communication as **codes**. These are not secret codes; rather, to be effective they depend on our ability to understand them. We assume that the codes we use will be understood by others. Every spoken language is a code because words are used as representations of things. The names we use to describe the objects in the world and the abstract ideas in our minds are all part of the code. Furthermore, body language and hand gestures are part of a cultural code in which all of the members agree upon meaning. There is no inherent meaning in the gesture of raising one's hand and waving it, but it has been agreed upon by our culture that this gesture means greeting and welcome. To communicate effectively, one must understand both verbal and nonverbal codes and must know how to make adjustments when the receiver has an imperfect knowledge of codes.

Influences on Communication

Denotative Meaning

Denotative meaning is the way in which a word indicates something else. Essentially, it is the definition of a word. The word "table," for instance, denotes a flat surface with three or more legs. A speaker must always be conscious of the denotative meaning of the words he or she uses. The denotative meaning is not decided on an individual basis. Rather, it is the product of unconscious agreements on meaning made by the members of a community. In other words, to ensure that he or she communicates effectively with the audience, the speaker must have a familiarity with the denotative meanings that will be known to the members of that audience. Effective speakers continually refer to a dictionary during speech composition in order to solidify their understanding of denotative meanings.

Connotative Meaning

Connotative meaning is any implication or suggestion connected to a word that extends beyond the denotative meaning of the word. The connotative meaning of the word, then, is not strictly the definition of the word. Connotative meanings are often quite emotional in character. For instance, the denotative meaning of the word *whale* is a large mammal that lives in the ocean. When the same word is used in a certain way, however, its connotative meaning may refer to someone who is overweight. Speakers need to be aware of both the connotative and the denotative meanings of the words they use. Otherwise, they run the risk of confusing or even offending the audience members. A detailed dictionary will often have explanations of the various connotative meanings of common words.

Role of Definitions in Communication

To be effective, a speaker must understand the basic definitions of the words he or she is using and make sure to share these definitions with the audience. If the audience members assume different definitions than those the speaker intends, there will be no possibility of communication. Speaker should always strive for clarity and precision in their choice of words. **Clarity** here means choosing words that directly convey the speaker's intended meanings. Clear language admits no confusion about the subject matter or intent. **Precision** in this context means selecting words that do the best job of denoting the exact meaning intended by the speaker. When the language of a speech is precise, the audience should not have to guess what is denoted by each word.

Abstract Terms in Communication

It is easy to discover the denotative meanings of simple nouns like *table*, *turkey*, and *television*. It is more difficult to determine the denotative meanings of **abstract nouns**; that is, nouns that describe feelings, ideas, or concepts. Some examples of abstract terms are *freedom*, *jealousy*, and *capitalism*. For the definitions of these words, a speaker must rely on a dictionary and on his own sense of how the word is used in a given community. For the most part, speakers who wish to present themselves as objective will try to make the denotative meanings of their words precise and minimize the connotative meanings as much as possible. Not only are connotative meanings more subjective for an audience, but they tend to induce a more emotional response. In other words, they compromise the speaker's objectivity.

Effective Naming in Communication

As much as possible, an effective speaker will try to choose the right words to describe his or her subject. In some cases, there may be several names for the same thing. For instance, the same car might be referred to as a sedan, an auto, or a jalopy. These three names all carry with them different connotations. Furthermore, whereas a word like *auto* suggests a certain objectivity or seriousness on the part of the speaker, a word like *jalopy* is more appropriate for a humorous or colorful speech. To maintain the right tone, then, a speaker will need to be able to select the appropriate terms. The only way to do this consistently is to develop a keen ear for language by reading widely and listening to the ways that people talk.

An effective speaker will be able to compose descriptions that clarify and illuminate his or her subject matter. For instance, consider the difference between describing a person as a "good man" and describing him as a "heroic, courageous inspiration to his community." Obviously, the second description is more colorful and paints a more comprehensive picture of the person. Indeed, it includes the information that the described person was valued for his effect on his fellow citizens. As much as possible, a speaker wants to include descriptions that combine engaging detail and vivid language, without being so colorful as to distract from the main point of the speech. A facility for effective description can be encouraged by paying attention to the way description is handled by great authors and speakers.

Effects That Cultural Background Can Have on Connotative Meaning

Members of any particular cultural group often have special connotative meanings for words. Because connotative meanings can carry such emotional power, it is especially important for a speaker to understand the connotative meanings shared by his or her audience before delivering a speech. The best way to acquire such a sense of connotative meaning is to spend time with the members of the community. Developing a feeling for what is appropriate language for a given audience is as much a matter of intuition as the acquisition of particular definitions. When in doubt, a speaker should avoid using any language that may have unpleasant or hostile connotative meaning to his audience.

Effects of Dialect on Communication

A dialect is simply a unique way of speaking that is common to a particular segment of a community. All Americans have a dialect of one sort or another. Individuals who have spent their entire lives within a given community, however, may not be aware that their mode of speech or of understanding language is different from that of any other American. To some extent, the widespread availability of television, radio, and internet has minimized the differences among American dialects. Nevertheless, a speaker needs to be aware of the dialects spoken by the members of his or her audience. Within certain dialects, common words may have unique connotative meanings that can confuse or even pervert a speaker's message. At the same time, the effective use of local dialect is a great way to endear oneself to the audience and to establish a firm channel of communication.

Avoiding Distractions While Delivering a Speech

As much as possible, an effective speaker will minimize distractions during a speech. Distractions can include things done by the audience as well as by the speaker. Of course, it is not possible for a speaker to control the behavior of an audience, but he or she can exercise self-control. Too many speakers challenge the patience of the audience by hemming and hawing over their words, making distracting gestures, or engaging in frequent vocal tics. For many speakers, making noises like "uh" and "er" while searching for the right word is natural and unconscious. It can be very distracting to an audience, however, so a speaker would do well to practice delivering his or her message without incorporating these filler sounds.

Speaking in a Manner Appropriate to the Topic and Setting of the Speech

Ideally, with experience a speaker develops the ability to deliver his or her message in a manner appropriate to the topic, the audience, and the setting. For instance, when speaking to a group of five or six people, it is inappropriate to use a booming voice and wild, dramatic gestures. Likewise, it takes a very sophisticated speaker to deliver an intimate, informal lecture to a group of two or three hundred. One of the best ways to develop a sense of what is appropriate for a given setting is to study effective speakers in various settings. Notice how they vary their vocal quality and nonverbal communication repertoire in different environments.

To gain the attention and respect of the audience, the speaker needs to deliver his or her message in a manner that will meet their expectations.

Nonverbal Communication in Establishing the Credibility of a Speaker

Many speakers underestimate the positive effects that nonverbal communication can have on their success in delivering a message. By making assertive and forceful gestures, a speaker can create an image of credibility and confidence. Similarly, by making easy gestures, a speaker can promote an image of relaxation and friendliness. The trick is to know which gestures are appropriate in which situations. Furthermore, an effective speaker will be able to modulate the volume and pitch of his or her voice in accordance with the requirements of the speech. A bombastic tone is not appropriate to an academic discourse, nor is a dry delivery appropriate for a political rally. A speaker needs to be aware of the expectations of the audience, and only challenge them when such a challenge is necessary.

Methods of Improving Voice and Articulation Problems

For many people, delivering an effective public speech is an uphill battle because they have never mastered the basics of vocal presentation. For instance, many people have not learned the proper manner of articulating complex sounds in English. Also, many people have not received enough exposure to effective oratory and therefore do not understand the essential rhythms of speech delivery. There are a few common ways to improve voice and articulation problems. Some articulation problems are the result of physiological issues and can only be treated by a doctor. Other issues, however, are behavioral and can be resolved with therapy and training. Increasingly, schools are staffing speech clinicians to help students resolve problems with articulation.

Procedure for Improving One's Own Public Speech

The process of improving one's public speech technique will vary depending on the individual's particular challenges. A few common remedies can be generally helpful however. For one thing, a person can record themselves and listen to the way they speak. Speakers are frequently unaware of their articulation problems until they review themselves speaking. With practice, speakers can train themselves to diagnose particular problems and can subsequently learn to self-correct them. Practice in producing the correct sound every day should result in almost immediate progress. After a while, the corrections will become habitual and will no longer need review or practice.

Effective Listening

Forms of Listening

Other Problems of Listening Besides the SUR Listening Style

SUR is an acronym for a listening style in which the audience is **self-absorbed**, **unfocused**, and **rules-driven**. Unfortunately, there are some other common obstacles to listening besides being self-absorbed, unfocused, or rules-driven. Many people simply do not pay attention or they allow their minds to wander off during a digression from the major ideas of the message. In scientific studies of listening behavior, researchers have observed that the human mind can process information much more quickly than information can be delivered in a speech. Thus, while a person is listening, his or her brain is often performing other tasks simultaneously. Obviously, these other tasks run the risk of hindering effective listening and concentration. Some research has suggested, however, that many individuals require a small amount of distraction in order to concentrate effectively. For instance, many people are able to study more intently when listening to music at the same time.

Intentional Listening

Ideally, when listening to a speech one will not simply sit back and allow the words being spoken to wash over him or her. Rather, an effective listener will engage in what is known as **intentional listening**, an active state of processing, interpreting, and thinking critically about a speech. It is always good for the audience members to ask themselves what they hope to gain from a speech before it begins, as this will focus their attention and give purpose to their listening. While the speaker is addressing them, audience members should be attempting to place each successive idea into an overall framework.

Appreciative and Therapeutic Listening

Speech communication researchers have identified five basic kinds of intentional listening: appreciative, therapeutic, discriminative, comprehensive, and critical. **Appreciative** listening is perhaps the most passive form of listening. An appreciative listener is simply seeking to obtain as much pleasure as possible from the words being spoken. Although the intention of many speeches is to entertain the audience, an appreciative listener may not pay enough attention to the actual message being delivered by the speaker. **Therapeutic** listening, on the other hand, is listening with the intention of obtaining as much emotional support as possible. Many times, those listening to sermons and motivational speeches are engaged in therapeutic listening. The message of the speech empowers them and makes them feel better.

Critical Listening

Critical listening is the most active form of audience behavior. It entails organizing and interpreting the information contained in a speech. While a speaker is giving his or her speech, the critical listener will be evaluating the arguments or ideas the speaker is presenting, weighing the evidence provided, and thinking of possible problems with the speech. As consumers, people engage in a form of critical listening every time they hear an advertisement. During a speech, however, many people sympathize with the speaker rather than critically evaluating the speaker's message.

Discriminative Listening

Discriminative listening focuses on the aspects of a speaker's message that are implied rather than spoken directly. A discriminative listener is paying attention to the speaker's voice, body language, and implicit argument. To a certain extent, everyone is always practicing discriminative listening, although some people engage in this style of listening more than others do. A sophisticated listener obtains information not only from the message but from the medium in which it is delivered.

Listening for Comprehension

Comprehensive listening, or listening for comprehension, is probably the most familiar form of listening. Students in a classroom are engaged in listening for comprehension when they take notes during a lecture. Whenever people listen to an informative or persuasive speech in order to gain information about a subject, they are engaged in listening for comprehension. The validity and accuracy of other forms of listening, such as critical listening and discriminative listening, depend on listening effectively for comprehension. If an individual is unable to understand the message being presented, he or she will not be able to critique it insightfully.

Importance of Detached, Intentional Listening

When speech communication instructors describe the ideal listener, they often refer to **detaching** or **decentering**. These terms refer to the process of considering the speaker's message on its own terms rather than in the context of the listener's experience and emotions. In essence, this simply means giving a speaker a fair hearing before applying critical thinking to his or her message. Too often, audience members prejudge a message based on their past experience or existing opinions. This not only prevents such listeners from acquiring a better understanding, but it significantly handicaps their ability to listen for comprehension. Even when a speech is being delivered on a subject with which a member of the audience is quite familiar, he or she should try to keep an open mind in order to gain as much as possible from the speech.

Purposes of an Audience Member May Change During a Speech

When speech communication instructors refer to the five kinds of listening (appreciative, therapeutic, discriminative, comprehensive, and critical), they do not mean to suggest that these forms of listening exist independent of one another at all times. On the contrary, the members of an audience may be engaged in several different kinds of listening at the same time. Furthermore, it is quite common for members of an audience to adjust their listening style during the course of a speech. For instance, whereas at the beginning of a speech an audience member may be strictly listening for comprehension, as the speech goes on, he or she may begin to listen more critically. Similarly, an audience member may at first pay attention strictly to the speaker's explicit message, but later may become more interested in the implications of the speech and may therefore engage more in discriminative listening.

RRA Technique for Active Listening

When speech communication instructors describe active listening, they sometimes refer to the **RRA** (review, relate, anticipate) technique. This technique breaks the process of active listening down into three easy steps.

1. To begin with, an active listener is constantly **reviewing** what has been said and placing new information into the evolving model of the message.
2. As the listener considers the speaker's argument or idea, he or she **relates** it to his or her foundational knowledge. In other words, the audience member tries to compare and contrast the speaker's message with his or her own knowledge of the subject.
3. Finally, an active listener tries to **anticipate** the rest of the speaker's message. Not only is this a good way to stay engaged with a speech, it provides an excellent measure of attention. When a listener is able to confidently predict the direction of a speech, he or she can be certain that his or her understanding of what has been said so far is sound.

How an Audience Member Should Consider the Content of a Speech

When considering the content of a speech, audience members should pay special attention to three basic areas: main ideas, organization, and supporting evidence. The **main ideas** of the speech are the fundamental arguments or concepts the speaker is trying to convey. If the speech is effective, the main ideas will be obvious. Audience members should be paying the most attention to the articulation and elaboration of these main ideas. The way in which the main ideas are expressed and supported is referred to as the **organization** of the speech. For a speech to be effective, the speaker needs to organize his or her ideas clearly and avoid long digressions that obscure the main points of the speech. Finally, the audience member must consider what supporting materials the speaker is using to provide evidence for his or her ideas or arguments and must determine whether these supporting materials are appropriate and credible.

How a Listener Should Assess the Situation in Which a Speech is Given

To get the most out of a speech, a listener needs to consider all of the various factors that contribute to the speaker's message. One of the factors that does not receive a great deal of attention is the **situation** in which the speech is delivered. Many times, the physical and interpersonal setting in which a speech is delivered has a great deal of influence on the message. For instance, an audience member might consider whether the speaker has been required to make his or her address more or less formal for the occasion. The audience member also might consider whether the occasion on which the speech is being delivered has influenced the quality of the speaker's message. Finally, the audience member should consider whether the physical environment in which the speech is delivered has been more or less conducive to understanding and appreciating the speaker's message.

How a Listener Should Assess the Characteristics of the Speaker

As part of the overall critique of a speech, an audience member should consider the **personal characteristics** of the speaker. For instance, the audience member might consider what he or she knew about the speaker before the speech and then determines whether this information has had any influence on his or her interpretation of the speaker's message. The audience member might also consider whether the speaker's personal presentation indicated credibility or made his or her message difficult to believe. Many times, a speaker with a good message and solid supporting materials can still come across as vague and disorganized because of his or her physical appearance and vocal mannerisms. Audience members should try to distinguish between weaknesses in the speaker's message and weaknesses in the speaker's personal presentation.

How a Listener Should Analyze the Message of the Speech

When a member of an audience listens to a speech, he or she should be paying attention to three fundamental factors: ideas, organization, and support. The most important thing to consider is whether the speaker's **main ideas** are logical and clearly expressed. If the ideas are comprehensible, an audience member can then consider whether the speaker has expressed those ideas in a **logical order** or in a disorganized way. Finally, the audience member needs to consider whether the speaker has adequately supported his or her main ideas by argument or **factual evidence**. Does the speaker provide enough support for his or her arguments to remain credible? Is the evidence provided relevant to the main ideas of the speech?

Benefits of Taking Notes During a Speech

One of the best things an audience member can do to organize his or her thoughts about a speech is to take notes. Taking notes during a speech allows the audience member to organize the speaker's message and mark down any questions or concerns he or she may have without becoming entangled in a long, digressive thought. Taking notes during a speech is a skill that every college student has to use on a daily basis. It is important for students to begin practicing these skills early in their academic careers. Many people believe they can accurately recall a speech in great detail, but few people actually can. Taking notes helps to refresh the memory so that an individual can accurately consider the message of the speech long after hearing it.

Process of Taking Notes on a Speech

The importance of taking clear and accurate notes during a speech cannot be overstated. Most people acquire a personal note-taking style over time. This style may be highly idiosyncratic, but it usually includes a few core features. For one thing, good note-takers usually develop a style of organization, so they can look back over their notes and discern the general structure of a speech. Indentations, margins, and numbers or letters are common ways of organizing a set of notes. It is always a good idea to leave some room on the margins of one's notes, in order to fill in any weak areas later on. Remember that notes are meant to be reviewed. After all, the primary goal of note-taking is to preserve an accurate record of the speech so that it can be recalled later.

Advanced Techniques in Note-Taking

Over many years of study, most students develop an efficient and organized way of taking notes. There are a number of common systems of organization that have proven beneficial for top students. For instance, many students use abbreviations and shorthand so they can condense a great deal of information into a relatively small space. Using symbols that substitute for common words or expressions can save time during note-taking. Another technique is color coding one's notes; that is, using a different color pen to indicate different types of notes. Some students create elaborate outline procedures to organize the main and supporting ideas in a speech or lecture. Whereas all of these methods of note organization can be effective, it falls to the individual student to experiment and decide which best promotes his or her own understanding.

Intercultural Contact as a Characteristic of Speechmaking

An effective speaker always keeps in mind the **cultural characteristics** of his or her audience. When a speaker is delivering a message to an audience whose culture is different from his or her own, he or she needs to be especially sensitive to the cultural mores observed by the group. For instance, excessive familiarity may be a sign of friendliness to the speaker, but it may demonstrate disrespect in the eyes of some audiences. It is a good idea to familiarize oneself with the basic manners appropriate to the intended audience. A failure to observe the customs of the group may prevent a message from being heard.

Differences Between Listening and Hearing

For most people, listening and hearing are synonyms. In the world of speech communication, however, a subtle distinction exists between the two. **Hearing** is simply receiving a sound in the ear. In other words, hearing is the physiological and neurological act of converting heard sounds into meaning. **Listening**, on the other hand, is the more active process of taking in what is heard and interpreting it. People are constantly listening to the words of those around them and using their knowledge of language and cultural values to determine the meaning of what is being said. Listening, then, is a more subjective act than hearing.

Three Listening Styles

Experts in speech communication distinguish among three listening styles: RRP, VAT, and SUR.

RRP includes reasons-oriented listeners, results-oriented listeners, and process-oriented listeners.

- **Reason-oriented** listeners are interested in hearing the logical support for a given argument.
- **Results-oriented** listeners, on the other hand, are interested in the overall intention of the idea or argument.
- Finally, **process-oriented** listeners are interested in the way a particular idea or argument was conceived. All of these types of listeners will be very interested in the specific details of a speech. To impress an RRP listener, a speaker must have his or her details in order and possess an extensive knowledge of the subject.

VAT listeners are so-called because their listening style emphasizes the visual, auditory, or tactile elements of a speech.

- A **visual** listener will focus on the aspects of the presentation that can be seen, whether it is the speaker's body language and physical presentation or any visual aids accompanying the speech. To engage an audience of visual listeners, the speaker should be sure to have sufficient visual aids on hand.
- On the other hand, an **auditory** listener will be most interested in the spoken words delivered by the speaker. Auditory listeners will not need the presence of visual aids to hold their attention during a speech.
- Finally, **tactile** listeners need some physical contact to truly appreciate what is being described. Physical demonstrations, handouts, and sample materials are all good ways to engage the attention of a tactile listener.

SUR listening style describes those who are self-absorbed, unfocused, and rules-driven.

1. **Self-absorbed** listeners are preoccupied with their own concerns and have a hard time paying attention to the ideas or interests of others.
2. **Unfocused** listeners are not skilled or knowledgeable enough to listen well and thus have a hard time understanding an argument or complicated idea.
3. **Rules-driven** listeners tend to obsess about minor points of reason and logic instead of paying attention to the most important aspects of a speech's message. In other words, rules-driven listeners "cannot see the forest for the trees."

Importance of Deciding to Listen

Although it may sound strange, it is actually a good idea to consciously decide to listen when involved in interpersonal communication. Most people fail to listen properly because, not being intentional listeners, they allow themselves to become distracted by secondary stimuli. When a person makes a conscious decision to listen, he or she naturally ignores all the other kinds of activity going on in the background. Also, once a person gets into the habit of consciously listening to others, he or she will find that his or her listening skills improve exponentially. Many people do not realize just how satisfying interpersonal communication can be until they make a conscious decision to listen.

Maintaining Proper Attention During a Speech

It is essential to maintain attention throughout the delivery of a speech. To get the full value of a speech, a member of the audience must understand the entire structure of the speech, and this can only be done by maintaining attention throughout. If a person misses the beginning of the speech, for example, he or she will not understand what all of the speaker's subsequent arguments and evidence are supporting. On the other hand, if an audience member listens to the beginning of the speech but allows his or her attention to trail off, he or she will come away from the speech not knowing the precise reasons why the speaker's thesis statement should be believed.

Concentrating on Message Structure During a Speech

An effective listener will be able to mentally outline the structure of a speech. The basic outline of a speech will include the main argument, supporting arguments, and supporting evidence and reasoning. Only by making sense of structure can an audience member truly assess the strengths and weaknesses of the speech. For instance, an audience member should be able to tell whether the speaker has done a good job of ordering his or her points. If the speaker makes the mistake of initiating the speech with minor points and only later working in more essential arguments, the audience members should be able to identify this error and determine whether it reflects poorly on the speaker or on the argument as a whole.

Relationship Between Good Listening and the Emotions

To be a good listener, an audience member needs to keep his or her emotions in check. Of course, this is not always easy. Sometimes a speaker's fiery rhetoric or sentimentality is designed to sweep the audience into a heightened emotional state. Audience members should try as much as possible to maintain control of their critical faculties, however, in order to accurately and objectively appraise the merits of the speech. Indeed, an objective and comprehensive speech analysis includes assessing the methods by which the speaker attempts to engage the emotions of the audience. If the audience member's emotions are roused by the speaker, he or she can say that the speaker's emotional appeal has been successful. This does not necessarily assume the merit of the speaker's argument, however.

Critical Listening as It Applies to Public Speeches

Critical listening is perhaps most important in the context of **public speeches**, since there will be less opportunity for each audience member to clarify the speaker's remarks through questions after the conclusion of the speech. In other words, each audience member will be on his or her own in the task of deciphering and evaluating the speaker's message. For this reason, many audience members try to take brief notes and chart out the structure of a speaker's argument. Speeches delivered to large crowds often involve appeals to the emotions. A speaker can get away with histrionic gestures and exaggerated vocal mannerisms when speaking to a large crowd, whereas these same techniques might seem ridiculous to a small group.

Principles of Rhetoric

Persuasion

Persuasion is the art of changing the attitudes, beliefs, or actions of other people. It can be used for any number of purposes: to sell a product, to make a friend, to advance a cause, or simply to win an argument. To a certain degree, even some primarily informative speeches contain an element of persuasion. The speaker is encouraging his or her audience to understand a given subject in the same way he or she does. To be persuasive, the speaker must have a clear idea of what he or she is trying to accomplish. Also, it is important to understand the best persuasive strategy for achieving the desired effect Persuasion can be styled as a direct argument or as a more indirect, maybe even subversive, suggestion.

Relationship Between Persuasion and Likeability

Students of rhetoric have long noticed the correlation between a **charismatic personality** and persuasion. Basically, if a speaker is able to establish strong personal relationships with his or her audience, he or she is much more likely to be an effective persuasive communicator. The most important thing a persuasive speaker can do is to establish trust from the outset. If a speaker can convince the audience that he or she has their best interests at heart and is a competent source of information, the work of persuasion is largely done. Establishing trust and respect with the audience is as much a matter of one's credentials as one's appearance and presentation. Speakers who can demonstrate expertise and empathy are likely to find success with their audiences.

Relationship Between Persuasion and Competence

To be persuasive, an individual must be perceived as **competent** by the audience. Competence manifests itself in a number of characteristics, such as preparedness, poise, thoughtfulness, and clarity. Competent speakers should be able to answer questions from the audience on a specific subject, or should at least be able to explain where the answers could be found. They must have supporting evidence for their arguments and must make this evidence clear to the audience. They will also be able to organize their message effectively, giving the audience the best opportunity to educate themselves. Finally, competent speakers will appear unhurried and calm.

Relationship Between Personal Conviction and Persuasion

Audiences seem to have a sixth sense for insincerity. They can tell when a speaker does not really believe his or her message. For this reason, effective persuasion is greatly benefited by the speaker's deep **conviction** in what he or she is saying. It is often said that before a speaker can persuade anyone else, he or she needs to be persuaded. When the strength of a speaker's convictions is evident in his or her delivery, the natural empathy of the audience will assist in persuasion. Historically, a survey of the great persuasive orators (Martin Luther King Jr., Abraham Lincoln, Pericles, etc.) confirms that strong belief is a boon to persuasive rhetoric.

Relationship Between Reputation and Persuasion

Another factor that can greatly influence a speaker's power of persuasion is **reputation**. When a speaker has a reputation for upright behavior and responsibility to the truth, an audience is much more likely to believe his or her message. The credibility of the speaker is imperative, regardless of the topic. If the content of the speech is highly specialized, the audience will want to know that the speaker has some advanced training in the subject. When an audience arrives for a speech already knowing the positive reputation of the speaker, the work of persuasion is almost complete. For many politicians and orators, building a reputation that encourages persuasion is the work of a lifetime.

Value of Direct Familiarity with Sources in a Persuasive Speech

Having direct knowledge of sources can be extremely beneficial to a speaker's power of persuasion. For instance, imagine a motivational speaker on the subject of weight loss. If that speaker has had the experience of being overweight and then successfully losing weight and becoming healthier, the audience will be much more likely to take his or her words to heart. When a speaker can claim direct experience of the topic on which he or she speaks, the audience is unlikely to attribute the speaker's motives to personal gain or manipulation. The most effective speakers are able to present their personal experience as a model for the examination and consideration of the audience.

Relationship Between Mimicry and Persuasion

Human beings have a natural tendency to imitate the behavior of those they perceive to be leaders or role models. People often adopt beliefs or act in ways uncharacteristic of who they really are in order to mirror the behavior of a leader. This phenomenon is due in part to the tendency of human beings to minimize differences between one another as a means of preventing conflict. Of course, to inspire imitation on the part of the audience, a speaker must appear competent and have a good reputation. The members of an audience should be particularly skeptical of speakers who encourage them to adopt a point of view simply because others are doing so.

Being Persuaded with Following Directions

Human beings have a natural tendency to believe what designated authority figures tell them. In part, this is an inherited characteristic. Early humans, in order to survive in the wild, often had to rely on the advice and guidance of their peers. In many cases, people will follow directions from an authority figure without considering the ramifications of their actions. This phenomenon was evidenced during the Nuremberg trials after World War II, as numerous Nazi officials defended their actions as "just following orders." The educational system also encourages people to trust authority figures and follow directions. Audience members should be aware of this tendency in themselves and should guard against blindly accepting the recommendations of a speaker.

Persuaded with Accepting a Suggestion

A persuasive speaker may sometimes use a **suggestion** rather than a direct command to achieve his or her goal. A suggestion is simply a less forceful recommendation; it implies that the audience has the ability to decide for themselves whether or not to accept the guidance of the speaker. Suggestion is a good strategy for dealing with naturally skeptical audience members, who will resist any overt attempts to change their minds. Because it is an indirect form of persuasion, however, suggestion requires a bit more subtlety on the part of the speaker. And since it gives the listener the impression that he or she has arrived independently at a conclusion, suggestion can be more effective than direction.

Relationship Between Persuasion and Dramatization

A persuasive speaker often employs the language and techniques of drama to capture the interest of the audience. In other words, the speaker will frame his or her arguments as part of a larger narrative. The speaker may introduce certain representative characters and may spend a short time describing their characteristics. The speaker may then introduce some conflict against which these characters must struggle. This kind of generic dramatic scenario gives the audience a sort of "hook" on which to hang its attention. Instead of being required to pay attention to dry statistics and formal arguments, the audience can become absorbed in the stories of the characters. Many speakers find this captivation to be a spur to positive persuasion.

Relationship Between Persuasion and the Motivation of the Speaker

When an audience is considering the elements of a persuasive speech, they will likely give some thought to the motivations of the speaker. For instance, when approached by a salesperson, a customer is likely to assume that the salesperson has a vested personal interest in making a sale and does not necessarily have the best interests of the consumer at heart. In other contexts, however, the motivation of the speaker may be harder to discern. In an academic speech, for instance, the audience will be aware that the speaker is attempting to promote a certain viewpoint, but they may not be able to determine exactly why the speaker supports that point of view. To the extent that the audience can discern the motivation of the speaker, they will be able to intellectually consider the merits of the speech and not be swayed by emotion.

Resistance to Persuasion

Audiences will naturally be resistant to persuasive arguments that attempt to take them out of their normal routine. People of all ages have a tendency to fall into habitual behaviors that can be difficult and even painful to interrupt. A persuasive speaker, however, is by nature one who attempts to convert an audience to a new way of living or thinking. He or she will therefore encounter the listeners' resistance, based on their entrenched habits. Habitual behavior can be attacked in a number of ways. One is to persuade the audience that these habits are detrimental. Another is to suggest the advantages that can be gained from a new way of living or thinking. In all cases, however, the speaker should remember that most behavioral change is incremental and not the result of sudden conversion.

Unique Qualities of a Speech that Persuades the Audience to Change

One of the most common kinds of persuasive speech is one in which the speaker attempts to persuade the audience to change something. The speaker may be asking the listeners to change their behavior, their opinion on some subject, or the way in which some issue is handled in their community. These kinds of speeches usually follow a similar arc: first, the speaker describes the disastrous state of affairs at present. Second, the speaker introduces his or her proposal for remedying the situation. Third, the speaker indicates the rewards that the audience will obtain by accepting the proposal of the speaker. If the speech is effective, by its conclusion the audience should be thoroughly enthralled by the expansive vision of a positive future the speaker has outlined.

Unique Qualities of a Speech That Persuades the Audience to Not Change

Another kind of persuasive speech is one in which the speaker attempts to persuade the audience to not change something. Like the speech in support of change, the speech against change has three classic components. First, the speaker argues that things are fine as they are. Second, the speaker argues against any proposals for change that have been made. Third, the speaker describes the negative consequences for the audience if changes are made. As with the speech in support of change, the speech against change begins by setting the general scene and only gradually works its way around to addressing the individual concerns of the audience members. In this way, the last impression the audience receives is that of the effects of change or stasis on their own lives.

Rhetorical Criticism

When speech communication theorists describe the process of breaking down and considering communication events, they often used the phrase "rhetorical criticism." This simply means the critical analysis of rhetoric, or spoken words. Rhetoric often refers specifically to persuasive messages delivered verbally or in writing, as in a political speech or an academic essay. The purpose of rhetorical criticism is to improve understanding of the strategies used by speakers. When speakers develop a greater understanding of rhetorical strategy, they can refine and improve their messages, and the audience can develop a healthy degree of skepticism. In other words, rhetorical criticism can help us to become better producers and consumers of communication.

Criticism Can Be Used to Advance a Cause

Individuals frequently use rhetorical criticism to promote a particular cause they are interested in. In a democracy, making change depends on rallying the support of the public, and this in turn depends on crafting an effective message. When a group of people wants to promote a particular social or political issue, they need to develop a communication strategy that will positively influence the opinion of the general public. Advocacy groups use mailings, television ads, print ads, and speeches to deliver their message to the general public. Individuals can advocate for a cause through letters to the editor, informal speeches, and just by talking with friends. For all of these channels, a careful study of rhetorical strategy will be advantageous.

Criticism Can Solve Problems in Society

Many people use rhetorical criticism as a means to solving problems. In particular, rhetorical criticism can be applied to various arguments, philosophies, and even societal problems. This is especially true in a democracy, where public debate generates most of the changes in laws and social conditions. To the degree that individuals with solutions can effectively communicate their message to the general public, they will be able to persuade citizens to give their votes and support to these solutions. Without effective communication, even the most logical solutions may not achieve the critical mass of public support required to be enacted. In a similar way, politicians are constantly self-critiquing and refining their communication techniques to increase their political capital.

Criticism Can Lead to Greater Knowledge

Rhetorical criticism is able to improve our general understanding of the ways human beings communicate with one another. Most universities have several professors whose job it is to theorize and teach rhetorical criticism. The academic study of rhetoric focuses on the ways that human speech drives social change, unifies groups of people, explains societal problems, and motivates social change. In particular, the study of rhetorical criticism focuses on the ways in which human speech develops and maintains individual and collective identity. Finally, rhetorical criticism takes a close look at persuasion, specifically the way in which language can motivate action in the real world.

Public Speaking

Speech communication instructors often refer to public speaking as a "transaction" to indicate the important active roles of both the speaker and audience. Too often, people consider speech-giving as a process in which one person actively provides information while another group of people passively receives information.

Instead, the ideal public speaking relationship is one in which the speaker presents a message and the audience presents feedback. Even when the audience is not given an opportunity to speak, they provide feedback in the form of attention or inattention. By referring to public speaking as a transaction, instructors emphasize the roles and responsibilities of both speaker and audience. In general, speech communication instructors would define a **transaction** as any communication in which information passes from speaker to listener and vice versa.

Purpose of Studying Public Speaking

There are a number of reasons for studying public speaking, but the most commonly cited are social, intellectual, and consumer motives. People need to learn to speak in public in order to function in society and to manage relationships, administrate social events, and minimize conflict. Intellectually, a study of public speaking gives insight into human thought, ethics, and persuasion. Public speeches can generate emotions and ideas in listeners as well as influence their existing thoughts and feelings. It is also important to study public speaking not only to improve one's own speaking skills, but to improve one's ability to analyze and interpret the speeches of others. Students need to be able to understand the forum of public expression, the rhetorical vocabulary, and the various methods of thinking critically about speech.

Basic Methods for Studying Public Speaking

An effective speech communication teacher will incorporate different pedagogical modalities into his or her instruction so that students receive exposure to a wide range of different methods. Students should practice giving different kinds of speeches in both formal and informal settings. Some of the different types of speeches include technical lectures, extemporaneous speeches, and entertaining monologues. Students should get some practice interpreting and analyzing different kinds of public speech, such as advertisements, political speeches, public service announcements, editorials, or other forms. It is also valuable for students to become familiar with acclaimed historical speeches.

Goals of Public Speaking

For most people, the obvious goals of public speaking are political victories and support for social movements. Both are common motives of public speech, but they are not the only recognized intention of public communication. Public speech is often used to define an individual or a community. For instance, people may use speeches to describe particular attributes of themselves or of the group to which they belong. People also use speeches simply to disseminate information. Speeches can be used to inspire other people to action. Famous addresses like the "I Have a Dream" speech of Martin Luther King, Jr. exemplify this kind of speech. Finally, public speaking can be used to introduce arguments and to debate controversial questions in a community. The presidential debates before the general election are a good example of this.

Speeches

Purpose of an Informative Speech

When one is delivering an **informative speech**, his or her primary goal is to instruct the audience on a particular subject. If the speech is effective, the audience members will leave with more knowledge and understanding. College lectures are great examples of informative speeches. Although informative speeches may be entertaining, the humor or "color" of the speech should not distract from the overall intention, which is to disseminate information. Informative speeches often contain specific statistical data and an organized set of arguments and supporting evidence. Many informative speeches contain mention of counter-arguments, including rebuttals.

Impromptu Speech

An impromptu speech is one delivered "off-the-cuff"; that is, one delivered with a minimum amount of preparation and in an informal style. Not everyone is capable of delivering an effective impromptu speech. Most people can give a successful **impromptu speech** only if the topic is one on which they have discoursed before or if they are extremely familiar with their topic. Of course, we all make impromptu speeches as a matter of course in our daily lives. Every time you are asked to give your opinion on a subject or to explain an idea, you are in effect making an impromptu speech. By studying speech communication, however, people can learn the elements of effective impromptu speeches and improve their ability to deliver them.

Extemporaneous Speech

An extemporaneous speech combines elements of preparation and improvisation. When one is delivering an **extemporaneous speech**, he or she is drawing on prepared research but not reading directly from a sheet of paper nor reciting the speech from memory. An extemporaneous speech is more conversational and informal than a written speech and is therefore more appropriate for casual gatherings. The colloquial and informal nature of an extemporaneous speech can be extremely helpful in cultivating a good rapport between speaker and audience. To deliver an effective extemporaneous speech, however, the speaker must be extremely familiar with his or her source material.

Eulogy

A **eulogy** is a speech that praises a particular individual and highlights his or her best qualities. Eulogies are often given at funerals as the speaker remembers the deceased in a positive light. Eulogies are not the appropriate form for criticism or objective analysis of a person's life. On the other hand, a eulogy may fail if the audience finds it so excessively laudatory that it is not believable. In some cases, a eulogy of sorts may be given in praise of a particular event, community, or culture. Typically, a eulogy is delivered to an audience that is already disposed to think favorably of the subject. The speaker is typically someone who has extensive personal experience with the subject of the eulogy.

Introductory Speech

It is common for a **speech of introduction** to precede a keynote speech, a presentation, or a public performance of some kind. For instance, a symphony director will often give a brief speech of introduction before a concert. The best introductory speeches do not simply list the achievements or characteristics of the person or event that is to follow. Rather, they engage the interest of the audience and whet their appetite for what is to come. A good speech of introduction should not include any criticism of what is to follow. It is always a good rule of thumb for the introductory speaker to confer with those who are to follow so that his or her message can be as appropriate as possible.

Welcoming Speech

A welcoming speech is often given at the beginning of a convention, meeting, or special event of some kind. Typically, the welcome will be delivered by a representative of the group or organization putting on the event. For instance, the chairman of a professional organization administering a business convention might deliver a speech of welcome to convention attendees. **Welcoming speeches** are typically light on substance and primarily provide an overview of the events to follow. Also, a welcoming speech typically includes a message of thanks to the organizers and administrators of the event. The speaker often indicates his or her personal goals for the event and may tell the audience how to make their questions and comments known to the event administrators.

Memorizing and Reading a Speech

When delivering a speech, the speaker may need to decide whether to memorize or read the text. There are advantages to each approach. When a speech is memorized, the speaker can make eye contact with the audience and use his or her hands to make illustrative gestures. Memorized speeches run the risk of sounding overly rehearsed, however, and the speaker may falter if he or she loses track of the speech. Some speakers prefer to read their speeches, often because they prefer to have a copy of the speech for reference. If the speaker plans to read his or her speech, he or she should become extremely familiar with the speech so it is not necessary to read every word from the paper. Regardless of whether a speech is memorized or read, the speaker should practice delivery to increase fluency.

Purpose of a Persuasive Speech

Persuasive speeches are designed to change the minds of the audience or motivate the audience to action. The precise goals of a persuasive speech are dependent on the particular cause promoted by the speaker. Moreover, the methods employed in a **persuasive speech** will depend on the subject matter and the speaker's rhetorical style. Some speakers employ a dry, data-driven style when making a persuasive speech. They hope to overwhelm their audience with the strength and breadth of information. Other speakers seek to beguile their audience by amusing and entertaining them. This kind of speech is appropriate for general audiences and non-technical subjects. When a persuasive speech is being delivered to an audience of experts, or is centered on a complex issue, it must include cogent reasoning and supportive data.

Purpose of an Entertaining Speech

The only goal of some speeches is to entertain and amuse the audience. Standup comedy is a type of **entertaining speech**. Many speeches that also contain information or persuasive content are primarily entertaining. The keynote speakers at conferences and conventions often cloak their arguments in witty anecdotes and jokes. Obviously, serious subjects are not appropriate content for entertaining speeches. However, many speakers will introduce some elements of an entertaining speech to first capture the attention of the audience and then persuade them to engage seriously with the weightier elements of the speech.

Importance of Having Specific Purposes for a Speech

The first step in preparing a speech is knowing the specific purpose of that speech. This enables the speaker to focus on what is important and to research efficiently for relevant material. The specific purpose of a speech might be informing the audience on a particular point, changing a few minds on a particular subject, raising some money, or simply entertaining the audience. It is a good idea to make the specific purpose of the speech explicit in the speech. Although you do not want to beat your audience over the head with your intentions, there should be no question as to what the speech is meant to accomplish. In general, the specific purpose of a speech is defined in terms of the desired reaction from the audience.

Elements of a Presentation

Over the last few years, the presentation has emerged as the most common speech form in the United States. Members of the business community frequently give presentations, but this form is also common to academic lectures, community discussions, and religious gatherings. One of the defining characteristics of a **presentation** is that it includes some form of media beyond simply a speaker. It is common for a speaker to include slide shows, photographs, brochures and handouts, short videos, and audio samples in a presentation. Because presentations are often designed to be given over and over again to different audiences, they may be complex, detailed, and highly coordinated.

Basic Presentation Aid

One of the defining characteristics of a presentation is the use of **presentation aids**. These aids can include supplementary audio or visual materials that elaborate or reinforce their presentation points. Currently, the most popular presentation aids are slide show presentations, a software program that allows speakers to assemble a collection of slides to accompany their speech. Speakers also frequently include video samples in their presentations. In business, tables and charts are frequently used to illustrate the points of a presentation. In the classroom, a teacher might use handouts or overhead projector transparencies as presentation aids. Basically, any media used by the speaker to supplement his or her spoken message is considered a presentation aid.

Increasing Importance of the Presentation in the United States

Most speech communication experts believe that presentations will increasingly become the most popular form of public communication. This is largely because the citizenry of the United States has been raised on television and radio commercials, and they are very familiar with multimedia presentations. For many people, a simple speech is boring. Presentation aids such as audio and video are often necessary to hold the interest of modern-day audiences. In the future, the most successful persuasive speakers will undoubtedly be those who can apply the traditional elements of direction and suggestion to a presentation containing enough multimedia to engage the interest of the audience.

PREMISE OF AUDIENCE ANALYSIS

In the study of speech communication, **audience analysis** is simply the practice of examining the characteristics and background of the audience in order to tailor a speech appropriately. For instance, one would want to know the general age, socioeconomic status, culture, and gender of the audience while preparing a speech. The type of speech appropriate to a group of elementary schoolgirls will be quite different from that appropriate to a group of older men, even if both speeches are on the same subject. The prejudices and pre-existing opinions of these two groups will be extremely different and thus, a speaker must tailor and deliver his or her message to each group in very different ways to be effective.

PRIMARY FACTORS OF AUDIENCE ANALYSIS

When a seasoned public speaker conducts an audience analysis, he or she focuses on a few specific characteristics of the audience. For one thing, the speaker wants to know the audience's background as it relates to him or her and the subject matter of the speech. Although much of audience analysis consists of determining the approximate ages and socioeconomic backgrounds of the audience, this is primarily because such information enables the speaker to estimate the audience's opinions and degree of familiarity with the subject matter and speaker. A speaker who is well-liked by the audience can employ a different rhetorical strategy than one with whom most of the audience disagrees.

IMPORTANCE OF REMEMBERING THE AUDIENCE'S CAPACITY TO ACT

When developing a speech, one should always remember the characteristics and capabilities of the audience. This is especially important when producing a persuasive speech. It does not make sense to encourage the audience to take an action they are not capable of taking. For instance, a politician would be foolish to make an impassioned plea for votes to a bunch of elementary school students, all of whom are years away from voter eligibility. When developing a persuasive speech, then, it is essential to remember the capacity of the audience to act.

AUDIENCE ATTITUDE

It is important for a speaker to gauge the attitude of the audience before delivering his or her speech. **Attitude**, because it is more subtle than age, ethnicity, or belief system, can only be determined through direct observation. Thus, if a speaker is able to observe the audience before delivering the speech, he or she can benefit greatly. Observing the audience beforehand can provide clues to what kind of general mood the audience is in, whether good or bad. If the audience is in a hostile mood, the speaker may want to avoid trying to joke with them. An audience that seems jovial and engaged, on the other hand, should not be alienated with strident rhetoric or harsh words. The job of the speaker is to establish and maintain a good rapport with the audience.

BELIEFS

To accurately assess what an audience might be thinking, one must understand that audience's core beliefs. Strictly defined, **beliefs** are the facts, ideas, and opinions that the audience holds to be true. Objectively, some of these beliefs may actually be untrue. However, to deliver an effective message, a speaker must take into account the sum total of the audience's beliefs. If the purpose of the speech is to adjust the beliefs of the audience, the speaker must appeal to either the reasoning skills or the emotions of his or her listeners.

FACTS AND OPINIONS

When considering the convictions of an audience, it is good to distinguish between facts and opinions. **Facts** are those convictions that can be proven in an objective sense. Scientific assertions, for instance, are considered facts. **Opinions**, on the other hand, cannot necessarily be supported by hard data. People often hold opinions for rather arbitrary individual reasons, such as those based on personal experience. The fact that communities hold collective opinions must also be considered when making a speech. In general, it is easier for a speaker to adjust beliefs or convictions based on opinion than those based on fact.

Fixed and Variable Beliefs

When describing the beliefs of an audience, speech communication instructors often distinguish between fixed and variable beliefs. The primary difference between the two is that **fixed beliefs** are harder to change. Typically, fixed beliefs have been held throughout an individual's life and most likely reinforced by his or her experience. **Variable beliefs**, on the other hand, may have been recently acquired and therefore may be less established in the individual's mind. A speaker is more likely to change variable beliefs and should therefore focus his or her attention on these. Variable beliefs are especially vulnerable to change when they are based on opinion rather than fact.

Fundamentals of Preparing a Speech

To successfully prepare a speech it is best to follow a basic set of established steps. By following these steps, the speaker or speechwriter can more efficiently develop an organized and effective presentation. The first step in preparing a speech is to select a subject, if the topic has not been predetermined. Next, the speaker should articulate to himself or herself the key ideas and arguments to be included in the speech. As he or she begins to formulate these ideas and arguments, it is important to take into account the characteristics of the intended audience. At this point, the speaker should begin gathering materials for the speech, whether through research or brainstorming. The next step is to outline the speech, and finally, write a draft of the speech. It is always a good idea to practice delivering the speech and to make revisions or adjustments where necessary.

Select a Subject for a Speech

Perhaps the most important component of an effective speech is an appropriate and interesting subject. When selecting a subject for a speech, one should look for a topic that is engaging to a general audience. While it is important for the speaker to have some familiarity with the subject, it is not necessarily a good idea to speak about a subject on which he or she is an expert. Too often, an expert delivering a speech to a general audience dwells too much in details and specificities, which has a tendency to bore the audience. It is a good idea for the speaker to have a passing familiarity with the subject, so that he or she will be able to find good research materials and judge what will be interesting to a general audience. However, the speaker should also make sure to emphasize the aspects of the subject that are relevant to the lives of the audience members.

Creativity Can Be Used to Select a Speech Topic

Sometimes it can be difficult to come up with a topic for a speech. All the "good topics" may seem to have already been covered, or there may be no one single subject on which a potential speaker has enough information to be effective. Effective speakers develop creative ways to come up with new speech topics. Being creative, however, does not mean sitting back and waiting for inspiration to strike. Creative speakers work proactively to develop new topics. They list their areas of interest and are constantly considering everything they see and read in terms of how it could be developed into a speech. Most creative speakers discard more ideas for speeches than they ever use.

Creative Analysis of a Speech Topic

After a speaker has decided upon a topic for a speech, the next move is to conduct a creative analysis of that topic—simply a detailed exploration of the topic. To begin with, the speaker assembles as much information as he or she can within the amount of time available. This may include interviews, books, and old periodicals. Experienced speakers will have a good working knowledge of the public or school library and will be able to acquire diverse basic materials in a short period of time. After all this information has been assembled, the speaker will sort through it, looking perhaps for an entry point for his exploration. An interesting narrative, a point of local interest, or a previously overlooked angle on the subject may all be ways for the speaker to engage the interest of the audience on a given subject.

Preparation Phase

During the **preparation phase** of speech composition, a speaker will begin to organize his or her research material. Once the speaker has decided upon the basic angle and structure of the speech, he or she may need to acquire more research materials for elaboration and support. Of course, it may take the speaker a while to find the appropriate flow of ideas. Speakers should not be discouraged by numerous blind alleys or false starts during the preparation phase. Even when it seems that progress is not being made, the speaker should remember that each false start eliminates a possible point of entry, bringing the ultimate goal closer.

Incubation Phase

During the **incubation phase** of creative speech analysis, the speaker actually does not engage in any direct work on the speech. Instead, the speaker allows his or her subconscious to mull over the content of the speech. Even though it seems like no work is being done during this period, the incubation phase is actually very important, as it is during this period that the most creative thinking on the subject occurs. Also, the incubation phase gives the speaker a chance to freely imagine the speech, associate various ideas, and try unique combinations. Many speakers say their most unique and powerful ideas often occur to them when they are doing something totally different than speech preparation.

Illumination Phase

After the incubation phase, the speaker should have a solid structure as well as a number of creative ideas for the speech. In the succeeding **illumination phase**, he or she will apply the ideas gained during the incubation phase to the basic outline constructed during the preparation phase. It is very common for a speaker to feel a burst of enthusiasm during the illumination phase, as he or she discovers the unique ways in which his or her original ideas will elaborate and improve upon the original structure. The illumination phase is still basically a brainstorming phase. Speakers are still experimenting with new ideas and combinations of materials.

Verification Phase

The fourth and final part of the creative analysis of a speech topic is the **verification phase**. During this phase, the speaker looks over his or her notes carefully. Occasionally, some of the ideas that seemed so brilliant during the incubation and illumination phases turn out to be inappropriate or implausible. Other times, a careful examination of the speech will uncover holes in the reasoning of the argument or reveal the necessity of adding or removing a particular part of the speech. The verification phase of creative speech analysis can be seen as a final polishing of the materials gathered and organized during the first three phases.

Necessity of Managing Creativity During the Development of a Speech

For the process of creative speech analysis to be effective, a certain amount of discipline needs to be brought to bear on the creative instinct. This is one reason why the process of creative speech analysis includes four distinct phases. By adhering to a set procedural pattern, the speaker will limit the amount of time spent in any one area and will move along toward completion at a predictable pace. Also, by following an organized analysis process, it is easier to avoid the procrastination that commonly occurs during the creative process. As much as possible, a speaker should try to work at specific times without interruption to allow the creative subconscious to do its work.

Basic Message Units in a Speech

In every speech, the content is divided into what are called **basic message units**. A basic message unit has two parts: the point the speaker is trying to make and the evidence or supporting material he or she has assembled. In order to be complete, a message unit needs to have both components. Otherwise, the speaker will be making points without offering any reasoning or evidence, or he will be giving factual information and argumentation without connecting the dots to make a larger point. The point stated by the speaker needs to be a complete and discrete thought. The supporting material must be pertinent and sufficient to convince a reasonable person.

Value of Making a Logical Analysis of a Speech Topic

A speaker should always perform what is known as a logical analysis before presenting his or her speech. This is simply an analysis of the message units that make up the speech, as well as the connections between these message units. To be effective, the logic of any speech must progress in a systematic and discernible manner and should include ample evidence and supporting materials. Speakers often create a brief outline for their speech, in which they sketch the basic structure of the speech's logic, leaving out the supplementary material. In any case, it is essential to make sure the logical skeleton of a speech is sturdy before focusing on other aspects.

Assess the Logic of a Speech Topic

As the speaker reviews his prepared speech and performs a logical analysis, he needs to be constantly asking himself whether each point and piece of supporting material is essential. Everything included in the speech should be there for a clear and explicit reason or else it must be considered superfluous. The speaker must also determine whether all of the evidence clearly and directly supports the points it is intended to support. Finally, the speaker must make sure every point in the speech follows a proper order, progressing logically to the speech's climax and ultimate conclusion.

Errors of Reasoning

Faulty Attribution of Causation

One of the most common errors of logic one can make in a speech is the **faulty attribution of causation**. This occurs when the speaker erroneously assumes that just because one thing followed another, the second thing was caused by the first. For instance, I may grab my umbrella on the way out the door before it starts raining, yet once it starts raining I cannot claim that bringing my umbrella caused the rain. If a speaker describes a major historical or social event and suggests such an event had only one cause, they are likely committing faulty attribution of causation. Major social and historical movements are simply too complex to be attributed to a single cause. At the very least, a speaker must provide detailed substantiation for any assertions of causation.

Circular Reasoning

A common logical error in speeches is **circular reasoning**. A chain of logic is described as circular when the assumptions made at the beginning of the argument depend on the conclusion of the argument being true. For instance, imagine a speaker declaring that the Tigers baseball team will certainly lose their playoff series. As evidence for this claim, the speaker declares that the Tigers always lose their playoff series. This reasoning clearly does not hold up. In order to believe the Tigers will lose their playoff series, we have to assume they always lose their playoff series, which we do not really know yet, and which depends on their performance in the upcoming playoffs series. In other words, the claims made by the speaker depend on the speaker's assumptions.

Contradictory Argument

Occasionally, a speaker will fall victim to the logical error known as the **contradictory argument**. A contradictory argument is one in which the speaker introduces information that directly contradicts his main argument. For the most part, this error should be easy to avoid. After all, a speaker will be careful not to include information that undermines his main point. Speakers do, however, sometimes include inconsistent arguments in a speech, and this can be highly detrimental to their purpose. Contradictory argument is especially problematic in a persuasive speech, in which the speaker is attempting to persuade the audience from their pre-existing opinions and hoping to sell them on the merits of an alternative view.

Use of Expository Supporting Material

Most speeches include expository supporting material. The word *expository* comes from the same root as *expose* and refers to information that sheds light on areas about which the audience may know little. Some of the common forms of expository information are examples, analogies, and narratives. **Expository supporting**

material is distinguished from argumentative supporting material in that it strives to remain as objective as possible When a speaker claims to be providing objective and impartial information, he or she will be held to that standard by the audience. For this reason, it is especially important for speakers who use expository supporting material to verify their sources.

Use of Examples, Both Real and Hypothetical

Successful speakers are likely to use both real and hypothetical examples in the course of a speech. Real examples are appropriate in speeches describing a particular historical or social topic that is grounded in reality. For instance, it would not be appropriate to use a hypothetical example in an argument about the Revolutionary War since there are plenty of real examples to illustrate points regarding that conflict. In more general speeches, however, it may be necessary to use a hypothetical situation as an example. When describing the possible results of some decision, for instance, a speaker might invoke the case of some hypothetical person as a means of dramatizing his or her argument. In general, real examples are treated with more respect by an audience and should be used whenever possible.

How a Good Speaker uses Examples

A good speaker knows that examples can be effective because they provide concrete case studies through which the audience can assess the arguments of the speech. Examples are also good for humanizing an abstract speech. For instance, an audience may have a hard time listening to a speech about water conservation, but if the speaker introduces examples of how drought can affect individual people, they will be more likely to stay engaged. A good speaker includes examples that are appropriate and interesting, but which do not distract from his or her main points. Also, examples should not dominate a speech; they should simply add interest to the body of the speaker's message.

Analogies in a Speech

An effective speaker will often elaborate and clarify his or her ideas with analogies. An **analogy** is simply an extended comparison between two things. For instance, a speech on economics might describe a current downturn in the economy as it relates to the Great Depression. In other words, the speaker is drawing an analogy between a current problem and a known historical event. The important thing to remember about an analogy is that the two things being compared will probably not be identical in all respects. The speaker should take care to indicate this and should not make claims that suggest the analogy is perfect. On the other hand, an effective analogy can be a useful predictive tool and can give the audience a way of engaging with the subject.

Narratives in a Speech

Speakers often incorporate narratives into their speeches as a way of engaging interest and indirectly making a point. A **narrative** is simply a story. Narratives can be either fiction or nonfiction. As with examples, narratives tend to have more impact on an audience when they are true. However, an artfully told fictitious narrative can also captivate an audience. Recent scientific research suggests that audience members are mentally programmed to pay attention to information when it is presented as a story. That is, the human mind is naturally receptive to a narrative. Good speakers take advantage of this tendency by delivering information in the context of a narrative.

Statistics in a Speech

Speakers often use **statistics** to provide numerical evidence for their assertions. Basically, a loose definition of statistics is any information that contains numbers. To be effective, statistics must be clear and accurate. Statistics can have a great deal of sway over an audience, since they carry with them the impression of objectivity and mathematical truth. That being said, audience members should keep in mind that statistics are often highly subjective. For instance, by manipulating sample size, information taken into consideration, and scope of a statistical survey, a speaker can present information to support his point no matter how incorrect it is. Audience members should always be wary of statistics and should press the speaker to provide more information on the origin and methodology behind any statistics he or she uses.

Numbers in a Speech

There are a few different ways to use numbers in a speech. One way is to use numbers as markers of evaluation. When we say a person weighs 120 pounds, for instance, we are using numbers to evaluate their weight. In a similar way, numbers can be used as a basis for comparison. By comparing the prices of two dishwashers, for instance, we obtain an important piece of information we can use in making a consumer decision. Numbers can also be used to make illustrative points. For instance, speakers often cite various statistics in support of an argument. It is important to emphasize that, although numbers suggest impartiality, they are calculated by human beings, who are highly subjective and whose intentions should be rigorously questioned.

Eyewitness Testimony in a Speech

Many speakers incorporate eyewitness testimony into their speeches to great effect. Of course, this kind of supporting material is only appropriate for certain kinds of speeches. For instance, when delivering a speech about the Battle of the Bulge, it might be very useful to quote some soldiers who fought in the battle. On the other hand, eyewitness testimony seems less appropriate to a speech about climate change, which is so widespread that no one person could view its entire effect globally. When using **eyewitness testimony**, it is important to establish the credentials of the person being quoted. Also, a speaker should take care to indicate the particular vantage point of the eyewitness, so the audience can consider his or her testimony in light of that point of view.

Expert Testimony in a Speech

Whenever possible, speakers attempt to incorporate **expert testimony** into their speeches. Any time a speaker can quote a well-known authority who agrees with his or her point of view, he or she will be eager to do so. Most members of an audience will probably feel relatively uninformed compared to the speaker and will be ready to listen to anyone who may be considered an expert. Of course, testimony is only expert and appropriate when it comes from an expert in that particular field. For example, most people would be less inclined to take seriously the political views of an expert in basketball than they would if those views came from a respected public servant. Nevertheless, an audience should remain skeptical about persuasive arguments, even when they are made by experts. The standards of logic required of experts apply to everyone else as well.

Ethics in Public Speaking

To be effective as a public speaker, one needs to maintain a high degree of ethics. This is true not only because of the inherent virtues of ethical behavior, but also because an audience will not trust a speaker whom they believe to be unethical. To promote good ethics as a public speaker, one should always be as honest as possible. One should also try to promote the interests of the audience whenever appropriate. It is important and ethical to give members of the audience responsibility for making up their own minds, rather than attempting to browbeat them into submission with one's argument.

Title of the Speech

It is very important to settle on a clear and appropriate title for a speech early on in the preparation process. The title should make explicit the central idea or concept to be discussed in the speech. The title should also indicate the intention of the speech. For instance, if the intent of the speech is to inform the audience about a particular subject, the title should clearly state the name of the subject. If the intention of the speech is to persuade the audience, the title should indicate the main arguments to be made by the speech. To be effective, a title should be succinct, clear, and, if possible, engaging.

Difference Between Immediate Aim and Ultimate Aim When Making a Speech

On occasion, a speaker will have a slightly different purpose for giving a speech than is apparent from the speech itself. In the field of speech communication, this is known as the distinction between **immediate aim** and **ultimate aim**. An example would be a particular speech intended to be a small part of achieving a long-term goal. A prominent businessman, for example, might make a speech about ethics in public policy. Whereas on its face the speech might seem to be a simple address about local community issues, it might be also be part of the businessman's plan to develop his reputation in advance of a political campaign. The immediate aim of the speech in this instance is to inform, while the ultimate aim is to advance the political ambitions of the speaker.

Location Should Dictate the Characteristics of the Speech

When preparing a speech, one should always keep in mind the occasion for which the speech is intended, as this will help determine what kind of speech is appropriate. Individuals who have gathered together for a summer picnic, for instance, will not be interested in hearing a long and complicated speech. A short, humorous address would be more appropriate for this setting. A convention of professors, on the other hand, will be receptive to a more substantive speech that might also include relevant technical information. On rare occasions, a speaker may decide it is necessary to deliver a speech not entirely appropriate for the setting; however, this should only be done when it is absolutely necessary.

Time Limits Influence the Preparation of the Speech

When preparing a speech, one must be aware of exactly how much time is available for presenting the material. The time limit will greatly influence the content of the speech. It is rarely possible, for instance, to effectively discuss a complicated subject in a short period of time. Nor will it be possible to hold an audience's interest over a long period of time without having a wealth of information and ideas. Giving an effective persuasive speech in particular requires sufficient time. This is especially true when one is trying to convert an audience's opinion on a subject with which they are unfamiliar or on which they already have firm opinions. Generally, it takes a strong argument, elaborated through a number of points, to alter an opinion already agreed upon by most members of the audience.

Elements of Setting a Speaker Should Consider When Preparing a Speech

When preparing a speech, a speaker should take into account any idiosyncrasies of the speech format or setting. For instance, in some situations a speaker will have specific guidelines and rules for his or her speech. When giving an address to the members of a particular religious or cultural group, for instance, one might need to abide by specific rules. Another thing to consider is the placement of the speech in the overall event. For instance, if other speeches are to follow, one might want to make sure there will be no overlap in speech content. Also, if the speech is to be given directly after a dinner, one should be aware that audience members will be less likely to pay close attention to the details of the speech. Finally, a good speaker will be aware in advance what the physical setting for the speech will be. That is, he or she will know beforehand such details as whether or not the speech is to be given standing or sitting and whether a podium will be available.

Research Required Preparing for a Speech

To adequately prepare for delivering a speech, one needs to assemble all pertinent information and create a complete outline. One of the reasons why it is a good idea to select a familiar topic for one's speech is that less research will be required. At the very least, one should know where to look to find the information necessary to deliver an informative and comprehensive speech. Speakers may need to consult with experts in their given subject or peruse newspapers, magazines, and books for extra information. Many local and school libraries have extensive databases for performing research, and a thorough internet search can often provide vast amounts of helpful material.

Composing a Speech Outline

Creating a detailed, comprehensive outline is the first step before actually writing the first draft of a speech. After assembling all the necessary material and information for the speech, the speaker can then begin organizing the main points of the speech and the arguments and evidence supporting his or her ideas and claims. It is important that all secondary ideas and claims also support the speech's main idea or claim. One should always introduce the most important claim, or thesis, at the beginning of the speech. The speaker can then spend the rest of the speech building a case for this thesis and elaborating other related points. When composing an outline, remember that the finished speech will ideally be much more colorful and engaging. An outline is not meant to entertain, but rather to clearly and succinctly indicate the organization of the speech.

Practicing Speech Delivery

Excellent speech delivery does not just happen. It is the result of extensive practice. After the speaker has outlined and drafted the speech, he or she needs to practice delivering it. Practicing a speech serves a number of purposes. For one thing, the speaker might not detect weak points in the speech until he or she actually speaks the words aloud. In addition, it is helpful to record oneself practicing the speech and then play back the tape to identify weaknesses in the delivery. It is often a good idea to practice delivering a speech in front of friends or family and have them critique the performance. Perhaps the most important point is that practice delivering the speech allows the speaker to further familiarize him or herself with the material, thus increasing the level of comfort and fluency in delivery.

Methods for Cultivating Self-Confidence While Giving a Speech

Most people struggle with some degree of anxiety when they are required to speak in public. One of the best things a person can do to reduce speech anxiety is to present a confident image. Naturally, one should always practice delivering a speech several times beforehand. Through repetition, the speaker becomes familiar with the appropriate gestures and rhythms of the speech, which gives rise to increasing confidence in his or her ability to deliver. Another good way to build confidence is to make eye contact with the audience during speech delivery. A forthright, steady gaze from the speaker connotes a feeling of confidence. Finally, confidence can be communicated through posture and body language. Standing up straight and emphasizing key points with hand gestures is a great way to communicate self-confidence.

Essential Points of Speech Evaluation

There are a number of things to look for when evaluating the quality of a speech. All effective speeches share a few essential characteristics, such as a good introduction—one that engages the audience and introduces the main idea or argument of the speech. The introduction also establishes the tone of the rest of the speech. The body of the speech should include clear exposition of ideas and appropriate supporting material. The conclusion of the speech should reinforce the main idea or claim and solidify audience understanding. The presentation of the speech should be appropriate to the audience and setting and should be fluent in its delivery.

Basic Elements of Speechmaking

To master the speechmaking process, one should clearly understand a few basic elements. The **central figure** is the speaker, the one delivering the speech. The speaker brings a self-conception as well as a conception or impression of the audience's general identity. In the study of speechmaking, the audience is sometimes referred to as the **receiver**. Like the speaker, the audience members will have a self-image as well as an impression of the speaker. The setting in which the speech is delivered is known as the **situation**. The speaker uses various channels of communication, including words and gestures, to communicate his or her message. The audience members will deliver their responses to the speech both verbally and through body language. This response to the speech is called **feedback**.

The Message of a Speech

The message of a speech is communicated not only with the words being spoken but also through the speaker's self-presentation. In other words, the quality of the speaker's voice and his or her body language contribute to the message as well. The message of the speech is generally considered to have three basic components: structure, content, and presentation. The **structure** of the speech is the order in which information is delivered. To be effective, a speech must have a logical and coherent structure. The **content** of the speech is the information it contains. Even an entertaining or persuasive speech must have good content. Finally, the **presentation** of a speech is the style in which it is delivered to the audience. Different kinds of speeches require different presentation styles. The most important thing is to match the presentation to the intention of the speech.

Most Important Attributes of a Speaker

To be an effective speaker, one must have a clear intention, a good attitude, and extensive knowledge of the subject of the speech, as well as a degree of credibility with the audience. The speaker should fully understand the intention of the speech, even if that intention is not directly expressed in the speech. Sometimes a speaker will have a hidden motive or a long-term goal that cannot be expressed in the speech. To establish credibility, the speaker should possess a solid working knowledge of the subject of the speech. When the speaker is fluent in the subject he or she is discussing, the speech will flow more naturally and the speaker will be able to tailor his or her message to the audience's level of understanding. Referring to a speaker's "attitude" simply means his or her self-conception; that is, the image the speaker has of himself or herself. If a speaker has a positive self-image, he or she is more likely to deliver an effective speech.

Characteristics of the Speech Listener

The individual or groups of individuals who listen to a speech bring their own characteristics to bear on the quality of the speech. For one thing, listeners will always have their own intentions. That is, they will always be seeking to obtain something from the speech, whether it is information or entertainment. Listeners will also have varying degrees of skill, meaning that some groups will be better at understanding complex messages. Listeners will also bring their pre-existing attitudes toward the speaker and the speaker's subject. To deliver an effective message, a speaker needs to perform an audience analysis to determine the characteristics of his or her listeners.

Basic Kinds of Feedback

Feedback is the response of the audience to the message delivered by a speaker. Although feedback is typically thought of as verbal responses to the message, it also includes body language, attention or inattention, and participation in dialogue after the speech. To be effective, a speaker must be attuned to all these kinds of feedback. In other words, he or she must monitor the audience throughout the speech to identify signs of boredom or engagement. The feedback a speaker receives while delivering his speech is called **immediate feedback**. The feedback the speaker receives after delivering the speech is called **delayed feedback**. Delayed feedback usually takes the form of critical comments, praise, or questions. A practiced speaker will use feedback to improve subsequent speeches.

Importance of Selecting a Subject Appropriate to the Time Limits of the Speech

Many speakers handicap themselves from the start by selecting a subject that is either too expansive or too narrow for their needs. To be effective, a speech subject must be appropriate for the amount of time available for giving the speech. Obviously, a half-hour speech can go into much more detail and tackle a wider range of issues than can a five-minute speech. A very short speech should have only one main idea, whereas in a longer speech the speaker may have time to deliver several important points and give supporting information for each. Although the best way to determine the appropriate subject for the time limit is to gain experience as a public speaker, beginning speakers can nevertheless help themselves by considering the parameters of a speech as they begin to consider possible subjects.

Tailoring the Subject of a Speech So That It Is Appropriate to the Audience

When deciding on the subject of the speech, the speaker must take into account the characteristics and ability level of the audience. The speaker should be aware of the audience's expectations. That is, whether they expect to be informed, entertained, or persuaded. Audience members may be annoyed if a speech has a drastically different tone from the one they were expecting. For instance, an audience expecting a serious speech will be impatient with a speaker who spends a great deal of time trying to make them laugh. In some cases, it may be necessary to thwart the expectations of the audience, as for instance when a serious moral point must be made instead of providing sheer entertainment.

Qualifications of the Audience

When deciding upon the subject matter of a speech, the speaker should take into account the audience's general intelligence level and subject-related knowledge. A speech will be ineffective if it is either too elementary or too advanced for the audience. If the speaker is unfamiliar with the knowledge base of the proposed audience, he or she should take steps to determine this knowledge before preparing the speech. For an unschooled audience, it is a good idea to focus on the most basic and important principles of a given subject. For an audience of experts in a given field, however, it is important to provide information that will be stimulating and informative.

Defining the Purpose of the Speech

In preparation for making a speech, it is important to strictly define the purpose of the speech. Without a firm idea of the intention of the speech, it will be too easy for the content to miss the mark. To begin with, the speaker should consider his or her own intentions as well as the intentions of the audience. As much as possible, the intentions of the speaker and those of the audience should be made to overlap. One should define the central argument or idea to be expressed in the speech and take care that this argument or idea is consistent with the intention of the speech. It is also important that the title of the speech indicates the intention as well as the central theme of the speech.

Difference Between an Idea and a Claim in a Speech

The goal of a speech is to disseminate information or persuade the audience. In other words, a speaker will either deliver **ideas** or make **claims**. A speaker who is delivering ideas is expressing information and opinions for their own sake, and not necessarily trying to change the minds of the audience. Informative speeches are usually on subjects about which the audience is not expected to know very much. The purpose of such a speech is to increase the knowledge of the audience rather than to convert them to any particular viewpoint. When a speaker makes claims, on the other hand, he or she is introducing opinions that may or may not be held by the members of the audience. The intention of this type of speech will be to provide arguments and evidence to support the speaker's claims.

Process of Phrasing the Main Idea of the Speech

It is important when giving an informative speech to lay out the **main idea** in a manner comprehensible to the audience. The main idea of an informative speech should be presented near the beginning of the address and therefore should not require an audience to understand any concepts that will be explained later in the speech. The audience should be able to understand the gist of the main idea before the speaker goes on to elaborate. In the preparation of a speech, the speaker should define the main idea early on, so that he or she can procure evidence and supporting arguments appropriate to that main idea. Too often, speakers introduce evidence and arguments not directly supportive of the main idea of the speech. This causes confusion among the audience and waters down the effect of the speech.

Process of Phrasing the Main Claim in a Speech

When a speech is designed to present or advance a particular viewpoint, the speaker will need to pay special attention to the phrasing of the speech's main claim. The **main claim** should be phrased in such a way that it will be comprehensible to a general audience and will not offend casual listeners with a harsh or controversial tone. The degree of intensity appropriate to the claim will depend on the audience. A more strident tone can be used with an audience of like-minded individuals, whereas a diverse group of uncommitted listeners requires a more evenhanded tone. When constructing the main claim of a speech, the speaker should be sure to present only ideas that can be supported by available evidence and reasonable argument. If the main claim of a speech is far-fetched or unsupportable, even the more rational elements of the speech may be dismissed by a skeptical audience.

Fundamental Qualities of a Well-Organized Speech

All well-organized speeches have certain qualities in common. For instance, a well-organized speech is comprehensible, meaning it can be understood by all members of the audience. A well-organized speech also has a formal unity, which means all of its parts contribute to the main idea. A unified speech has no extraneous parts. A well-organized speech is also comprehensive—it covers all the issues an audience member would expect to be addressed by a speech on the given subject. Finally, a well-organized speech does not have any repetition. Every major point should be covered in its entirety, but no points need to be repeated once they have been clearly delivered.

Process of Speech Organization

The process of speech organization entails selecting the elements that will comprise the speech, placing them into a coherent order, and arranging the supporting material for each message unit. During the organization process, a speaker will often summarize each message unit in a simple sentence. This gives the speaker simple building blocks that can be easily rearranged. In general, a speech should include a coherent introduction, body, and conclusion. The introduction should engage the interest of the audience and summarize the main points to be made. The body should contain the central points of the speaker's argument, as well as the supporting evidence. The conclusion should summarize the argument and give the audience food for thought.

Outline for a Proof Speech

Speech communication instructors often refer to a proof speech. This is a common type of speech, in which the speaker introduces his or her argument and then attempts to prove it. **Proof speeches** follow a consistent pattern. In brief, a proof speech has four components: introduction, argument, development, and conclusion. A speech that follows this pattern allows the audience to become acquainted with the thrust of the speaker's arguments before substantiation is offered. The lengths of the various components of a proof speech will vary, depending on the speaker's interests and the knowledge level of the audience. For instance, an audience already familiar with the subject matter may not require as much supporting material to be convinced.

Impromptu Speech Pattern

Any relatively informal speech on a light subject can be referred to as an impromptu speech. An impromptu speech may be given on very short notice and will therefore give evidence of much less preparation. Even so, impromptu speeches tend to follow a similar pattern. There are four basic steps in a typical impromptu speech: an engaging introduction, a brief overview, elaboration, and summary. Notice that the four components of an impromptu speech directly parallel the components of a proof speech. The only real difference is that the delivery will be looser and the style of delivery will endeavor to be more entertaining. An impromptu speech often begins with a humorous or intriguing anecdote and often ends with a light touch as well.

Problem-Solving Pattern of Speech-Making

In a problem-solving speech, the speaker outlines a particular problem, attempts to diagnose the cause, and then suggests a potential solution. **Problem-solving speeches** are at their heart persuasive speeches, since they attempt to convince the audience of the merits of adopting a particular strategy to solve a given problem. To be effective, however, a problem-solving speech needs to follow a logical pattern. These speeches typically begin with an introduction and a definition of the problem in question. The speaker will then summarize the possible causes of the problem and discuss some of the possible solutions. Following this, the speaker will make a case for one of the solutions and provide supporting evidence and argumentation. Finally, the speaker will attempt to rebut some of the possible counterarguments to the proposed solution.

Appropriate Outline for a Call-to-Action Speech

When speech communication instructors describe a call-to-action speech, they are referring to a speech that intends to inspire the audience to follow some recommended course of action. A **call-to-action speech** has five typical components: engaging the audience, describing why the audience should want to change something, explaining the best way to change, describing the positive consequences of making the change, and directly indicating how change can be made. It is not really possible to rearrange the steps in a call-to-action speech. Unless the argument is delivered in this order, the speech will likely be ineffective. It is important to end by outlining the positive consequences of change and making an emotional plea, as this leaves the audience on a high note, which is most likely to translate into direct action.

Body Language in Public Speaking

Posture in Public Speaking

Many speakers fail to recognize the significance of proper posture in the delivery of a speech. As much as words or gestures, a speaker's posture transmits information about his or her attitude, credibility, and confidence. To present a message effectively, a speaker should stand up as straight and tall as possible. Slouching forward or bending over one's notes indicates a lack of interest and preparation. This kind of advice may seem trivial, but an audience will subconsciously pay closer attention to anyone whose posture indicates command and authority. Effective speakers pay close attention to their own posture and make sure that poor posture does not disrupt the transmission of their message.

Facial Expression in Public Speaking

The facial expressions made by a speaker can have a significant impact on the effectiveness of message delivery. The facial expressions of the speaker can either reinforce or contradict his or her words. If the words being spoken are amusing or colorful, it is appropriate for the speaker to be smiling and have a relaxed facial expression. If the speaker is addressing a serious subject while grinning, however, the audience will most likely discount what he or she is saying. A speaker needs to match his or her facial expressions to the subject matter and to the expectations of the audience. A large audience can expect the facial expressions of the speaker to be slightly exaggerated, while a small audience may be put off by what seems like a leering or grimacing speaker.

Eye Contact in Public Speaking

Speakers should never underestimate the importance of eye contact during message delivery. For one thing, it is very difficult for an audience member who is making eye contact with the speaker to lose interest. An effective speaker will often shift his or her gaze around the room, making eye contact with as many people as possible. Under no circumstances should a speaker look up in the air, stare at his or her notes, or fix his or her eyes on some point in the distance. At the same time, the speaker should not constantly move his or her eyes around the room, as this may be perceived as anxious behavior. Eye movements should be calm, regular, and smooth.

Gestures in Public Speaking

A public speaker should make sure that his or her gestures are in harmony with the subject matter of the speech and the expectations of the audience. Many people are in the habit of either moving their hands frequently during speech or keeping their hands stationary. Both of these approaches are only appropriate in certain circumstances. When delivering a speech to a large audience, or delivering a speech with a high emotional content, a speaker may be advised to incorporate wide, energetic gestures. These kinds of motions are not appropriate for a more somber subject, however. And although gestures can amplify the meaning of the speaker's words, they should never become a distraction from the message of the speech.

Proper Way to Use Notes During a Speech

Many speakers will require notes, but they should rely on these notes as little as possible during delivery of the speech. For one thing, notes tend to prevent a speaker from making effective eye contact and using his or her hands expressively while speaking. Also, speakers who become reliant on notes may not be able to orient themselves in a speech if something goes wrong with their notes. Notes should only be used as a reference point of last resort. They should be kept down in front of the speaker, preferably out of view of the audience. They should not be held and should be on as few pieces of paper as possible, to prevent excessive shuffling during a speech. Finally, a speaker who requires notes should carefully look them over before a speech to make sure they are understandable and arranged properly.

Skills Required for Making a Speech

To deliver a successful speech, an individual needs to have acquired certain skills. For one thing, the speaker must understand in depth the topic about which he or she is speaking. He or she must also be able to address the topic from a number of different points of view and to answer any questions the audience might have after the speech. More generally, a successful speaker must have an air of authority, so the audience will pay attention and trust his or her words. A speaker should also have what is known as rhetorical sensitivity, or the ability to adapt his or her message to different audiences. Successful speakers know that a given style of speaking may be very effective with one audience and ineffective with another. A successful speaker will be able to modulate his or her voice and gestures appropriately.

State Apprehension as a Component of Speech Anxiety

To some extent, everyone grapples with speech anxiety. The fear of embarrassment or public disclosure can be overcome only with significant practice at public speaking. There are a couple of different kinds of speech anxiety. **State apprehension** is defined as speech anxiety that is only felt in specific situations. For instance, an individual who is comfortable talking in class but becomes anxious when required to speak informally with peers is experiencing state apprehension. Many people experience state apprehension in relation to delivering formal speeches in front of a group. State apprehension has both physical and mental symptoms, including vocal tics, sweaty palms, and a trembling voice.

Trait Apprehension as a Component of Speech Anxiety

Some people experience speech anxiety to a greater degree than others. Those aspects of speech anxiety that are unique to an individual are known as **trait apprehensions**. For instance, someone might have an aversion to public speaking because of a past experience. People who have an unnaturally high level of trait apprehension tend to avoid situations in which they will be required to speak to a large group. The good news for these individuals is that trait apprehension can be overcome with experience. Unfortunately, however, this means practicing public speaking until it becomes natural.

Interpretation of Speech Anxiety

Speech anxiety is a common malady but not one that should cause a person to lose heart. Even the most successful speakers have a bit of anxiety when delivering a message. In a way, this anxiety is a positive thing, because it focuses the attention and encourages concentration. Speech anxiety is a natural response to confronting an uncertain and unfamiliar situation. Research suggests that those who suffer from severe speech anxiety are often the most effective public speakers. Also, most speakers report that the anxiety they feel before delivering a speech is much greater than the anxiety they feel when actually in the process of speaking.

Using Speech Anxiety Productively

The abundance of nervous energy felt before delivering a speech can be used to the speaker's advantage. For one thing, many people find that speech anxiety sharpens their senses and focuses their concentration on the task at hand. Human beings are naturally inclined to focus their attention when they perceive a threat. The good thing about speech anxiety is that the attention is sharpened even though the threat is not significant. Many accomplished speakers use speech anxiety to increase their level of excitement and dynamism while delivering a speech. Indeed, many speakers say that without speech anxiety, they would not be able to achieve the rhetorical effects that have made them successful speakers.

Four Basic Channels of Public Communication

Normally, speech delivery is considered a simple transmission of words by one person to a group. However, this is only one of the channels through which information is delivered during a speech. In the technical language of speech communication, the speaker's words are said to pass through the **verbal channel**. At the same time, the speaker's tone of voice indicates his or her attitude through the **aural channel**. Some speakers use visual aids, which transmit information through the **pictorial channel**. Finally, a speaker transmits information about his or her attitude and self-image through gestures and facial expressions. This transmission is said to pass through the **visual channel**.

Importance of Physical Setting in the Delivery of a Speech

The physical setting in which a speech is delivered exerts significant influence over the expectations of the audience and should therefore be taken into account by the speaker beforehand. For instance, an audience that is required to stand during a speech will have less patience for a long-winded and complex oration. On the other hand, if the audience is seated in soft, plush chairs, they may be too relaxed to pay attention to a serious lecture. When the subject of a speech requires a fair amount of technical detail, it is a good idea for the audience to be seated in upright chairs and for the room to have sufficient light. In any case, the speaker should consider how the physical setting will influence the mood of the audience and should adjust his or her speech accordingly.

How Social Context Can Influence the Delivery of a Speech

When speakers consider the characteristics of the environment in which they will deliver their speech, they sometimes neglect to consider the **social context**. The social context is the set of relationships between the members of the audience and the speaker and between the members of the audience themselves. The speaker should know beforehand how he or she stands in relation to the audience. For instance, a speaker may be recognized as an expert, an entertainer, or an intriguing fraud. Also, the speaker should understand how the members of the audience stand in relation to one another; they could be friends, colleagues, or strangers, for instance. The information gained by this consideration of social context should inform the construction and delivery of the speech.

How Communication Rules Can Influence the Delivery of a Speech

Sometimes a speech will be delivered in a particular environment or to a particular group that is governed by specific communication rules. For instance, a speech delivered in church is unlikely to be followed by a question-and-answer period. As another example, some debating societies have strict rules for the presentation and critique of a speech. In more informal situations, some groups will have different expectations for speaker behavior. For instance, a gathering of senior citizens is unlikely to respond well to coarse humor. In other words, communication rules may be explicit or implicit. While preparing a speech, the speaker needs to address the formal considerations that will influence his or her message.

Principles of Argumentation and Debate

Basics of a Formal Debate

A **debate** is simply an organized communication event in which two or more parties offer opposing views on the same subject. A debate is not a synonym for an argument. Debates are meant to be civil and constructive. A typical debate format has two sides: affirmative and negative. A statement known as a proposition is read and the affirmative side argues in favor of it. The negative side then argues against it. It should be noted that the hosting sides of the debate are not trying to persuade one another, but rather are trying to convince some third party, whether it is a judge or the audience. The terms of the debate are usually set ahead of time. These may include time limits and order of speaking.

Characteristics of a Good Proposition

In a debate, the statement to be discussed is called the **proposition**. Some propositions are better than others at inspiring good debate. A proposition that has an obvious answer, for instance, will not be very good for debate because one side of the argument will be much stronger than the other. A proposition should be limited to a reasonable scope of application, so that the debaters can focus on a few key issues. Also, the wording of the proposition should be simple and clear. The debate should be centered on the topic indicated by the proposition and not on the meaning of the words in the proposition.

Propositions in Formal Debate

In a formal debate, propositions begin with the words "resolved that" followed by the statement. There are three basic kinds of proposition: propositions of value, propositions of judgment, and propositions of policy.

A **proposition of value** makes a statement about the correctness or practical utility of something. For instance, a proposition of value might state that eliminating summer vacation in favor of year-round schooling is a good idea. The affirmative position will then argue in favor of this proposition and the negative position will argue against it. Propositions of value usually require statistical evidence to be supported or opposed effectively.

A **proposition of judgment** states that something is true or exists. For this reason, propositions of judgment are often referred to as propositions of fact. For instance, a proposition of judgment might state that men generally earn more money for the same labor than women earn. This is an unfortunate fact, and it will be up to the affirmative position to provide the argument proving it to be so.

A **proposition of policy** declares that a particular course of action should be taken. Propositions of policy usually include the words "ought" or "should." For instance, a proposition of policy might read: "resolved, that teachers should be required to eat lunch with their classes." Propositions of policy often make for the liveliest debate because there is no way of absolutely knowing whether a proposed policy will be effective.

Process of Finding a Debate Topic

The first step in the planning of a debate is to find an appropriate topic, or issue. The best issues are those that are controversial without being potentially offensive and which provide equal opportunity for both sides to make a convincing case. Of course, the responsibility of proving a proposition is borne by the affirmative side. Debate instructors have isolated three common issues in a policy proposition debate. First, the debaters will need to determine whether there is a pressing need for immediate change. They will also have to decide whether there is a plan that provides the appropriate change. Finally, the affirmative side will have to prove that the proposed plan is the best available plan. The negative side is not required to win all three of these issues, but the affirmative side is required to win all three in order to hold sway.

Defining Terms in a Debate

For a debate to be successful, any unclear or abstract terms must be defined at the appropriate time. Debates are not meant to be inquiries into the meaning of the words in the proposition. Rather, the propositions should be clear enough to be understood without a problem by both the affirmative and negative sides. If the proposition includes any troublesome language, it is usually the responsibility of the first speaker in the debate to define the terms. Since the affirmative speaker is the one who is responsible for proving his or her case, it makes sense for him or her to define the terms of the proposition.

Constructing Debate Cases

The process of constructing a debate case is very similar to constructing an outline for a speech. It is common for both sides in the debate to compose what is known as a debate brief, in which their case is outlined point by point. These debate briefs are prepared ahead of time; as the debate proceeds, each side will outline the argument made by the other side in what is known as a flow sheet. A debate brief usually begins with a thesis statement and, if necessary, definitions for any problematic terms in the proposition. It then goes on to list the major points to be made as well as rebuttals to potential counter-arguments made by the other side.

Finding Proof in a Debate

The ability of either side in a debate to claim victory will depend on each one's ability to produce adequate proof. In a debate, proof consists of two basic components: evidence and reasoning. **Evidence** is factual information. **Reasoning**, on the other hand, is the set of inferences or judgments drawn from evidence. To provide adequate proof, then, a debater will need to have both evidence and reasoning. The debater must also have this information organized so that he or she can use it to greatest effect during the course of the debate and so it can be produced in direct contrast to the argument made by the opposing side.

Evidence as It is Used in a Debate

In a debate, evidence is the factual information used to support an argument. To be successful, a debater must have substantial evidence to support his or her case. It is a good idea to record this information on paper before the beginning of the debate. The most important pieces of evidence should be used in the first speech made by each side, known as the **constructive speech**. As a debate progresses, minor pieces of evidence can be used in the various **rebuttal speeches**. Also, a debater should recognize which evidence is appropriate for supporting his or her main case and which evidence is better suited to rebut possible counterarguments by the opponent. Debaters should be able to identify the sources of their evidence.

Common Tests of Evidence for a Debate

During preparation for a debate, each side will gather as much evidence as possible to support their case. They will need to apply strict guidelines in their evidence-gathering in order to make sure they only select evidence that will stand up to their opponent's scrutiny. The four most important qualities of good evidence are relevance, consistency, timeliness, and the ability to be verified. A piece of evidence needs to pertain directly to the argument being made. It needs to hold up in a number of different conditions and be the same from different sources. It needs to have been produced recently enough to remain believable. Finally, it needs to be susceptible to verification so that the debate judge does not have to depend on the word of the debater.

Common Kinds of Evidence Used in a Debate

A few different kinds of evidence are commonly used in debates. Perhaps the most common form of evidence is documented statistics. Statistics can be obtained from a variety of books, trade journals, and other publications. Sometimes debaters will introduce the testimony or writings of acknowledged authorities on the subject. It is important to establish the credentials of the authority when this kind of evidence is used. Finally, debaters will often rely upon what they believe to be commonly accepted facts. These are matters of truth generally accepted by a reasonable audience and therefore do not need further support.

Inductive Reasoning in a Debate

Debaters frequently rely upon inductive reasoning in making their points. **Inductive reasoning** is the process of beginning with a group of specifics and gradually working toward a general idea. In other words, inductive reasoning begins by looking at the trees and eventually broadens the scope to take in the whole forest. For instance, someone debating from the affirmative view might begin by citing a number of statistics. He or she could then make a general point that is supported by all those statistics. Inductive reasoning is a good way to utilize pieces of evidence that can stand alone.

Deductive Reasoning in a Debate

In the process of **deductive reasoning**, a debater transitions from a general rule to a specific instance of the rule. The debater first offers what is known as a premise. For example, a premise might be "All teachers love summer vacation." The debater will then offer an example of this premise in what is known as the minor premise: "We are all teachers." The debater will then give the conclusion that stems from the information so far provided: "We love summer vacation." This process is known as a **logical syllogism**. For a syllogism to be logically correct, all of the premises must be true. This example of deductive reasoning, then, would be easy to argue against, since there are probably teachers who do not love summer vacation.

Refutation in a Debate

The negative side in the debate is primarily responsible for **refutation**, or the act of damaging the opponent's case. The process of refutation has a few general components. First, the argument to be refuted is defined. Next, the importance that this argument has to the opponent is emphasized. The debater then presents his or her counterargument, along with evidence in support of it. Finally, the debater summarizes his or her refutation and makes any necessary clarifications. Refutation does not necessarily need to constitute a direct attack on the opponent's position. Instead, it is possible to refute an opponent's argument by simply offering a stronger argument for one's own side.

Rebuttal in a Debate

The process of rebuttal is a formal element in a debate. A **rebuttal** gives the debater an opportunity to counter any refutation of his or her argument that has just been made by the opponent. During the rebuttal, the debater is allowed to introduce new evidence but may not make a new argument. To begin a rebuttal, the debater will restate the arguments that have been made so far. The debater will then restate the refutation offered by the other side. Then, the debater will attempt to demonstrate problems with the opponent's arguments. He or she will then give any additional information to strengthen his position and will conclude by summarizing his or her original argument.

Traditional Form of Debate

In a **traditional debate**, also known as a standard debate, there are two sides composed of two individuals. The affirmative side speaks first and the negative side speaks second. A traditional debate generally lasts for about an hour and begins with a ten-minute speech by the first affirmative speaker. This is followed by a five-minute rebuttal from the first negative speaker. The first negative speaker is then given ten minutes to make a constructive speech, followed by a five-minute rebuttal from the first affirmative speaker. This arrangement is then duplicated with the second members of each team.

Cross-Examination Form of Debate

In a **cross-examination debate**, the affirmative side and the negative side both have two members. Unlike in a traditional debate, where debaters are given lengthy amounts of time in which to make their cases and counter-arguments, a cross-examination debate encourages each side to directly question the other.

1. It begins with a constructive speech by the first affirmative speaker, followed by a few minutes in which the second negative speaker can question the first speaker.
2. The first negative speaker then makes a constructive speech, followed by a few minutes of questioning from the first affirmative speaker.
3. The second affirmative speaker then delivers a message, followed by questioning from the first negative speaker.
4. The second negative speaker delivers a message and is then questioned by the second affirmative speaker.
5. The first negative speaker issues a rebuttal speech, followed by a rebuttal speech from the first affirmative speaker.
6. Finally, the second negative speaker issues a rebuttal, concluding with a rebuttal from the second affirmative speaker.

Lincoln-Douglas Form of Debate

The common format for a two-person debate is typically referred to as a **Lincoln-Douglas debate**, in reference to the celebrated debates between Abraham Lincoln and Stephen A. Douglas in Illinois in 1858.

- In the contemporary arrangement, the debate begins with a topic being introduced by the moderator.
- The affirmative speaker then has six minutes to deliver his or her constructive, followed by a three-minute cross examination from the negative speaker.
- The negative speaker is then given seven minutes to deliver their negative construction (which almost always include a negative rebuttal), followed by a three-minute cross examination from the affirmative speaker.
- The affirmative speaker is then given four minutes to issue a rebuttal and is then followed by a six-minute rebuttal from the negative speaker.
- The affirmative speaker then concludes with a final three-minute rebuttal. Lincoln Douglas debates often end with the floor being opened to questions from the audience.

First Affirmative Constructive Speech in a Traditional Debate

In a traditional debate, the first affirmative constructive speech should be the only one that can be fully organized ahead of time. It is during this speech that the main argument of the affirmative side is advanced. The speaker should also clear up any problems with language that may exist in the proposition and deliver any important background information required to understand the topic. The speaker will then outline the major points of the affirmative case and will give as much evidence as possible within the time constraints. At the conclusion of the first affirmative constructive speech, the speaker will summarize his or her main argument.

First Negative Constructive Speaker in a Traditional Debate

After the first affirmative constructive speech has been made in a traditional debate, the first negative constructive speech will be given. In this speech, the negative speaker issues his or her basic response to the arguments advanced by the affirmative side. He or she may call into question the definitions offered by the affirmative side. For the most part, however, the first negative constructive speaker is likely to attack the premises and evidence given by the first affirmative speaker. If appropriate, the first negative constructive speaker may want to advance an alternative to the argument proposed by the first speaker.

Second Affirmative Constructive Speech in a Traditional Debate

In a traditional debate, the second affirmative constructive speech follows the first negative constructive speech. In this speech, the affirmative speaker directly addresses the counter-arguments made by the first negative constructive speaker. The affirmative speaker may wish to clarify any problems that have been raised about the language in the proposition. The affirmative speaker should address all the counter-arguments made by the first negative constructive speaker. It is best to address these points in a systematic manner.

Second Negative Constructive Speech in a Traditional Debate

In a traditional debate, the second negative constructive speech follows the second affirmative constructive speech. The second negative constructive speech is a brief period in which the negative speaker can summarize the debate to this point, strengthen his or her own case, and then attack the major arguments of the second affirmative speech. This is the final constructive speech in the debate, so the second negative speaker will want to make every argument he or she has available since new arguments will not be allowed in the rebuttal sections. It is a good idea to conclude the second negative constructive speech with a simple but forceful counter-argument to the affirmative case.

The First Negative Rebuttal Speech and First Affirmative Rebuttal Speech

The second negative constructive speech is the final constructive speech in a traditional debate. At this point, the rebuttal speeches begin. The first negative rebuttal speech serves as a reminder of the major weaknesses in the affirmative case. The first negative rebuttal speaker will also take this opportunity to re-state the arguments made by the negative side. Next, the first affirmative rebuttal will review the high points of the affirmative case and will attempt to counter any arguments that were made during the first negative rebuttal. The first affirmative rebuttal speech will also include a response to the second negative constructive speech.

The Second Negative Rebuttal Speech and the Second Affirmative Rebuttal Speech

The arguments made by the negative side in a traditional debate will conclude with the second negative rebuttal speech. In this speech, the negative side will conclude their argument, resolving any questions about their side, and pleading with the debate judges to agree with their point of view. A traditional debate concludes with the second affirmative rebuttal speech. In this speech, the affirmative side summarizes their argument and response to the previous rebuttal speech. Finally, the affirmative side delivers their own plea for the support of the debate judges. These judges may be specially chosen or may simply be the audience at the event.

Basics of Extemporaneous Speaking

In an **extemporaneous speaking** event, students select one of three questions and then prepare and deliver a speech within 30 minutes. During the 30-minute interval, students are given a selection of articles from magazines and newspapers. The extemporaneous speech is usually required to be approximately seven minutes long. It must be delivered without notes or other visual aids. Speakers are expected to deliver their message in a way that is informative to the audience as well as entertaining. Moreover, an extemporaneous speech must have a discernible structure; it must an introduction, body, and conclusion.

Two Common Types of Extemporaneous Speaking Events

The two common types of extemporaneous speaking events are **foreign extemporaneous speaking** and **domestic extemporaneous speaking**. The only real difference between these two events is that foreign extemporaneous speaking takes foreign issues as its subject, whereas domestic extemporaneous speaking concentrates on issues particular to the United States. Both of these events have a similar format. Students are required to prepare and deliver a speech within a short amount of time, typically 30 minutes. Each round of competition contains between five and eight students. Judges rank the performances in order from first to last.

Structure of an Extemporaneous Speech

To be effective an extemporaneous speech must follow a discernible structure. At the beginning of the speech, the speaker will try to engage the attention of the audience with a memorable quote or statistic. The speaker will then show how this interesting piece of data relates to his or her larger point. At this point, the speaker will fully introduce his or her topic. The speaker may need to define any words that may be unknown to the audience. After clarifying his or her thesis statement, the speaker will continue to substantiate this point with supporting arguments and evidence. Extemporaneous speaking competitions typically require the speaker to use a certain number of sources. In the conclusion of an extemporaneous speech, a speaker should make sure to restate his or her thesis and create a memorable or intriguing image or anecdote for the audience.

Basics of Original Oratory

Original oratory is probably the most popular event in a traditional high school forensic competition. In this event, each competitor is required to prepare and deliver a speech on a factual subject. Typically, the speeches are not allowed to be more than ten minutes long. The speeches delivered in an original oratory competition are often persuasive in nature. Each competitor is judged on the effectiveness of his or her speech, body control during delivery, the evidence marshaled on behalf of his or her argument, and the overall truth of his or her message.

Rules and Judges for an Original Oratory Competition

Original oratory competitions tend to abide by the same rules. First, orations are usually required to be between seven and ten minutes long. Each speaker has to memorize his or her oration and is not allowed to use note cards. Similarly, speakers are not allowed to use props or charts. Each oration may contain no more than 150 words or 30 seconds of quoted material; the rest must be original. The judges in an original oration contest are usually former competitors, speech and debate coaches, sponsors of the tournament, or parents of other students. Family and friends of students participating are forbidden from judging.

Basic Structure of an Original Oration

Original orations tend to follow a basic structure. An oration will begin with an introduction in which the speaker attempts to engage the attention of the audience and introduce the main components of his or her message. Next, during the body of the oration, the speaker will attempt to show the audience why the subject is important to them. The speaker will need to maintain a balance between factual exposition and interesting detail. A good oration will simultaneously entertain and inform the audience. Finally, in the concluding section of the oration, the speaker will reiterate his or her main points and attempt to leave the audience with a lasting positive impression.

High School Policy Debate Competitions

High school policy debate competitions are a great opportunity for beginning debaters to get some experience in a tournament setting. It is typical for these debates to be held over two days. On the first day, the preliminary rounds of the policy debate competition are held. All of those students who qualify will participate in what are known as "out rounds" on the second day of the tournament. In these out rounds, debaters are judged against one another by a set of official judges, who eliminate one debater in each round. Eventually, the two best debaters will be pitted against one another in the final.

National Speech and Debate Tournament

Every year in early June, the National Forensic League hosts the **National Speech and Debate Tournament**. It is a weeklong tournament held in a different city every year. Only the best high school debaters are invited to compete in the national tournament. Every year, only about 3,000 students participate. The tournament contains the following events: domestic extemporaneous speaking, duo interpretation, foreign extemporaneous speaking, humorous interpretation, dramatic interpretation, Lincoln-Douglas debate, original oratory, policy debate, public forum debate, and student congress.

National Forensic League

The **National Forensic League** administrates hundreds of high school competitive speech events. This group also coordinates changes to the rules of speech and debate competition. Every state has a subsidiary organization that pledges to abide by any rule changes made by the National Forensic League. Perhaps the most important function of the organization is to host the annual National Speech and Debate Tournament. The NFL also publishes a monthly magazine, the Rostrum, on the subject of debate education. High school students who participate in speech and debate competitions are awarded points by the NFL.

General Objectives of a School Forensics Program

A school **forensics program** has a number of objectives. Perhaps most importantly, it aims to provide students with the opportunity to develop their public speaking and oral interpretation skills. To be effective, a school forensics program needs to offer frequent opportunities for all student members to practice these skills. Teachers should aim to develop in their students both verbal and nonverbal communication skills. They should also teach their students how to apply critical reasoning skills to the arguments and ideas of others. Students should learn how to organize their own ideas effectively. Finally, students should be able to dramatically interpret the literary works of others.

Social and Intellectual Benefits for Students Who Participate in a Forensics Program

Students can expect to benefit in a number of ways from participation in a forensics program. By joining such a program, students develop their skills in oral and nonverbal communication and learn to effectively present an argument to a group. Forensics programs also give students the chance to develop strong research skills, which underlie the ability to construct a clear argument. Students will also build relationships among themselves and with students from other schools who participate in debate and speech competitions. Finally, for many students, participation in a forensics program is a springboard to other leadership opportunities.

Effect of Forensics Competition on School Relations

Perhaps the most overlooked benefit of school forensics programs is the strong relationships that develop among participating schools. During speech and debate competitions, students from various schools get to know one another through their shared interest in forensics. Many school teams travel overnight to participate in forensics competitions and through this experience are encouraged to make friends with people from different parts of the state and country. The National Forensics League is the umbrella organization under which all school forensics programs operate. This organization strives to cultivate relationships between schools through speech and debate.

Parliamentary Procedure

Purpose of Parliamentary Procedure During Meetings

Parliamentary procedure is a system of administrating meetings. These rules were developed for formal situations, but they are often used by informal organizations to keep business on track and provide structure to professional interactions. One of the benefits of parliamentary procedure is that it gives every member of a group an opportunity to participate in making proposals and voting. Also, parliamentary procedure limits the control that can be exercised by any person or group of people and therefore makes decision-making a more streamlined process. Parliamentary procedure can be used by very large and very small organizations.

Parliamentary procedure has its own set of terms, which include:

1. Abstain: to opt not to vote on a particular proposal.
2. Amend: to change the words in a particular proposal.
3. Chair: the person who is designated to preside over the activities of the group.
4. Floor: the authority to speak.
5. Majority: the position supported by a larger group of people; in parliamentary procedure, the majority holds more influence than the minority.
6. Minority: the position supported by a smaller group of people; certain rights of the minority are guaranteed by parliamentary procedure.
7. Minutes: the written report of the happenings at the previous meeting.
8. Motion: a proposal that the group will consider.
9. Pending: in the process of being considered, as in "the motion is pending".
10. Second: approve a motion publicly; to be introduced for discussion, a proposal must be seconded.
11. Table: set aside a motion until a later time; this is done when more information is likely to be obtained, at which point it will become more appropriate to discuss the given motion.

"Majority Rules" Principle of Parliamentary Procedure

In parliamentary procedure, decisions are made on a democratic basis. In other words, the will of the majority drives the decision-making process. The success of an organization relies on the ability of the minority to accept the decisions of the majority. In parliamentary procedure, a simple majority is defined as any more than one half of the voting individuals. Those who do not vote (that is, who abstain from voting) are not counted in the calculation of simple majority. For important decisions, an organization might require a two-thirds majority vote, as this means the decision will require a greater consensus in order to be made.

Rights of the Minority in Parliamentary Procedure

Although the decisions made within the framework of parliamentary procedure favor the majority, the minority is accorded certain rights. Within parliamentary procedure, there are numerous opportunities for the members of the minority to make their voices heard in an attempt to persuade other members of the group. Even after a decision has been made, the minority is given a chance to declare its sentiments. Moreover, the chairperson is responsible for not favoring or showing undue influence on behalf of the majority. One of the resulting benefits of parliamentary procedure is that no one becomes alienated or feels excluded from the process.

Principle of Equal Rights and Responsibilities in Parliamentary Procedure

In parliamentary procedure, all members of the organization are given equal rights in all responsibilities. Certain members of the organization may be designated as leaders or may be given other special roles, but this is only done with the consent of all the members. Within a parliamentary organization, every member is given the right to vote and the right to speak his or her mind. It should be noted, however, that parliamentary procedure frames these actions as responsibilities as well as rights. That is, in order for an organization to be healthy, all of the members need to participate by voting and making their opinions known.

Emphasis on Discussing One Problem at a Time in Parliamentary Procedure

One of the things that parliamentary procedure emphasizes is that discussion should be organized in order to minimize digressions and confusion. It is the job of the chairperson to introduce issues to the group and to make clear transitions between discussion topics. The most important issues before the group should always be discussed first. Usually, an issue will be discussed for a limited amount of time, at which point the group will decide whether to vote on it. It is only after a vote has been held or the issue has been tabled that the group can move on to the next issue. The best chairpersons are those who limit discussion to the matter at hand and efficiently move through the agenda of the group.

Emphasis on Maintaining Focus in Parliamentary Procedure

For a parliamentary organization to function effectively, the members need to limit their discussion to the issues currently on the floor. In part, this is the responsibility of the chairperson, but each member needs to be careful to limit his or her speech to the issues at hand. Every motion requires a second in order to be discussed. If some members of the group feel that discussion has gone on too long, they may call for a two-thirds vote to end discussion and hold a vote. If they do not achieve the two-thirds majority, discussion may continue. A chairperson can cut members off if they begin to speak on subjects other than those on the floor.

Chair's Objectivity in Parliamentary Procedure

To administer a parliamentary organization in a fair manner, a chairperson must remain objective at all times. A chairperson cannot be seen to favor either side in the debate. This is especially important because the opinions of the chairperson have the ability to sway the opinion of the members. The important consideration for members, however, should be the quality of the arguments on either side and not the opinions of the chairperson. In order to be viewed as objective, a chairperson needs to allow equal time to both sides.

Order of Business

Quorum, Call to Order, and Reading Minutes

Parliamentary procedure outlines a specific order of business. First, a certain number of members must be in attendance before business can be introduced. This minimum number of members, which is usually one more than half of the total members, is referred to as a **quorum**. Once a quorum has been reached, the chair will **call the meeting to order**. At this point, the meeting has begun. The secretary will then **read the minutes** from the last meeting. After the minutes have been read, the chair will ask if any members of the group have any additions or corrections to make to the minutes. If not, the minutes will be approved.

Officer Reports, Unfinished Business, and New Business

After the minutes have been approved, the group may hear various **officer reports** from committee heads. For instance, the treasurer often makes a report at this point in the meeting. An organization may have standing committees, which exist in perpetuity, or special committees, which are created to accomplish specific purposes and disbanded after the purpose is accomplished. Once the committees have reported, the chair will ask if there is any **unfinished business** in front of the group. If there is, it must be resolved before moving on. Once unfinished business is complete, the chair will open the floor to new business. Upon opening the floor to new business, the chair may briefly describe the agenda for the current meeting. The chair may also ask if any member of the group has items to be added to the agenda. At this point, members of the group can propose motions.

Announcements, Adjournments, and Voting

It is during the introduction of new business that elections for new officers in the group are held. The chair will call for nominations and seconds and then voting will occur. After new business is complete, the chair may ask the group if they have any particular **announcements** to make. After all business is complete, the chair may ask if there is a motion to **adjourn**. If so, the group can vote on whether or not to end the meeting. According to parliamentary procedure, voting can take place in a number of different ways. The most common form of vote is a **voice vote**, in which all those in favor of the motion say "aye" and all those opposed to the motion say "nay." Voting can also be held by having members stand up or raise their hands to indicate their approval or disapproval of a motion. In a **roll call vote**, the names of the members of a group are called out loud one by one and each member indicates his or her vote. Finally, a **secret ballot** can be held when members prefer anonymity.

Types of Motions Made According to Parliamentary Procedure

Main Motions and Subsidiary Motions

According to parliamentary procedure, a motion can be made in a number of different ways. A **main motion** is used to introduce the topic for discussion. If a main motion gets a second, the motion will be discussed and will require a majority vote for passage. A **subsidiary motion**, on the other hand, is introduced to alter or eliminate some other motion. Subsidiary motions are issued after a main motion. They must be voted on before the attention of the group can return to the main motion. Subsidiary motions include the motion to table, to postpone debate, or to amend the main motion.

Privileged Motions, Incidental Motions, and Unclassified Motions

According to parliamentary procedure, a motion can be made in a number of different ways. A **privileged motion** has to do with the requirements of the members. For instance, a privileged motion may be made to adjourn at a certain time or to set a date for a future meeting. An **incidental motion** has to do with the way business is conducted in the meeting. An incidental motion may be made to withdraw a motion, for instance, or to object to a certain idea. Incidental motions refine motions that have already been made. Finally, an **unclassified motion** attempts to recall issues that have been tabled or dismissed earlier.

Motion to Fix Time to Reassemble

In parliamentary procedure, a **motion to fix time** to reassemble is a privileged motion. Indeed, in the table of motions used in parliamentary procedure, it is the most privileged motion, meaning that it is more important than any other motion. This motion is typically made directly after a motion to adjourn has been seconded. It is made, however, before the motion to adjourn has been voted on. This is because the motion to adjourn will then be voted on taking into account the proposed time for future meetings. No debate takes place on a motion to fix time to reassemble, although the motion may be amended. A simple majority is required to pass this motion.

Motion to Adjourn

In parliamentary procedure, a **motion to adjourn** is the privileged motion that usually ends a meeting. If some members of a group feel that debate has gone on too long, or if they do not like the way the debate is tending, they may call a motion to adjourn as a way of stopping discussion, if the motion is seconded, it must be voted on immediately. A motion to adjourn requires a simple majority. It is not debatable or amendable. It should be noted that a motion to adjourn does not eliminate the subject under discussion for good; on the contrary, because the issue under discussion has not been resolved, it will be taken up again at the next meeting.

Motion to Recess

In parliamentary procedure, a **motion to recess** is a privileged motion in which one member moves to suspend a meeting for a brief period of time without fully ending it. For instance, a member might make a motion to recess for lunch. One of the advantages of going into recess rather than adjourning a meeting is that after a recess, the regular order of business does not need to be repeated. This can save a great deal of time. A motion to recess requires a second and is debatable and amendable. It requires a simple majority for passage.

Motion to Rise to a Question of Privilege

In parliamentary procedure, a **motion to rise to a question of privilege** is a privileged motion in which a member asks permission to make a request regarding the safety, comfort, and convenience of the group. In other words, this is a motion that briefly interrupts discussion to take care of some environmental distraction. For instance, a member might make a motion for a question of privilege if he or she wants to adjust the air-conditioning in the meeting room. The passage of this kind of motion simply depends on the will of the chairperson. A motion to rise to a question of privilege does not require a second and is neither debatable nor amendable.

Motion to Call for the Orders of the Day

In parliamentary procedure, a **motion to call for the orders of the day** is a privileged motion in which a member asks that attention be paid to the predetermined order of business in a meeting. This kind of motion is typically made when a member feels that the agreed-upon order has been abandoned or that the group has forgotten its original intent in a discussion. A motion to call for the orders of the day can interrupt a speaker and does not require a second. It is neither debatable nor amendable. The chairperson decides whether or not this motion will be passed.

Motion to Appeal a Decision

A **motion to appeal the decision** in parliamentary procedure is an incidental motion in which a member disagrees with the decision made by the chair and asks for a vote of all the members. This motion is typically made after a motion decided solely by the chairperson. It is debatable but not amendable. Before voting on this motion, both sides are allowed to briefly state their cases. It is acceptable to interrupt a speaker with this motion, but the motion requires a second in order to come to a vote. For passage, this motion requires a simple majority.

Motion to Rise to a Point of Order

In parliamentary procedure, a **motion to rise to a point of order** is an incidental motion in which a member seeks to indicate that a procedural error has been made. A member might make this motion if he or she feels that discussion has wandered off-topic or that the order of business has not been followed. A member may interrupt discussion to make this motion and it does not require a second. A motion to rise to a point of order is neither debatable nor amendable. Its passage depends on the will of the chairperson.

Motion to Call for a Division of the Assembly

A **motion to call for a division** of the assembly is an incidental motion in which a member declares that a voice vote has been too close to call and that a more precise vote should be taken. Specifically, a motion for a division of the assembly calls for a vote by show of hands or by standing. This motion may be made as an interruption to current discussion and does not require a second. It is neither debatable nor amendable. A motion to call for a division of the assembly requires a simple majority for passage.

Motion to Object to a Consideration of a Question

A **motion to object to a consideration of a question** is an incidental motion used to stop discussion of a particular topic. This motion may be made for any number of reasons. In some cases, a member may feel that the discussion is fruitless or that it has wandered too far away from the original topic. A member might also feel that the meeting has run on too long. A motion to object to consideration of a question can be made as an interruption to discussion and does not require a second. It is not debatable or amendable. Because it is such an important motion, in that it has the ability to stop discussion, it requires a two-thirds majority.

Motion to Ask Permission to Withdraw a Motion:

In parliamentary procedure, a **motion to ask permission to withdraw a motion** is an incidental motion in which a member tries to remove a motion that has been previously made. For instance, a motion might seem like a good idea at the time but after subsequent discussion may be discovered to be weak or wrongheaded. In such a case, the member who made the motion may ask permission to withdraw it. A motion to ask permission to withdraw a motion cannot interrupt a speaker and does not require a second. It is neither debatable nor amendable. It requires a simple majority for passage.

Motion to Suspend a Rule

A **motion to suspend a rule** is an incidental motion used when a group wants to temporarily remove the restrictions placed on it by a certain rule. For instance, in some cases it might be appropriate to alter the normal order of business in order to obtain an important piece of information from a committee report. A member could then move to suspend that rule in this particular case. This motion cannot be made as an interruption to a speaker and it requires a second. It is neither debatable nor amendable. Because it calls for a fundamental change in the rules of the group, this motion requires a two-thirds majority for passage.

Motion to Table a Motion

In parliamentary procedure, a **motion to table a motion** is a subsidiary motion that is made when a member seeks to postpone further discussion of the topic. This motion is often made when a member of the group feels that more and better information about a subject will be available in the near future and that it is not incumbent upon the group to make a decision immediately. This motion does not stop discussion, but rather postpones it to a later date. This motion cannot be used to interrupt a speaker and it requires a second. It is neither debatable nor amendable. It requires a simple majority for passage.

Motion to Move the Previous Question

A **motion to move the previous question** is a subsidiary motion meant to conclude discussion on a particular topic. This motion is often made when a member of the group feels that the group has fully discussed a topic and is only repeating previously made arguments. If this motion is passed, the chairperson will then have the right to cease discussion on anything other than new points on the designated topic. This motion is neither debatable nor amendable. It cannot interrupt a speaker and it requires a second. It requires a two-thirds majority for passage.

Motion to Limit or Extend Debate

A **motion to limit or extend debate** is a subsidiary motion whose purpose is to define how much time will be allowed for discussion of the topic. This motion is made when a group is under particular time constraints or when the members of the group feel that discussion has the potential to continue for an impractically long time. This motion may limit the number of speeches, may designate a time limit for each speech, or may limit the total amount of time to be spent in discussion. A speaker may not be interrupted with this motion. This motion requires a second and is both debatable and amendable. It requires a two-thirds majority for passage.

Motion to Postpone to a Definite Time

A **motion to postpone to a definite time** is a subsidiary motion that is made when a speaker wants to table discussion until a designated point in the future. This motion is slightly different from the motion to table, in that it specifies when discussion will be resumed. It is typically made when a member feels the meeting has gone on too long or that discussion has become unprofitable at present. The motion to postpone to a definite time cannot interrupt a speaker and it requires a second. It is both debatable and amendable. It requires a simple majority for passage.

Motion to Refer to a Committee

A **motion to refer to a committee** is a subsidiary motion in which a special committee designated by the group is asked to study a particular problem and report back to the group at large at a later date. This motion often contains a recommendation as to who should be on the committee as well as the designated time at which the committee will report to the group. This motion is often made to prevent a regular meeting from running on too long. It may not be used to interrupt a speaker and it requires a second. It is both debatable and amendable. It requires a simple majority for passage.

Motion to Amend

A **motion to amend** is a subsidiary motion made to alter a previously made motion. It may amend the previous motion in the following ways: adding more language, subtracting language, substituting language, or substituting an entirely new motion. Main, subsidiary, and privileged motions may all be amended. A motion to amend must be discussed and voted on immediately, before any other business is handled. These motions cannot be used to interrupt a speaker and they require a second. They are both debatable and amendable. They require a simple majority for passage.

Motion to Postpone Indefinitely:

A **motion to postpone indefinitely** is a subsidiary motion made to prevent a vote on a pending main motion. If this motion is passed, discussion on the topic in question must cease for the rest of the current meeting. Also, the passage of a motion to postpone indefinitely suggests that most of the members of a group are not really interested in passing the main motion. A motion to postpone indefinitely cannot be used to interrupt a speaker and it requires a second. It is both debatable and amendable. It only requires a simple majority for passage.

Concepts of Oral Interpretation

Basics of Oral Interpretation

Although oral interpretation is a type of public speaking, it is very different than the delivery of a speech. For one thing, oral interpretation does not require the speaker to have written his or her own words. On the contrary, an **oral interpretation presentation** is a reformulation and expression of words written by someone else. In a sense, oral interpretation is a public and social form of storytelling. The work being interpreted may be a dramatic text, a work of prose, or a poem. Before the advent of radio and television communication, oral interpretation was the predominant form of information and entertainment. It is still very prevalent, although much more oral interpretation occurs through other media than in person.

Selecting a Text for Oral Interpretation

Perhaps the most important step in oral interpretation is selecting a proper text. Works of prose, poetry, and drama are acceptable texts for oral interpretation. It is important to choose a text that is appropriate for the audience. For instance, storytellers often take fairytales as their text, this is appropriate for an audience of children but may be too simplistic for an adult audience. Also, it is important to make sure the text is of an appropriate length given the time constraints. An effective oral interpretation may require significant dramatic pauses and periods of nonverbal communication. All of these features should be taken into account when determining whether a text is the right length.

Composite Recital

In the form of oral interpretation known as **composite recital**, two or more people will interpret various texts. All of the texts interpreted by the performers will have some common thread, whether it is the author, theme, cultural background, or subject matter. Typically, an introductory speech precedes a composite recital. In this speech, the unifying thread will be presented and the various pieces to be interpreted will be introduced. In a typical composite recital, all of the performers will be grouped together on a stage and will take turns interpreting their material. Oral interpretation presentations usually require minimal set dressing.

Choral Speaking

In the form of oral interpretation known as choral speaking, a group of people joins their voices together to pronounce a single text. Perhaps the most famous example of choral speaking is the dramatic chorus in Greek drama. Only texts with a regular meter or rhythm can be used in choral speaking; other, more varying texts are too difficult to recite in unison. Different kinds of poetry have been incorporated into choral speaking with great results. Sometimes an individual speaker will deliver the verse and the group as a whole will deliver the chorus. In other cases, each individual will read a line and then the group as a whole will read the refrain.

Basics of Reader's Theatre

Reader's theatre is a form of group oral interpretation in which two or more individuals present a dramatic interpretation of a literary work. The presentation of reader's theatre is similar to that of a play, except the text is a work of prose or poetry rather than of drama. Also, reader's theatre typically has little set direction and scenery. Participants in reader's theatre often use elements of pantomime to suggest props. Because there are so few accessories in reader's theatre, the presenters tend to make exaggerated movements and display broad emotions. Reader's theatre is similar to the run-through performed by actors during the rehearsal of a play.

Dramatic Texts in Reader's Theatre

On occasion, the participants in reader's theatre will use a work of drama rather than one of poetry or prose. Obviously, works of drama lend themselves to oral interpretation and therefore will require much less use of suggestion to indicate costumes and scenery. On the other hand, plays often have elaborate set directions, which may be beyond the scope of reader's theatre. When this is the case, the participants should either select another text or should include an introductory speech in which the potentially confusing aspects of the presentation are explained. In a more formal presentation, the participants may hand out a program that gives this information.

Folklore

Any story passed on by word of mouth until it becomes ingrained in a culture may come to be known as **folklore**. In other words, folklore is the set of narratives that circulate among the members of a community through oral interpretation rather than through writing. Various categories of folklore include legends, jokes, fairy tales, and fables. Even though people usually associate folklore with a bygone age, there is a great deal of modern folklore as well. Although most scholars declare that folklore must be fictitious, it is often based on themes and issues common to everyday "real life." For instance, there is a great deal of folklore surrounding the figure of Davy Crockett. Even though most of this folklore is exaggerated or untrue, it is based on events that actually happened to a real person. Many scholars concentrate solely on the characteristics of folklore in various cultures.

Review Video: Myths, Fables, Legends, and Fairy Tales
Visit mometrix.com/academy and enter code: 347199

Folklore in Performance

Because it is an oral exercise, the creation and dissemination of folklore is by definition an act of performance. Folklore is traditionally allied with storytelling, though there are other ways in which it can be delivered. For instance, one of the most common forms of folklore at present is joke telling. Whenever someone tells a joke to a friend, he or she is engaged in a form of performance. This performance can be subjected to as much scrutiny and evaluation as a formal dramatic presentation. Indeed, all of the elements that define a successful performance (vocal control, nonverbal communication fluency, rapport with the audience) are essential to the delivery of folklore.

Storytelling

Storytelling is the craft of using words, gestures, and sounds to convey a narrative to an audience. At one time in human history, storytelling was the predominant form of information, entertainment, and self-knowledge for communities. Societies defined themselves based on the stories they told about themselves. By studying the stories that have been told in the past, scholars can gain insight into which qualities were particularly valued by a culture and the particular issues that caused the most anxiety for those people. Many people assume that storytelling is a dying art, though in fact it continues to thrive in various media. Television, movies, and radio, for instance, all use traditional elements of storytelling to develop powerful narratives.

Storytelling in Performance

Storytelling as a type of oral interpretation remains a popular form of entertainment even in this modern age of computers and televisions. Storytelling requires a narrative, which means it must have characters and a plot. Outside of these requirements, the storyteller has a great deal of creative freedom. Many storytellers incorporate sound effects and simple props into their performances. In any case, a speech communication instructor can assess a storytelling performance in the same way as he or she would any other oral interpretation. The success of the performance will depend on the fluency, preparation, and rhetorical skills of the storyteller.

Oral History

Oral history is any account of past events that is transmitted through the human voice rather than through writing. In the distant past, many cultures developed their self-identity primarily through oral history because they did not have the means to maintain a written history. At present, many historians focus on oral histories that are tape-recorded or videotaped. Many historians claim that oral history is a good way to give a voice to members of a society who, because of their marginal status, would otherwise not be able to make their voices heard. Also, oral history lends a human element to large, formerly impersonal historical events.

Oral History in Performance

Because it is a serious source of scholarly information, it sounds strange to speak of oral history as performance. However, in the broad sense of the word "performance," meaning any presentation involving speech and other forms of communication to an audience, it is clear that oral history fits the definition. Indeed, oral history is an important supplement to written history because information can be conveyed through the speaker's tone of voice and vocal mannerisms that cannot be expressed through printed language. Oral historians make a point of emphasizing those aspects of vocal performance that differentiate oral history from other forms of record-keeping.

Principles of a Text

Theme and Mood

To present an effective oral interpretation of a piece of literature, one must be able to discern the predominant theme and mood of the work. To discover the **theme**, one must read the text in its entirety and consider the general point the author is trying to get across. Even if the selection to be interpreted is only a portion of the entire work, one needs to understand how the selection fits into the work as a whole. This comprehensive reading should also reveal the mood of the piece. The **mood** is essentially the emotional content of the text. Naturally, the predominant mood of the text will have an enormous impact on the interpretation. Note that the mood of a text can change.

Characterization

When interpreting a work of literature, one is often required to assume the point of view of a character in the text. To do this effectively, or to provide appropriate emotional emphasis in the portrayal of a given character, one needs to pay special attention to the author's use of characterization. **Characterization** is simply the way the author describes a character. Characterization may be direct, as in descriptions of the character's appearance and personality, or it may be indirect, in which the character is revealed through his or her actions or the ways in which other characters react to said character. It is important not to take whatever a character says about himself or herself at face value because authors often create "unreliable narrators," or characters whose words are not necessarily to be trusted.

Structure

Structure is a combination of plot elements used to give shape and form to a text. These basically include the beginning, middle, climax, and ending. With experience, a reader will develop a sense of the structure of a literary work. This sense of structure is invaluable when developing an oral interpretation. A sophisticated reader will be able to identify the climax, or most intense emotional point, in the text. Identifying the text's climax allows the reader to structure his or her interpretation to properly emphasize this peak dramatic moment. A reader should also be able to identify when an author is attempting to build tension in the text. The interpreter will want to convey this mounting emotion in his or her delivery.

Dialogue

If a selection for oral interpretation includes dialogue, the interpreter will have to make some important decisions about how he or she will handle this dialogue. For instance, the interpreter might decide to use different voices for the different characters in a conversation. Also, the interpreter will need to practice adjusting his or her voice to accurately represent the various moods of the characters involved in the dialogue.

It is important for a speaker to understand these characters' motivations as well, as this information will allow him or her to produce a more sophisticated, nuanced interpretation of the words. Conversations have their own rhythms, frequently increasing and decreasing in tension. A good interpreter will be able to capture these rhythms in his or her presentation.

Diction

Diction is the unique style in which an author uses words and expressions. To interpret a work of literature effectively, one must understand both the denotative and the connotative meanings of the words an author uses. If necessary, the interpreter should look up all questionable words in the dictionary. Most importantly, the interpreter needs to understand how to properly pronounce each word. A dictionary will provide pronunciation guides as well as definitions. Besides understanding the pronunciation and definition of each word in the text, the interpreter also needs to know which words deserve special emphasis. Identifying key words in the text allows the interpreter to convey the appropriate meaning and correctly reflect the author's diction.

Punctuation

Although it is easy to pay little attention to it in a literary text, punctuation is an important element in oral interpretation. For instance, punctuation such as periods, colons, semi-colons, dashes, spaces, and spaces between sections of text all require pauses of varying duration. Also, when posing a question, it is typical to lift the voice to a higher register at the end of the sentence. Quotation marks in a sentence, of course, indicate that a character is speaking. In the case of such direct quotations, the interpreter will have to decide whether or not to use a different voice to represent each character who speaks.

Point of View in the Oral Interpretation of a Work of Prose

In the interpretation of a work of prose literature, it is especially important to have a sense of the point of view. The **point of view** is simply the perspective from which the story is told. For instance, in first person point of view, the story is told by one of the participants. First person perspective is distinguished by words like "I," "me," and "mine." When a story is told from the third person point of view, however, the narrator stands outside the story. Such a text is often told from an omniscient point of view, meaning the narrator knows everything, including the thoughts of all the characters. A limited omniscient point of view refers to a narrator who only knows certain information.

Treatment of Rhythm in the Oral Interpretation of Poetry

In the oral interpretation of poetry, one needs to be conscious of the rhythms and repetitions of the poem. Poetry is almost always written in a meter, or rhythm. Rhyming poetry will have what is known as a rhyme scheme, or a pattern of rhyming that occurs in the last word of each line. Also, many poems frequently repeat a single word, phrase, line, or set of lines. An interpreter needs to pay attention to these repetitions and vary his or her reading of the repeated words. The enunciation of the repeated words should evolve throughout the performance, so that the audience gets a sense of progress within the interpretation.

Technique of Emphasis in the Oral Interpretation of Poetry

In the oral interpretation of poetry, it is essential to recognize which words in a line deserve special emphasis. Too often, interpreters simply emphasize the last word in each line. Not only does this give their performance a repetitive and boring quality, it is also incorrect in cases where the line does not end with a comma, semi-colon, or period. When there is no punctuation at the end of a line of poetry, the interpreter should continue reading to the next line with no special emphasis. It is only through close study of the language and punctuation of a poem that an interpreter can learn the proper points of emphasis.

Oral Interpretation of Dramatic Works

Occasionally, a single individual will attempt the oral interpretation of a dramatic work. The obvious advantage of doing so is that the text has been designed for public performance, so the language and points of emphasis should be fairly clear. On the other hand, works of drama may call for elaborate staging and costumes beyond the scope of an individual oral interpretation. The interpreter will have to study the text to determine whether it can be adapted for oral interpretation. If too much action is called for in the stage directions, or if understanding the text depends on the presence of other characters, the interpreter would do well to look for another text.

Condensing Selections for Oral Interpretation

For a literary selection to be of an appropriate length for oral interpretation, it may be necessary to condense or cut the work. When editing a selection, it is important to leave all text that is essential to the meaning. For instance, when condensing a selection from a work of prose, it is a good idea to trim any references to characters or events that do not appear in the selection, unless these references have bearing on the meaning of the selection. The best rule of thumb is to always review the selection after the condensed version has been performed. If it still makes sense and conveys the same thematic meaning as the original, then the process of condensing the work can be considered successful.

Writing an Introduction to an Oral Interpretation Presentation

In some cases, an oral interpretation presentation will be preceded by a short introduction. If a selection is being taken from a larger work, or if a selection requires some context in order to be understood, it will be especially important to provide some guidance to the audience. There are a few key components to this kind of introduction. First, the presenter should outline the selection, including the major characters, back-story, and any other information necessary to understand the selection. A speaker will likely explain why he or she has picked that particular selection and why it might be of interest to the audience. If the selection has any relevance to current events or to the lives of the audience members, this information would be meaningful to an introduction.

Necessity of Practicing for an Oral Interpretation Presentation

It may seem obvious, but it is absolutely essential to practice before an oral interpretation presentation. Practice begins with learning the text inside out, but it is not complete until the performance has been fully rehearsed several times. During these rehearsals, the performer should be timed to make sure his or her delivery does not exceed the time constraints. If possible, the performer should rehearse in front of an audience (perhaps of friends or other performers) so he or she can practice making good eye contact and directing his or her voice to the different parts of the room. Multiple rehearsals also give the performer a chance to experiment with different deliveries and gestures.

Analysis and Interpretation of Dramatic Presentations

During the preparation for a dramatic presentation, the director and the crew will need to analyze and interpret the text. The director must identify the central character, or protagonist, as well as the supporting characters and the main conflict in the text. The director should also identify the mood and theme of the play, as these factors will influence all of his or her other decisions, from casting and staging to vocal emphasis and lighting. The director should outline the general structure of the play in order to bring the action to its appropriate climax and resolution.

Analysis of Rhythm

One of the aspects of drama that receives less attention than it should is rhythm. Every play has a natural **rhythm**, or periods of intense action followed by lighter action. To avoid overtaxing the audience, a dramatist has to mix moments of high and low intensity. Typically, a play will have several small climaxes before reaching its most dramatic point, the major climatic scene toward the end of play. A period of resolution, known technically as the denouement, usually follows the climax. During the analysis of a play, the director and his or her staff should pay close attention to the rhythm of the text so they can bring that same rhythm into the dramatic presentation.

Analysis of Character

During the planning phase of a dramatic presentation, the director and his or her staff should pay close attention to the relationships between the various characters. Each actor should note the attitude of his or her character toward all the other characters in the play. In some cases, the relationships between even distantly-related characters will change subtly during a performance. The director needs to be able to point out these slight changes to the actors so they can be conveyed in the performance. Also, a dramatic performance will convey the unique relationships between characters, such as that of a father and son or brothers.

Benefits of Group Oral Interpretation

There are a number of advantages to performing group oral interpretation. First, it encourages more than one person to familiarize themselves with the text. Also, group members can motivate one another to higher achievement. It is easier for a group to perform works having more than one character since it can be very difficult for one person to express all the different voices required by some texts. Group interpretation is also a good venue for people to gather and share their various ideas of interpretation and of literature. Finally, rehearsals tend to be more productive when there are other people present to critique one another's performances.

Use of Scripts in Choral Speaking

Typically, all of the participants in choral speaking use a script during the performance. Each participant should indicate on his or her script those lines that he or she will be required to speak. If there are any stage directions, these should be indicated on the script. It is a good idea to print the text in a double-spaced format and to number the lines so the cast can easily find their places. Additionally, the scripts should be distributed in advance of rehearsal so cast members can become familiar with where their lines occur throughout the script.

Motion and Position in Choral Speaking

For a choral speaking performance to be effective, the cast members need to practice speaking in unison. Only by beginning and ending each word at the same time can they achieve the clarity necessary to be understood. Also, if the cast is required to make any synchronized motions, these should be practiced as well. The intended effect will be successful only if the motion is performed precisely in unison. Finally, the director of a choral speaking group needs to organize the group by voice. Typically, any soloists will be positioned toward the front of the group. Those with deeper and stronger voices are usually placed in the back.

Memorization for an Actor

To be truly expressive, an actor needs to memorize his or her lines. This is in large part because the actor's concentration needs to move from the recitation of the mere words to the development of nonverbal communication methods and interpretation of character. If an actor is looking at cue cards or holding a copy of the script, he or she will not be able to gesture or move freely about the stage. Furthermore, he or she will not be able to make eye contact with the other actors or with the audience. It is most important to memorize lines before rehearsals begin in earnest. Even if an actor forgets some of his or her lines and requires a prompt during rehearsal, it is still better to start working without a script as soon as possible.

Motivation for an Actor

An actor's **motivation** does not mean his or her reason for participating in the play. Rather, it refers to the actor's identification of the motivations of the character he or she is playing. To effectively interpret a role, an actor needs to understand why the character behaves as he or she does. Without the right motivation, an actor will not be able to demonstrate effective emotion. Even the nonverbal aspects of a character's interpretation are dependent on the character's mood and motivation. Therefore, in order to transmit the right thematic message to the audience, the director and the actors need to have a good sense of each character's motivation.

Establishing Character Background for an Actor

Actors often talk about developing a character's background, or back-story. By this they mean establishing what the character's life and history were prior to the point at which the play begins. By understanding where a character is "coming from," an actor can gain insight into that character's motivation and emotional range. Sometimes this information can be discerned from the author's description of the character for instance, if a character is handicapped, it might be assumed that he or she has been in an accident in the past. Actors also get information from the character's dialogue and behavior. The director and actors need to collaborate to establish character background in order to accurately determine the characters' motivations.

Vocal Control

To effectively interpret his or her role, an actor must have excellent **vocal control**. An actor needs to be able to pronounce words clearly, so that every member of the audience will be able to understand the dialogue. In some cases, an actor may need to incorporate a regional dialect and have it be both credible and comprehensible. Some characters have particular vocal mannerisms, like a stammer or a lisp, which must be interpreted accurately. Finally, an actor must be able to convey the appropriate emotion with his or her voice at different times during a play. An actor who has a sense of his or her emotional vocal range can thereby save his or her most exaggerated vocal techniques for the climactic sections of the play.

Projection

Actors often refer to the vocal quality of **projection**, by which they mean the level of force in volume with which words are delivered. To perform in front of a large audience, an actor needs to have enough projection so that everyone in the audience can hear and understand all the lines. Actors cultivate strong abdominal muscles and lungs so they can maintain their ability to project. Also, actors constantly work on combining clarity of expression with volume. A specific technique that actors use to increase the quality of projection is called **pointing**. This is the technique of emphasizing particular words in a sentence, either by pausing before them or extending their enunciation. Pointing helps the actor's words to be understood.

How an Actor Handles Nonverbal Communication

An actor can handle nonverbal messages during a dramatic presentation in a number of different ways. It is important for the gestures to be appropriate, consistent, and tailored to the audience. Any nonverbal communication used must be appropriate to the character being portrayed; in other words, the gestures and vocal techniques need to be such that they seem right for the character. Also, a character's mannerisms must remain consistent from the beginning of the play to the end of the play. Finally, the ways in which an actor uses nonverbal communication must be expressive enough to be seen by everyone in the audience. When performing for a small audience, an actor can get away with more subtle nonverbal communication than he or she can when performing for a large audience.

How Movement Is Used in a Dramatic Presentation

There should be no random movements during a dramatic presentation. That is, all the positioning of the actors should be choreographed ahead of time. The entrances and exits of the characters are usually indicated in the text, but the proxemics may be at the discretion of the director. A sophisticated director can convey information about the characters and their interrelationships through their positioning onstage. At all times, however, the director needs to keep in mind the necessity of making the actors visible to the audience. Positioning should be one of the main focuses of rehearsal, and the director should experiment with different arrangements.

Basic Parts of the Dramatic Stage

A basic dramatic stage includes a single floor and an arch that extends from one side to the other. The section of the stage closest to the audience is referred to as downstage. The section of stage farthest away from the audience is known as upstage. When the stage directions call for movement to the right or left, this means from the perspective of the actors. Although most of the major set directions are included in a dramatic text, a director will have to come up with supplementary directions. These supplementary directions are known as **blocking**.

Choosing an Appropriate Dramatic Script

When selecting a dramatic script for presentation, a producer needs to keep in mind the makeup of the audience. For instance, when a work is to be presented to a group of children, it should not deal with mature or violent themes. One of the best places to find a dramatic text is the local library. Most libraries have numerous anthologies containing famous plays. Once a play has been chosen, the producer needs to procure playbooks for all the members of the cast and crew. It may be necessary to pay royalties to the author or publisher of the play.

Process of Holding Auditions for a Dramatic Presentation

When holding auditions for a dramatic presentation, directors should have a basic idea of what type of actor they prefer for each role. At the same time, they should keep an open mind. Sometimes an actor will give a unique performance during the audition, thus changing a director's mind about what he or she needs for a given role. If an audition is **open**, that means anyone is allowed to show up and try out. A **closed** audition means only invited actors are allowed to attend. If particular qualities or abilities are required of an actor to fill a given role, such as the ability to sing or play an instrument, these should be made known before the audition.

Typical Policy for Making Casting Decisions

When making casting decisions, directors adhere to a general policy. First, everyone who participates in an audition fills out a form with contact information. This audition form should also include space to indicate any conflicts of interest that might interfere with an actor's ability to appear in the dramatic presentation. During the audition itself, actors may read from a script or be asked to improvise. Sometimes actors will be instructed to prepare a short scene ahead of time. If an actor is going to be required to sing or dance during the presentation, these skills should be tested during the audition. Usually, a committee that includes the director and producers makes its casting decisions once all the auditions have been completed.

Feedback During Rehearsal

During rehearsal of a dramatic presentation, it is essential that the director and producers provide constant and specific feedback to the cast and crew. Rehearsals are a valuable opportunity for everyone involved in the performance to experiment with different techniques, so it is important for the director to let the actors and crew know what is working and what is not. In some cases, it may not be appropriate to give feedback immediately. To provide a venue for feedback, the director will set up regular meetings with each member of the cast and crew. By the time the dress rehearsal and first performance take place, the director should have already fully reviewed and approved the performances of the cast and crew.

Responsibilities of the Student Director and Stage Manager

A student director (also known as assistant director) helps make the director's job easier. He or she may transcribe notes dictated by the director during rehearsal, may help to implement the director's blocking plan, and may coordinate activities with the costuming, lighting, and sound departments. The stage manager has a number of practical responsibilities, including overseeing construction of the set and making sure that any set changes can be accomplished quickly. He or she is also responsible for organizing and managing the crew. A stage manager needs to be intimately familiar with the light and curtain cues in the play and must also have contingency plans in case things go wrong.

Responsibilities of the Business and House Managers

In a dramatic presentation, the business manager is responsible for overseeing all financial aspects of the performance. These include ticket sales, the cost of promotions, and the costs of production. In the case of professional presentations, the business manager also handles wages paid to cast and crew. The house manager, on the other hand, is responsible for handling the admittance and seating of the audience members. The house manager runs a crew of ushers, who help audience members find their seats. Ushers also clean up the auditorium after each performance. The house manager is responsible for maintaining the heat or air conditioning system in the auditorium as well.

Necessity of Makeup, Costumes, and Props

To be performed professionally, a dramatic presentation needs makeup, costumes, props, and crews. Makeup is necessary to counterbalance the effects of bright stage lighting. The members of the makeup crew will need to practice applying makeup to each cast member before the first performance, so they can get a good idea of what makeup scheme is appropriate. Costumes are important for fostering believability in the performance. The costume crew acquires the necessary wardrobe and makes sure it fits the cast. The props crew is in charge of acquiring, caring for, and storing all the movable items used in a performance.

Interpersonal Communication Skills

Self-Concept

Self-concept is simply an individual's sense of himself or herself. Voluntarily or involuntarily, every person brings his or her self-concept to bear during interpersonal communication. Some of the aspects that make up a **self-concept** include personality, roles, aspirations, and past achievements. To a large degree, a person's self-concept is defined by his or her interactions with others, especially by their responses to what he or she says and does. Personality traits and other aspects of one's self-concept may become more pronounced if they are reinforced by the comments of others, since people often internalize the compliments and criticism they receive. Some individuals construct their self-concept in relation to someone they admire or despise. For instance, an individual might model himself or herself after some famous person and therefore evaluate his or her own words and deeds in comparison with those of that other person.

Changing Self-Concept Through Communication

Although it is a nebulous, complicated process, self-concept does change over time. One of the main factors that influences change in self-concept is interpersonal communication. Individuals largely determine their self-concept in relation to how they see others, and their views of others are primarily developed through communication. Although specific interactions—compliments and criticism in particular—can have a major impact on self-concept, it would be wrong to isolate a particular communication event as the sole determining factor in individual self-concept. The development and maintenance of self-concept is too complex and long-term to be traced back to one particular communication. Occasionally, interpersonal communications can cause an "identity crisis," or the radical questioning of one's self-concept. Even in its most extreme form, however, an identity crisis is simply a slight acceleration of the normal changes in self-concept.

Self-Concept Applies to Interpersonal Communication

During interpersonal communication, all the participating parties filter information through their own self-concept. Everyone naturally applies new information to their own self-concept. Often, however, self-interested concerns can make it difficult for a listener to get a true sense of what the other person is saying. As much as possible, listeners should strive to understand and take into account their own self-image, so they can be as objective as possible when evaluating an incoming message. Although a slight degree of egotism or self-centeredness is natural, these traits can hinder accurate and insightful listening. Therefore, the goal of speech communication education is to mitigate these distorting factors.

When two individuals have a conversation, their self-images and the images they hold of each other exert a great influence on the course of the conversation. For instance, imagine you are talking to your teacher. You have a self-image and an image of the teacher. You also have an image of how you hope your teacher sees you. Finally, you have an image of how you think your teacher actually sees you. Similarly, your teacher holds his or her own set of four images in mind. Obviously, then, even carrying on a simple conversation becomes a complicated event. Speech communication theorists assert that conversations tend to go better when there is less discrepancy between these various images. For instance, if your self-image is similar to the image you imagine your teacher has of you, you are less likely to have trouble coming up with appropriate things to say. Similarly, if your impression of what the teacher thinks of you is similar to what you hope the teacher would think of you, you are less likely to make outlandish claims or try to justify yourself.

Self-Disclosure

According to speech communication theorists, conversations work best when both parties are as honest and forthcoming about themselves as possible. In other words, when engaged in conversation, a person should strive to be as accurate as possible in revealing his or her self-image. This process is known as **self-disclosure**. To the degree that we hide information about ourselves, we prevent others from truly understanding us. There are a number of reasons why a person might not engage in total self-disclosure. Propriety, pride, and fear are probably the most common reasons for hiding information about oneself. Difficulty can also arise when one individual in a conversation has information about the other without the other party being aware of it. This kind of asymmetrical knowledge can create underlying but unexpressed tension in a conversation. Ideally, people should attempt to continually increase their level of self-disclosure while encouraging their interlocutor to do the same.

Supporting Self-Disclosure

If we assume that self-disclosure is a positive value in conversation, we can then consider the ways in which it can be promoted. Obviously, it will not always be appropriate to simply demand that our interlocutor be entirely open and honest. Instead, the best way to encourage self-disclosure is to establish a comfortable, nonjudgmental environment for conversation. If a strong rapport and level of trust are established between the interlocutors, self-disclosure will follow naturally. When trying to promote self-disclosure in others, we should refrain from negative comments and harsh criticism. We should also remember to smile and be as warm as possible with our interlocutors, so they will become more comfortable about truly revealing themselves.

Alienation Can Influence Interpersonal Communication

If a supportive environment is the ideal state for self-disclosure, a state of alienation is the exact opposite. **Alienation** is a feeling of estrangement from other people. Alienated individuals view the world around them as cold and frightening, and they are therefore less likely to engage in self-disclosure. Many sociologists feel that the United States has an abnormally large number of alienated individuals. It should be noted that people with a long history of alienation will be especially unreceptive to efforts at honest and open communication. The natural response of someone who feels alienated is to retreat into him or herself and avoid exposure. For this reason, it is especially important to develop a supportive and welcoming environment, one that promotes self-disclosure. Over time, people who feel alienated can learn to trust others and experience the value of healthy self-disclosure.

Trust Can Improve Interpersonal Communication

For effective interpersonal communication to exist, the parties involved must trust one another. Note that trust does not necessarily connote affection. In fact, most people can think of others whom they do not particularly like but do trust. For the most part, the ability to trust develops in the early years of childhood and is based on the child's relationship with his or her parents. When parents honor commitments they make to their children and take care of their responsibilities, those children ordinarily begin to develop trust in the correspondence between words and actions. Although it can be dangerous to be too trusting, interpersonal communication is generally improved when one has a natural trust of others, tempered by some measure of healthy skepticism. Furthermore, by becoming more trustworthy ourselves, we allow others to respond to our communications more openly and appropriately.

Selecting Criteria for the Evaluation of Interpersonal Communication

There are three steps in the evaluation of an interpersonal communication event: selecting the criteria for evaluation, describing the event, and making the evaluation. The first step, **selecting the criteria for evaluation**, establishes the qualities of communication that will be scrutinized. The particular criteria used to judge the quality of a communication event will vary depending on the kind of event. For instance, when evaluating a casual conversation, you might focus on warmth, clarity of expression, and comprehensibility. When evaluating a public speech, on the other hand, you might place more emphasis on audience analysis, appropriate gestures, and argument structure. In an informal setting, we would not expect a speaker to have his or her message rigidly organized. On the other hand, we would be surprised if a public speaker did not have a firm grasp and orderly delivery of his or her subject.

Describing an Interpersonal Communication Event

After selecting the criteria that will be used in the evaluation of an interpersonal communication event, one can turn to the task of **describing the event** itself. Naturally, the description of the communication event will emphasize those aspects, or channels, of the communication that correspond with the selected criteria. For instance, in the description of a public speech, one will naturally be more concerned with the structure of the speaker's argument and will therefore pay considerable attention to this subject when describing the event. When describing a casual conversation between friends, on the other hand, one might pay more attention to describing tone of voice and body language, as these communicate openness and ease. It is important for a description to mention all the communication channels the speaker uses.

Evaluating an Interpersonal Communication Event

After the criteria have been selected and the communication event has been described, one can set about **evaluating the interpersonal communication event**. This simply means using the information from the description to decide whether the speaker has done an adequate job of meeting the standards set by the selected criteria. For instance, if it has been determined that effective argument structure is an important criterion for a successful public speaker, it will be necessary to evaluate whether a particular speaker has met this criterion. The evaluation is important because it enables progress to be made in communication. In a way, the process of evaluating communication is similar to the response to feedback made by the speaker. Consciously or unconsciously, a speaker is constantly evaluating the effectiveness of his or her communication and making adjustments based on these observations.

Critics Function as Consumers of Communication Information

To be successful in interpersonal communication, one needs to become a conscious critic. This does not mean hunting out the flaws in other people, or emphasizing the negative aspects of communication events. On the contrary, being an effective critic means paying attention to both the strengths and weaknesses of a communication event. Whether we realize it or not, we are all, to a greater or lesser degree, critics of communication. For instance, from a young age we are all inundated with advertisements. Over time, we become less and less susceptible to advertising because we begin to identify and discount its communication strategy. We implicitly understand the intentions of the advertiser and are therefore skeptical of the message. Speech communication education seeks to expand this healthy skepticism into everyday interpersonal interactions.

Study of Nonverbal Communication

The study of nonverbal communication is divided into three categories: paralinguistics, kinesics, and proxemics.

Paralinguistics

Paralinguistics, a term that means "beyond language," emphasizes vocal productions and sounds not strictly considered language. So, **paralinguistics** includes all those noises a person can make to express meaning, as for instance grunts and snorts. In addition, paralinguistics includes elements of linguistic expression such as tone of voice, cadence, and pitch. A great deal can be communicated through the paralinguistic elements of speech. Indeed, the tone of a speaker's voice can either reinforce or contradict the words he or she is saying. Paralinguistics looks at the ways in which these elements contribute to communication.

Kinesics

Kinesics emphasizes the motions of the body that support and elaborate verbal communication. Gestures, facial expressions, and gesticulations are all considered in the field of **kinesics**. More generally, posture and overall body language are studied as part of kinesic observation. Note that the body motions of a speaker may either contribute to or detract from his or her message. For instance, an individual's facial expression may contradict what he or she is saying. As an example, consider an individual who is using strong language yet standing with his shoulders slumped and head down. Such an individual will be detracting from the confident message expressed by his language.

Proxemics

Proxemics focuses on the relative positions of the individuals who are taking part in a communication event. The dynamics of a communication event are different depending on the proximity and relative positions of the speaker and his or her audience. For instance, if a speaker is delivering his or her message from a raised platform, the effect is different than if he or she were casually strolling through the audience during the speech. Because of the subtle effects of positioning during a communication message, proxemics is frequently invoked by stage managers. For speech communication teachers, however, proxemic study will focus on unrehearsed and informal arrangements of people during communication.

Ways in Which Nonverbal Communication Patterns Are Learned

One of the main issues in nonverbal communication study is the degree to which nonverbal communication patterns are learned or inherited. Researchers are especially interested in whether or not particular gestures hold the same meanings throughout different cultures. In general, they have discovered that people learn basic nonverbal communication patterns from their parents and the other senior members of their community. At the same time, each individual develops his or her own idiosyncratic nonverbal mechanisms, which reinforce that individual's identity. Interestingly, people tend to use more individualized nonverbal communication techniques at moments of high excitement or stress.

Common Paralinguistic Factors

The three most important paralinguistic factors are pronunciation, articulation, and voice quality. **Pronunciation** is the ability to effectively make vocal sounds that achieve communication goals. Proper pronunciation is relative to an individual's culture. **Articulation** is the ability to make distinct sounds that are intelligible to another person. **Voice quality** is an individual's ability to pronounce the vowels and consonants that are common in a given language. For the most part, voice quality is directly tied to the pronunciation of vowels, since these sounds last longer and are therefore more responsible for an individual's characteristic sound. The collection of vowels and consonants that make up the tonal repertory of a culture are known as the set of **phonemes**.

Articulation of Consonants

Consonant sounds are created by stopping or redirecting a sound. For instance, an "s" sound is formed by pressing the tongue to the palette to slow down an escaping sound. Because consonants often depend on a percussive motion, it is usually not possible to draw them out for a long time. Consequently, consonants do not have as much effect as vowels on the quality of an individual's voice. Because consonants are articulated quickly, they are often more difficult to hear. For this reason, speakers need to be especially sure to clearly articulate them. When a conversation is heard at a great distance, often all that can be discerned is a long string of vowels sounds. Similarly, individuals who mumble are doing a poor job of articulating consonants. Many individuals focus on pronunciation, but clear articulation of consonants is a prerequisite for this skill.

Major Errors of Articulation

As a child learns a new language, he or she has a tendency to omit sounds from words. Over time, the child will include all of the sounds, but may not be able to effectively articulate some of the more difficult consonants. For instance, the "t" sound is one that is often omitted from words, as for instance in the contraction "don't," which is often pronounced as "don'." As an individual begins to speak more quickly, he or she is even more likely to omit these common consonant sounds. To a certain extent, these errors of articulation are not a problem. When they become chronic and extreme, however, they can make speech extremely difficult to understand.

Vocal Pitch

Vocal pitch is the measure of the frequency of a human voice. When the frequency is extremely high, we might say that a person has a whiny or nasal voice. When the frequency is extremely low, we might say that a person has a rumbling or deep voice. Individuals vary the pitch of their voices in order to emphasize or deemphasize certain words in a sentence. For instance, people often raise the pitch of their voices in the last word of a question. Speech communication instructors consider changes in pitch to be a form of nonverbal communication, since the changes in pitch do not themselves contain a linguistic message. Changes in pitch are often made during the pronunciation of a single vowel sound, or between syllables in a word. In some languages, as for instance Chinese, pitch variations actually communicate meaning and cannot be considered nonverbal communication.

Volume and Vocal Delivery

The **volume** of an individual's voice is simply the relative loudness or softness of it. The primary requirement of vocal volume is that it must be loud enough for the intended audience to hear it. As long as this requirement is met, a speaker can utilize varying levels of volume in order to emphasize or deemphasize words and phrases. Obviously, using a higher level of volume draws special attention to what is being said, whereas speaking softly tends to diminish the perceived importance of the message. In the employ of a trained and skilled speaker, however, changes in volume can be quite artful. For instance, a speaker who has fully engaged the attention of his or her audience may lower the volume in order to force the audience to listen closely.

Speed and Vocal Delivery

Speech communication instructors consider vocal speed to be a subdivision of paralinguistics. **Vocal speed**, or rate of speech, is simply a measure of how fast an individual articulates syllables. In most cultures, a rapid rate of speech indicates excitement or urgency, whereas a slow rate of speech suggests calm and thoughtfulness. However, some cultures have a naturally fast or slow rate of speech. For instance, Spanish is typically spoken quite rapidly, even when the speaker is communicating information that has a normal level of urgency. English, on the other hand, is a more slowly-spoken language, especially by the citizens of the United Kingdom. In part, these varying rates of speech are determined by the characteristics of the language. The fact that Spanish words tend to end in a vowel makes it easier to string them together rapidly.

Functions of Pauses in Vocal Delivery

Human speech is not just a constant stream of syllables. The placement and use of pauses during speech also plays an important role in forming meaning. The study of **pauses** in human speech is a subcategory of paralinguistics. A short pause is often used to denote the end of a sentence or clause. In many ways, short pauses are used like commas. Long pauses, on the other hand, are more similar to periods or the ends of paragraphs. When a speaker takes a long pause, he or she may be allowing what has been said to sink into the minds of the audience. Individuals often pause as they search for the right word. Other times, individuals will insert a slight pause into a sentence to create a level of suspense before the thought is finished.

Nonverbal Communication

Enhance Spoken Words

Nonverbal communication is the ability to enhance or elaborate on the words of the speaker. In particular, hand gestures and changes in vocal rhythm and volume have the ability to add expressiveness to what is being said. Many times, the gestures and vocal mechanisms of the speaker simply emphasize his or her message; however, at other times the speaker may detract from or undermine his or her message with contradictory gestures. Hand gestures and gesticulations have the ability to dramatize a communication event. By giving the audience things other than words to concentrate on, the speaker engages and entertains them.

Feedback

Although nonverbal communication is typically thought of as supplementary to the words being spoken during a communication event, it can also serve a vital purpose as **feedback**. The gestures, eye movements, facial expressions, and posture of the audience often indicates their level of engagement more accurately and honestly than verbal criticism. It is very difficult to hide extreme boredom or rapt attention. The nonverbal communication of the audience will indicate their level of interest and acceptance of the message of the speaker. The speaker can then adjust his or her message accordingly.

Alter the Meaning of Spoken Words

At times, the nonverbal communication produced by a speaker will give a slightly different message than that of the speaker's words. This is often the case when a speaker is attempting to introduce an element of irony into his or her message. For instance, if at the conclusion of a bad movie one friend says to another, "Well, that was a good use of my time," but smiles while saying the words, the other friend might assume that the message is being delivered with sarcasm. In other words, the speaker does not literally mean that the movie was a good use of time, but rather wishes to indicate that it was a waste of time. A message is being delivered, but the nonverbal communication accompanying the words creates a complex message different than the mere words being spoken.

Can Create Contradictory Communications

Sometimes, a speaker's nonverbal communication is contradictory to the words he or she is speaking. This can often create confusion and conflict. For instance, imagine a person is in distress. In some cultures, it is not considered dignified to ask another person for help, even in emergency situations. So a person in dire need of assistance might be saying he or she does not need help, even though observation of nonverbal signs says otherwise. Obviously, this will create conflict in the mind of the audience, who will want to obey the wishes of the person but will also want to lend assistance to a person in need. When an individual directly contradicts his or her words with his or her nonverbal communication, it becomes much more difficult for the communication message to be interpreted.

Four Proxemic Distances

Speech communication theorists distinguish four essential proxemic distances: intimate distance, personal distance, social distance, and public distance. **Intimate distance** is the degree of separation common to individuals who know each other very well and are comfortable being physically intimate, for instance parents and children or mates. Intimate distance is at most 2 feet. **Personal distance**, meanwhile, is around 2-1/2 feet. It is the distance maintained between two individuals who know each other and are engaged in a friendly, casual conversation. **Social distance**, usually defined as being from 4 to 7 feet, is the appropriate distance for impersonal and formal conversations. **Public distance** is 12 feet or more and is the amount of distance appropriate for the delivery of speeches to a group of people. Public distance is great enough to focus the attention of the audience on an individual speaker.

Emphasis on Geographic Relationships in Proxemics

In their study of proxemics, speech communication theorists place a great degree of emphasis on geographic location—that is, the relative positions of the participants in a communication event. To begin with, the distances between the various parties are important; the closer the participants in a communication event, the more intimate with one another they can be assumed to be. If one individual is placed above the other members of the communication event, he or she can be assumed to have some sort of elevated status or authority. When individuals are placed around a round table, on the other hand, we may assume that they are equal in importance, and that a democratic discussion rather than a lecture will take place.

Proxemics Can Define Boundaries

The proxemics of a communication event often indicates the boundaries of the parties involved. Individuals have a concept of personal space and territoriality, and tend to be defensive if they believe another person is encroaching on their area. A teacher who lectures from a podium at the front of the class, for instance, would be made uncomfortable if a student got out of his or her chair and stood next to the podium. Similarly, an informal conversation might become uncomfortable for one of the parties if there is too little distance between him and the other participants. For the most part, the appropriate distances between people during a communication event are indicated without explicit mention. In part, the appropriate distance is a cultural designation. However, participants in a communication event can indicate their preferred position through gestures, or simply by moving forward or back.

Proxemics Can Define a Communication Event

The relative positions and distances between the participants in a communication event can indicate a great deal about the quality of the event, even when none of the content of the message is known. For instance, when two people are standing very close to one another during a conversation, we can assume that they are intimate with one another and are discussing a subject of personal interest to each. On the other hand, if two individuals are standing at a considerable distance from one another and avoiding eye contact, we can assume that they either do not know each other very well or they are not well disposed to one another. If one party attempts to close the distance with the other party and the other party resists, we can assume that the first party desires a greater degree of intimacy than does the second.

Proxemics Can Define Interpersonal Relationships

The evolution of interpersonal relationships can be charted by the changes in proxemics. When two people first meet, they are likely to maintain a social distance, between 4 and 7 feet. This distance indicates formality and impersonality. If the two people develop a closer relationship, however, they will likely begin to stand closer to one another during communication. Another scenario in which proxemics denotes interpersonal relationship is when the parties have varying degrees of power. For instance, communication events in which one person is positioned by himself or herself while the others are facing him or her indicate that the isolated individual has a greater degree of power than the others.

Importance of Listening

For most students, the vast majority of information is obtained through listening. Despite the large amount of reading that most students have to do, they still take in more information through their ears than through their eyes. Good listening is an essential part of the communication process because it advances the interests of both the speaker and the listener. Obviously, the listener needs to understand and remember what he or she hears in order to consider the information accurately. At the same time, the listener protects his or her own interests by developing an accurate impression of what the other person has to say. Meanwhile, the ability of the speaker to have his or her message be effective depends on the listening skills of the audience.

Listening for Comprehension

Although listening appears to be a passive process, it must be active in order to be effective. Indeed, the listener should have a purpose for listening. The precise purpose of listening need not be conscious in the mind of the listener. Speech communication teachers generally distinguish four intentions of listening: comprehension, criticism, empathy, and appreciation. These intentions are often intermingled in the same act of listening. When we listen for **comprehension**, we are trying to understand the message the speaker is communicating. In order to listen for comprehension, we need to know the standards of grammar and punctuation in English as well as the common forms of argument. We also need to have an understanding of the context in which the words are spoken so we can understand the relationship between message and context.

Listening for the Purposes of Criticism

Most speech communication teachers will say that in order to listen for the purposes of **criticism**, one must also be listening for comprehension. It is true that to accurately assess the quality of a verbal communication, one must understand the content of the communication first. To a certain degree, however, we all apply critical listening skills to communication we have yet to fully understand. For instance, when we hear an advertisement on the radio, we know immediately that the speaker is trying to sell us something, which makes us naturally receptive or skeptical of the message, depending on our preexisting interest in the product or service. In such a case, our critical listening skills are influencing our listening even before we have begun to comprehend the content.

Listening for Empathy

People often listen to one another as a demonstration of empathy. **Empathy** is the ability to understand and appreciate what another person is going through despite not having the same experience oneself. One of the ways a person can express understanding and compassion for others is simply by listening to them. Listening to someone indicates that his or her problems are worth your time. Most people find that not only is listening a good way to demonstrate empathy, but it is also a good way to develop empathy. It seems that when we listen to one another, we gradually develop a sense of each other's internal worlds, and we come to treat each other with more compassion.

Listening for Appreciation

In many cases, people listen not necessarily for information but simply to **appreciate** the quality of what another person is saying. Many conversations are designed for the entertainment of the listener so it is not absurd to say that one listens to another person talk with the same appreciation one would have when listening to a piece of music. At the same time, it is important to take the speaker seriously on his or her own terms. If the speaker is trying to be gravely serious, it may not be polite to simply listen for appreciation. In many cases, though, and especially when listening to a speaker who is exceptionally fluent or interesting, it is appropriate for a listener simply to appreciate the sounds and meaning the speaker is conveying.

Physical, Mental, and Emotional Obstacles to Listening

A number of things can prevent a person from listening effectively. Perhaps the most common is an external distraction, like background noise or confusing motion. A listener may also be experiencing internal distractions, however, such as anxiety or other preoccupations. Many people are desperate to express themselves and fail to listen to other people because they are so focused on what they themselves want to say. Also, many people have personal biases regarding what the other person is saying that prevent them from listening effectively. Any of these problems can prevent effective interpersonal communication.

Listening for Content in Interpersonal Communication

In almost every listening situation, the audience is required to listen for information. A communication can only be considered effective if the message communicates the information intended by the speaker. The feedback from the audience indicates the degree to which the information has been received accurately. When the audience is required to ask for clarification or repetition of the message, it is possible that the speaker has been ineffective in delivering his or her information. Moreover, if the audience provides no verbal feedback about a delivered message, it is possible that they either did not understand any of the message or are simply not interested in the message. Of course, when there is no verbal feedback it is also possible that the audience simply understood the transmitted message perfectly and they require no clarification or elaboration.

Problems Created by Unwillingness to Listen

Communication can be significantly obstructed when the intended receiver is unwilling to listen. This is a common situation on television talk shows, when all the guests and the host try to talk at once. When this occurs, no one is listening and therefore no messages can be considered complete. In order for a communication event to take place, all the parties involved must accept that there can only be one speaker at a time. Frequently, the unwillingness to be a receiver is a symptom of a poor interpersonal relationship.

Unwillingness to listen is a classic sign of disrespect. Sometimes, however, a failure to listen is simply the product of unfamiliarity between two parties. With a little patience and practice, this obstacle can be overcome and complete communication events can take place.

Interpersonal Communication

For a communication event between two people to be effective, both parties need to alternate the roles of speaker and receiver. Moreover, each receiver should ensure that the message of the speaker is fully understood before delivering his or her own message. Through the use of feedback, such as clarifying questions and comments, the speaker's message can be elaborated and made plain. A conversation cannot really move forward until both parties understand what has been said. This is not to say that the two parties are required to agree on what has been said. On the contrary, some of the best conversations are those in which two parties calmly and descriptively elaborate their differences. To be effective communicators, people need to be able to play the roles of both the speaker and the receiver with skill and dexterity.

Nonverbal Feedback

To be an effective receiver of communication, a person must be able to give clear nonverbal feedback. In particular, facial expressions are a key way of signaling interest and understanding— or the lack thereof. If a person can display subtle gradations in understanding and interest with his or her face, he or she is much more likely to receive a refined and well-adjusted message. Traditionally, smiles and head nods are good indications that the message is being understood, and that the listener agrees. On the other hand, a shake of the head or a frown tends to indicate disagreement with the speaker's message or, sometimes, an inability to comprehend the content. Many people forget that the receiver in a communication event must be as active and engaged as the speaker for the event to be considered a success.

Verbal Feedback

To be an effective receiver, a person needs to be able to issue timely and thoughtful verbal feedback. For instance, a receiver needs to be able to ask pertinent questions if he or she does not understand a particular aspect of the delivered message. At the same time, the receiver needs to be able to describe his or her reaction to the delivered message, whether it be confusion, agreement, or disagreement. Questioning that encourages the speaker to elaborate and refine his or her message often leads to new insights not contained in the original message. In pedagogy, this is known as the **Socratic Method**. In terms of verbal feedback, however, a receiver's most important function is to continually indicate his or her level of understanding of the delivered message.

Process of Creative Listening

Speech communication instructors often use the phrase **creative listening** to describe extremely engaged receivers who are constantly encouraging the speaker to develop and specialize his or her message. An extremely good listener can often discern implications and ideas inherent in the message that may not have been known even to the speaker. In this way, a creative listener can actually add value to the content of the message. Some of the best conversations involve interplay between speaker and creative listener, as each plays ideas off the other until new and exciting conclusions are reached. Creative listening also demonstrates the receiver's interest and respect for the speaker. Often, this has the effect of encouraging the speaker to improve and expand his or her message.

Psychological Effects of Listening

Simply listening to another person can have profound psychological implications. Indeed, the entire field of psychoanalysis is largely based on the idea that having a sympathetic audience for one's problems is profoundly therapeutic. Many people pay a great deal of money simply to have a sympathetic listener who can offer some professional advice. Psychoanalysts are especially skilled at creative listening. That is, they are able to "unpack" the message of the speaker and discern new, possibly hidden meanings. Numerous studies have indicated that the process of verbally elaborating and describing personal issues eases the burden of stress on the mind, regardless of whether the interpretation of these issues is accurate or constructive.

Relationship Between Defensiveness and Good Listening

Defensiveness can be extremely limiting to an individual's ability to listen properly. When a person is **defensive**, he or she is overly concerned with protecting his or her own interests. Defensiveness is especially prevalent in interpersonal communications in which the two parties do not trust one another. However, some paranoid individuals may be naturally more inclined to defensiveness than others. The problem with defensiveness is that it indicates that the attention of the listener is on his or her own concerns, rather than on the content of the message being delivered. To the degree that a listener is not focusing on the message being delivered, his or her ability to understand and respond to the message will be impaired.

Various Ways that Defensiveness can Impair Communication

Speech communication theorists identify a number of ways in which defensiveness can impair effective and accurate communication. These ways are basically defined by the attitude of the listener. For instance, some defensive listeners adopt an overly evaluative posture, in which they indicate that it is up to them to decide whether the speaker is competent or not. Other defensive listeners adopt a self-consciously apathetic attitude, as if to indicate that they are above being interested in the message of the speaker. Another common listening attitude for a defensive individual is certainty, or the assumption that he or she already knows the content of the message. This attitude draws the speaker up short and makes it difficult for him or her to continue communicating.

Active Listening

Active listening is a technique of communication reception in which the listener tries to develop an empathic relationship with the speaker. Proponents of this form of listening declare that a great deal of listening contains an unhelpful evaluative aspect, to the extent that the speaker continually feels in danger of being criticized by the listener. In **active listening**, on the other hand, the listener makes an effort to fully experience the thought process of the speaker before even beginning to judge. Perhaps most importantly, active listening is a skill that is developed over time. To fully engage with what someone is saying, the listener must practice subverting his or her own ego and focus instead on the perceived interests of the speaker.

Cultural Demographics

One way of looking at culture is through the lens of category distinctions. The process of dividing people into categories is commonly known as **demographics**. The most common demographics are age, gender, sexual orientation, religious affiliation, ethnicity, and socioeconomic status. When an individual considers his or her own culture, he or she typically considers it as a set of memberships in these various categories. Those who study and teach speech communication are constantly considering the prejudices and values that influence speech and the interpretation of the spoken word. Part of the process of speech communication instruction is to bring the implicit cultural information in speech to light so that it can be analyzed and critiqued.

Identification with Demographic Categories

In speech communication, one is required to view speech through the lens of received and lived culture. In other words, one is required to consider how elements of culture influence the medium and message of speech, as well as the interpretation of the spoken word. One of the most important aspects of an individual, then, will be the extent to which he or she identifies with various demographic categories. Some people, for instance, have a strong identification with their ethnic or religious background, whereas others base their self-concept more on their gender or age. Age, of course, is a demographic identification that changes with time. Indeed, all demographic identifications may change with time, as an individual acquires more information and critically evaluates the prejudices and values of his or her culture.

Cultural Ideology

Whether consciously or not, every individual has adopted certain ideas, patterns of thought, and prejudices from his or her native culture. This native worldview is known as a **cultural ideology**. The cultural ideology of a particular group permeates every aspect of the group's existence. It defines what is important in the group, what is right or wrong in the group, and how members of the group should behave. The aspects of an individual's native ideology are often so ingrained that they are considered "common sense" and never really held up to scrutiny. Ideologies are important because they provide individuals with a moral compass and a sense of pattern in the world; however, it is important to develop an ability to think clearly and objectively about one's own ideology.

Cultural Hegemony

Cultural hegemony is any relationship in which one party is dominant and one party is submissive and in which both roles are agreed upon by the participants. Every culture establishes basic hegemonies, in part as a way of organizing the populace. For instance, in Asian cultures it is typical for the husband to impose his will on the wife, although she may subtly exercise power in her own right. Both partners agree that this is the proper hegemonic relationship between married couples. The hegemonies are not necessarily bad; in fact, they are useful ways of distributing power and responsibility in a society. However, students of speech communication need to be conscious of the ways in which language establishes and reinforces hegemony. Over time, it may be necessary for a culture to modify its hegemonies in response to the repressed needs of certain people.

Cultural Enactment

Cultural enactment is the process in which an individual fulfills the expectations of his or her culture with his or her words or behavior. In other words, cultural enactment is the "acting out" of cultural values. All of us are engaged in cultural enactment throughout our lives. When we get up in the morning, go off to work, and fulfill our roles as professionals, we are adhering to the expectations of our society. When we relate in a certain way to our family members, we are fulfilling our roles as mothers, fathers, brothers, sisters, etc. In speech communication, we study cultural enactment as it is performed in language. Whether consciously or not, we are constantly adhering to the expectations of society with our manner of speaking and with the message we present. Speech communication seeks to analyze this process.

Cultural Embodiment

Although every person grows up and develops with a particular cultural background, very rarely do we take the time to objectively consider it. In part, this is because it is very difficult to put into words the ideology that supports our worldview. Nevertheless, through our speech we are constantly producing and reinforcing the values shared by the members of our community. This process of expressing cultural assumptions is known as **cultural embodiment**. In literal terms, "cultural embodiment" means giving a body to the unconscious values and beliefs held by a particular culture. In speech communication studies, we are particularly interested in cultural embodiment through language. One of the goals of studying speech communication is to acquire an objective understanding of one's own culture as it is reflected in speech.

Demographic Analysis

Before delivering a speech, a speaker should, if possible, engage in some basic demographic analysis. The following are the most important demographic categories: age, education, gender, group membership, and cultural background. In many groups, all the audience members will be of the same general age, and the speech can therefore be tailored to their maturity level. As far as education, it is important to know about the audience's experiences and knowledge regarding the topic before the speech begins. Many times, the members of the audience will all belong to a specific group, such as a school class or a civic organization. Finally, the cultural background of a group should be considered because the group's values, taboos, predilections, and ethics could be offended by the speech.

Nonverbal Communication

Nonverbal communication is the set of ways in which humans send and receive messages without using words. For teachers, it is just as important to be effective nonverbal communicators as verbal communicators. They are essential aspects of the teaching process and can sometimes even be more effective than a verbal reminder. Nonverbal communication includes gestures, facial expressions, proximity, humor, posture, body orientation or touching. Being aware of the ways students communicate nonverbally can also assist teachers in getting messages about how their students are learning. Sometimes sending signals can reinforce learning more effectively, because they are implicit. Students will learn how to react to your nonverbal communication more readily because it tends to be less confrontational than direct statements.

Group Communication

Purpose of a Discussion Group

One special form of interpersonal communication is the **discussion group** in which a small number of people gather together for a particular purpose. The purpose may be to solve a problem, to organize a collective effort, or simply to elaborate and analyze a controversial issue. Sometimes, discussion groups are held in a ritual fashion, as for instance in the case of book clubs or Bible study groups. Speech communication theorists assert that regular and organized discussion groups typically have better communication. Also, discussion groups seem to function better when there is a clear and explicit hierarchy among the members, whether there is one leader of the discussion or none at all.

Characteristics of a Positive Discussion Group

For a discussion group to function effectively, a good sense of rapport and understanding must exist among the members of the group. These positive sentiments are more easily cultivated in groups that meet regularly. For new groups, establishing a positive environment for discussion is the responsibility of the chairperson, leader, or moderator. Unless a comfortable discussion environment is established, it will be difficult for the group to accomplish its goals. Time and again, research studies suggest that relationships between people have far-reaching effects on the progress and ultimate success of organizations both great and small. Discussion groups are no exception to this tendency.

Importance of Morale and Efficiency for a Discussion Group

For a discussion group to be effective, the group needs to have a high sense of morale. **Morale** is a general expression used to describe the attitude of the members of the group in regard to the activities of the group. If the members of the group enjoy one another's company and feel like the group meetings are worthwhile, morale will be high. Morale is also linked to situations in which the members of the group know their respective roles. When everyone knows his or her job and responsibilities, there is much less resentment and blaming for unaccomplished work. Similarly, the degree to which a discussion group is productive in pursuit of its goals will determine the effectiveness of the group. If, after several meetings, the members of the discussion group observe that progress is being made toward long-term goals, they will be more likely to commit themselves to the group and make any necessary changes to promote its effectiveness.

Importance of Togetherness for a Discussion Group

Research into discussion groups suggests that a sense of togetherness is essential for the promotion of discussion group goals. When the members of the group feel tied to one another, they are more likely to go out of their way to help one another and promote the progress of the group. In other words, the members of a cohesive group subvert their own goals in the interest of promoting the group goals. Also, the members of a cohesive group are more likely to communicate any personal problems that may affect the progress of the group. Communication becomes highly efficient and constructive criticism does not derail group activities. Cohesiveness can be built by creating an atmosphere in which the group members take an interest in one another and are respectful of each other's feelings.

Building a Positive Social Environment for a Discussion Group

Discussion group leaders can actively promote a positive social environment in a number of different ways. One easy thing to do is to allow the members of a group to get to know each other during the first group meeting. Many group leaders begin with a few "icebreaking" activities, in which the members of a group share a little bit of information about their personal lives and therefore become more comfortable. It is especially useful to have all the members of a discussion group describe what they are hoping to get out of the group work, as this establishes a climate in which all group members are openly working toward communal goals. It is natural for the members of a new group to feel a bit apprehensive during the first meeting. As much as possible, the group leader should seek to mitigate this apprehension by promoting warmth and positivity.

The Relationship Between Disagreement and Cohesiveness in a Discussion Group

It may seem like a paradox, but groups with a high level of cohesiveness tend to have a higher incidence of disagreement. The simple reason for this is that in a cohesive group the members feel comfortable enough with one another to disagree. In other words, the group members do not worry that a disagreement will destroy the group. Also, a cohesive group has likely established positive channels for constructive disagreement, so members are assured that conflicting opinions will not be viewed harshly by the other group members. Furthermore, cohesive groups often discover that frequent disagreement can be a stimulus to improve effectiveness in group discussion. When all the group members agree with one another, they do not raise pertinent objections and do not subject ideas to enough scrutiny.

Establishing Roles in a Discussion Group

For a group discussion to be effective, it is important that the group members have established roles. Speech communication research suggests that even if roles are not made explicit at the beginning of the discussion, after an hour or so individuals will naturally assume specialized roles. For instance, once the discussion gets rolling, it is natural for one or two leaders to emerge. Similarly, a discussion usually has two or three individuals who do not advance the discussion but offer insightful critiques of what has been said by others. The formation of an individual's role within a group is a constantly evolving process in which the individual's personal desires and thoughts are combined with the needs and reactions of the group.

Basic Principles of Role Emergence

The emergence of individual roles in a group discussion is the result of interplay between the individual and the group. In other words, an individual is not solely responsible for his or her role, and neither is the group solely responsible for designating that individual. Once the members of the group have assumed tentative roles, the other members of the group assess the value of each role. That is, a hierarchy begins to develop within the group. Those individuals who have emerged as the leaders of the group are given a higher status. Group members look to them for direction, their opinions carry more weight, and the other group members tend to listen to them more closely. Lower status group members, on the other hand, may feel that their opinions are not valued and that they are not really being given the full attention of the group. Over time, however, group roles can shift, and individuals can gain or lose status.

Characteristics of a Leader

Perhaps the most important role within a discussion group is the leader. Research suggests that most people, given the option, would prefer to be the leader. Indeed, most people lead in at least one area of their lives, whether at school, at home, or at work. However, some people have a natural gift for leadership. In a discussion group, these individuals tend to speak more, be more forthright with their opinions, and project more confidence with their nonverbal communication. Of course, individuals can also develop leadership traits over time. Some people do not really blossom as leaders until they reach adulthood. Although our society values democracy, it seems clear that discussion groups function most effectively when there is some form of leadership. Perhaps the essential point is that leadership must be a designation agreed upon by all members of the group in order to be effective.

Characteristics of a Central Person in a Discussion Group

Speech communication instructors often refer to a "central person" in a discussion group. A central person is one who has such a strong personality that he or she cannot help but influence the group. A central person may have a positive or negative effect on the group. Central people are often funny, charming, and charismatic. However, their charisma may distract the attention of the group from its intended goals. Speech communication instructors are interested in central people because of their random and destabilizing effects on groups. At times, the presence of an influential central person can lead a group to high achievement; at other times, the manipulations and distractions of the central person can negatively affect the group.

Effects of Changing Membership on a Discussion Group

The effect of membership changes within a discussion group is destabilizing. When new members are added to a group, they must quickly assume roles in order to avoid obstructing the current progression of group work. If a group member is removed, on the other hand, the remaining members must try to fill the void by assuming different responsibilities. In general, it seems that when the members of a group change, the roles of every other group member are affected to a greater or lesser degree. Afterward, a brief period of instability ensues, in which the group is less effective than before. It is important for discussion groups to recognize the inevitability of this down period, and to be patient as roles are reestablished.

Basic Principles of Formal Leadership

Sometimes the roles in a discussion group are determined ahead of time. Speech communication instructors refer to this kind of group as having a formal organization. A formal organization will almost always have a designated leader. Furthermore, the other members of the group will probably have their relative status designated over time, as well. Unlike a free-form group, in which roles emerge and evolve over time, a formal discussion group features static group roles. At times, this can create inefficiencies in the group, as for instance when the designated leader is ineffective at discharging his or her duties. Similarly, group members with lower status may gradually develop skills that would otherwise lead to an increase in the importance of their role. The rigid nature of a formal hierarchy, then, can inhibit discussion if it is not managed properly.

Characteristics of Group Discussion

When speech communication instructors use the phrase **group discussion**, they are referring to a single meeting or group of meetings of a small number of people who have a similar, agreed-upon set of goals. The minimum number of people required for a small group discussion is three, and whereas the maximum number is not set in stone, it is generally agreed that a group of more than fifteen will have a hard time managing a democratic discussion. Ideally, a small group discussion will have about five members. This seems to be the maximum number of people who can participate fully in a discussion. When a group has more than five members, it is common for the extra members to remain silent for the most part.

Characteristics of an Isolated, One-Time Meeting

In some cases, a small group discussion meeting will be held only one time. The dynamics of this kind of meeting are slightly different than those of a set of meetings held regularly over a period of time. For instance, a one-time meeting does not provide enough time for roles to develop and emerge, so it is beneficial if a group organization is established beforehand. As much as possible, the members of the group should become familiar with one another rapidly so the business of the discussion can begin without delay. Effective leadership is especially important when administrating a one-time meeting, as there will be no time to waste on role development and making acquaintances.

Characteristics of an Ad Hoc Meeting

Small group discussions are sometimes organized to address a particular problem. Speech communication instructors refer to these meetings as **ad hoc groups**, from the Latin phrase meaning "for a particular purpose." An ad hoc group may meet only once or it may meet several times until the intentions of the group have been realized. It is likely that the members of an ad hoc group will not have met each other before the first group meeting. However, unlike the members of the one-time meeting, the members of an ad hoc meeting group can assume they will be in contact with one another until their mission is complete. This tends to encourage a bit more solidarity. Also, an ad hoc discussion group provides more opportunity for role emergence and development.

ROLE OF A CHAIRPERSON IN LEADING AN ISOLATED MEETING

A discussion group that meets only once requires effective leadership more than any other kind of group. To swiftly and effectively lead a one-time discussion group, a chairperson must establish ahead of time the precise purpose of the meeting. This purpose should be known to all group participants. The discussion should be structured to achieve the goal and, as much as possible, environmental distractions should be minimized. Any preparatory materials required for the discussion should be procured ahead of time. It is also important to determine the necessary outcomes of the meeting. The chairperson needs to know what sort of information constitutes a conclusive decision by the discussion group. He or she needs to know what details have to be decided upon before the group can adjourn. Finally, the chairperson needs to know and explain the mechanisms for putting into place the decisions made during the discussion.

STRUCTURE FOR LEADING A ONE-TIME MEETING

Although every one-time meeting will be slightly different, depending on the structure, membership, and intentions of the meeting, there is a basic structure a chairperson can follow. First, the chairperson should call the meeting to order and announce the intentions of the discussion. The chairperson should then lead the discussion, heading off any digressions and maintaining the group's focus on its overall goals. After a sufficient amount of discussion, the chairperson may need to stimulate decision-making by calling for a vote. If there are time constraints on the meeting, the chairperson should be aware of these and truncate discussion when necessary. The chairperson should occasionally summarize what has been decided to that point and indicate what the group has left to do. When all the goals of the discussion have been reached, the chairperson needs to be able to summarize them and indicate what will then happen in the future.

PARTICIPATION IN A ONE-TIME MEETING

Individuals who participate in a one-time meeting need to be conscious of the particular characteristics of this kind of discussion. They should not waste any time worrying about their personal concerns or role within the group, but should focus their efforts on the achievements of group goals. Participants need to maintain an open mind during discussion and keep their own contributions on topic. In a one-time meeting, it is important that all perspectives receive an airing, so participants should avoid dominating discussion. In general, participants should maintain a civil and respectful tone in their remarks, as a one-time meeting group is typically made up of individuals who do not know each other very well and they must necessarily maintain a decent rapport in order to achieve their mission

GROUP DISCUSSION

ATTENTION SPAN OF A SMALL GROUP

One of the obstacles any small discussion group will face is the limited attention span of its members. Sometimes a discussion veers off in a direction only interesting to one or two of the group members, causing the other members to lose interest and become disengaged from the discussion. If a designated group leader exists, it is his or her job to make sure digressions are avoided and all members of the group are engaged. After the group has fully discussed a subject and can no longer continue with the topic, the group leader needs to summarize the positions of the group members and introduce a new topic for discussion. This is especially true when a group has only limited time for discussion or numerous things on the agenda.

RELATIONSHIP BETWEEN FREEDOM AND STRUCTURE IN SMALL GROUP MEETINGS

In their consideration of small group discussions, speech communication instructors often focus on the balance between freedom and structure. To be effective, a discussion needs to have a discernible and appropriate structure. On the other hand, to be engaging, a discussion needs to allow group members to follow their own ideas and interests. How effective a group leader is at maintaining the balance between freedom and structure will spell the difference between success and failure. With experience, discussion leaders can learn to moderate in such a way that the goals of the group are accomplished without repressing the interests of the participants. Occasionally, a group leader must refer members of the group back to the original goals, or at least reframe the current discussion in light of the avowed intentions of the group.

Benefits of Small Group Conversation

Small group conversation has a number of potential benefits. For one thing, information can be exchanged during these discussions. Small group discussions are also a useful forum for individuals to share their ideas and experiences. People are often able to convey emotion much more effectively in a small group discussion setting than through writing or communication with a larger group. A small group discussion is an excellent way to develop individual speaking and listening skills, since it is likely that each member of the group will be called upon to contribute frequently. Furthermore, a small group discussion is an ideal environment for persuading others of something because the intimacy afforded by the limited membership is conducive to building rapport.

Certain individuals seem to thrive in small group discussions. Although the charismatic qualities that make for effective small group discussion may seem abstract to many people, they are actually quite simple. For one thing, good discussion members are always sincere in what they say. They do not make the other members of the discussion group guess whether they are being serious or not. Good discussion members are also versatile and can adjust their comments and questions depending on the flow of conversation. Good discussion members exercise tact and courtesy in regard to their peers. Finally, good discussion members are good listeners, capable of demonstrating through their actions and responses that they take all the other members of the group seriously.

Group Discussions Can Help Provide Information

Group discussions are a useful source of information. The various members of a group discussion will naturally have different levels of experience and expertise on the subject at hand and will hopefully be able to fill in gaps in each other's knowledge base. Indeed, many discussion groups are organized simply for the purpose of assembling a comprehensive body of knowledge on a particular subject. It is always useful to ask participants to prepare for group discussions that have information-gathering as their explicit purpose. Sometimes a group discussion will begin by compiling all the information on the subject, after which it will move into the analysis and evaluation phases.

Group Discussions Can Yield Solid Evaluations

Group discussions are often used to evaluate a given subject. This is especially the case when the members of the group discussion are attempting to solve a particular problem. In this scenario, the group may outline the problem, describe the various proposed solutions, and then evaluate them. A small group discussion is most effective at evaluation when all the members have equal standing. Also, evaluation is most effective when all the members have a similar body of knowledge on the subject. If only a few people in the small group truly understand the problem, they may be the only ones who can contribute meaningful evaluations of the proposed solutions.

Decisions Are Made in a Group Discussion

Group discussions are often used to make decisions. Often, a group will gather and compile a body of information, evaluate potential solutions to a problem, and then decide on a course of action. Group discussions that are intended to end with decision-making seem to work best when there is an established and agreed-upon format for this process. For instance, many groups adopt parliamentary procedure as a way of organizing a discussion. For many groups, though, this may be excessively formal. In a small group, any system of decision-making is fine as long as it is agreed upon by the members. In small groups, there is enough time and space for all members to contribute their opinions before holding a vote.

Panel Discussion

Panel discussions are probably the most common form of small group discussion. They typically consist of between four to eight individuals, one of whom is designated by the others as a leader. The members of a panel discussion do not prepare formal speeches in advance of the meeting. In addition, there is no prescribed order to the proceedings beyond the fact that the discussion will be led by the designated individual. **Panel discussions** are typically organized to discuss a specific problem or theme. They are not really the best format for decision-making. Panel discussions often occur at conferences. When this is the case, a small group may discuss an issue before a large audience and then open the floor to questions.

Lecture Format for Group Discussion

A group discussion held in a **lecture format** always includes a clearly defined leader. The leader will deliver a long, prepared speech on a given topic. Before the meeting, various members of the discussion will have been given assignments. During the course of the leader's presentation, he or she will call on the various group members to elaborate on key points or provide specific information. During the leader's presentation, group members will have the opportunity to interrupt and ask questions. Once a subject has been covered in its entirety and is understood by all discussion members, the leader will move on to another topic.

Roundtable Discussion

In a **roundtable discussion**, there is very little hierarchy among the members. There may be an acknowledged leader, but he or she is often not responsible for providing more information or direction to the group than any other member. All the members of a roundtable discussion are expected to have done some preparation before the beginning of the meeting. This kind of meeting format is especially appropriate for groups in which all the members can be assumed to be reasonably informed and competent in the area to be discussed. Also, groups whose members have different areas of expertise often hold roundtable discussions. When this is the case, a leader might informally direct the conversation to various members as different points in the overall subject are being discussed.

Progressive Group Discussion

In a **progressive group discussion**, a large group is divided into several smaller groups. These smaller groups simultaneously discuss the various components of a larger problem. For example, one group might focus on the roots of a problem while another group might look at the consequences of possible solutions. Each member of the discussion group may be asked to be ready to discuss all subjects or each may be assigned in advance a particular aspect of the subject to discuss. Once all the small groups have come to a general consensus, the group as a whole will reconvene and one representative from each small group will present his or her group's findings to the rest of the people.

Symposium Format for Group Discussion

In a **symposium**, the participants in the discussion are allotted a certain amount of time and are placed in order ahead of time. It is typical for a symposium to have a designated leader. This leader will introduce each of the participants in the discussion. All speakers in a symposium will be discoursing on the same subject or theme. The leader will often take a moment between speakers to provide a cohesive overview of what has been covered to that point. At the end of the symposium, the speaker will offer some concluding remarks. There is no prearranged interaction between the participants in a symposium, although the leader is free to open the panel to discussion at his or her discretion.

Steps of a Successful Group Discussion

To be productive, a group discussion must follow a logical sequence. Speech communication instructors have delineated five basic steps in successful group discussion:

1. The group defines the problem or topic to be discussed.
2. The group compiles all the information they have on the subject.
3. The group evaluates the possible solutions to the problem or possible insights to be gained from evaluating the topic.
4. The fourth step is selecting the best solution, which may require deliberation and even voting.
5. The group will outline practical ways that the agreed-upon solution can be put into action.

Introduction of New Material Can Improve Group Discussion

One sure way to improve the quality of a group discussion is to assemble a greater amount of information. One of the common fallacies of participation in a discussion is that it does not require preparation. On the contrary, discussions are only successful to the degree that the participants can offer reasoned, well-considered examples and evidence. If necessary, group members should bring published material that is relevant to the discussion. Also, group members may want to consider how the subject or problem to be discussed has impacted their personal lives. Although group members do not want to spend a great deal of time discussing their personal lives, in some cases personal experience may have a direct influence on the discussion.

By listening more carefully and creatively, participants can improve a group discussion. In a sense, group discussion is a creative, collaborative enterprise. Group members expand upon, elaborate, and modify one another's ideas until a group consensus is reached. By listening attentively, group members achieve a good understanding of what is being said by their fellow participants, and will improve their ability to modify and embellish ideas. At any given time, every group member should be able to summarize the general topic of discussion as well as what has been said so far in the discussion.

Discussion Leadership

Although group discussions are basically a democratic arrangement, it can be useful to designate a discussion leader. A leader is someone who has the special responsibility of being prepared and keeping the business of the group on track. There are three basic kinds of leaders: non-directive, directive, and supportive.

A **non-directive leader** participates in the group discussion like any other member. This kind of leader exercises very little control over the actions of the group. Mainly, a non-directive leader is designated just in case the group needs help getting the discussion back on track or coming to a conclusion. If the discussion flows smoothly, a non-directive leader will not have to assert him or herself.

A **directive leader** is assertive in controlling the activities of the group. Unlike a non-directive leader, who only leads when the discussion gets off track, a directive leader is constantly arranging the activities of the group. A directive leader initiates discussion, calls upon members of the group to speak, and suspends discussion when he or she believes it is time. Directive leaders are more appropriate in situations where group participants are unfamiliar with one another or unfamiliar with the general dynamics of group discussion.

A **supportive leader** exhibits elements of both directive and non-directive leadership. The supportive leader is a bit more hands-on than a non-directive leader but is less assertive than a directive leader. Basically, a supportive leader is responsible for suggesting possible solutions and discussion strategies to the group. A supportive leader does not attempt to influence the course of discussion or the decisions made by the group, but rather seeks to aid the group in whatever direction is chosen. Supportive leaders are appropriate for groups that understand the topic thoroughly but may need some help coming to a decision.

Discussion Leader

A **discussion leader** is responsible for opening and closing a discussion meeting. The leader should first introduce the topic or problem to be discussed. If the members of the discussion group do not know one another, the leader should take a moment to introduce all members or allow new members to introduce themselves. The discussion leader should always make sure that every member of the discussion group fully understands the problem or topics to be discussed. Once a resolution to the problem has been found or the topic has been fully discussed, the leader should close the discussion. At this time, the leader should offer a brief summary of what has been discussed as well as the agreed-upon solution. The leader should also ask if there are any remaining questions from members of the group.

To lead a discussion group effectively, the group leader must be well prepared. Of course, all members of the discussion group need to be prepared in order to contribute in a positive way to the discussion, but this is even truer of the group leader. A leader needs to be able to summarize the topic at the beginning of the meeting and should have a rough idea of the potential solutions or conclusions the group will come up with. A leader must also be fluent enough in the discussion topic to summarize it to the group at various points during the discussion.

It is imperative for a group leader to maintain the focus of the group on the task at hand. All too often, a group discussion goes off down a blind alley or ends up in unproductive digressions. Even a non-directive leader needs to be capable of stepping in and refocusing the attention of the group one easy way to do this is by restating or summarizing what has been discussed so far. This tends to draw the attention of the group members back to the original task at hand. A group leader may also indicate discussion topics that still need to be addressed or try to refocus the group by asking a general question about the central issue of the discussion.

Discussion Critique Can Be Performed

After a discussion is over, it is advantageous to spend some time considering which aspects of it were successful and which were not. To this end, many people find it useful to complete a discussion critique. A discussion critique is simply a standardized form on which people can indicate their opinion of the discussion. Sometimes, participants are asked to grade the quality of the discussion in a number of different areas on a scale of one to ten. Some discussion critique forms ask participants to grade the individual performances of their fellow group members. When this is the case, it may be appropriate to make the forms anonymous.

Use of Interaction and Participation Diagrams

People who study group discussion often use participation and interaction diagrams as tools for analysis and evaluation. These diagrams indicate how many times every participant in a discussion has spoken, on what issues they spoke, and to whom they directed their comments. The members of the group are represented in boxes or circles on the form. Lines drawn between the participants indicate interactions during the discussion. These diagrams can be useful because they indicate when certain members of the group are primarily talking amongst themselves as opposed to involving all the members of the group. Sometimes a group leader will study interaction and participation diagrams and realize that conversation has been unfairly dominated by a few members of the group.

Oral Communication Builds Community

Public speaking is an act that creates and reinforces the bonds of a community. When a person speaks in public, he or she is expressing his or her own opinions and beliefs, which may echo or stand in contrast to those of the community. In either case, public speech requires the listeners to consider their own shared beliefs. Public speech draws attention to the similarities and differences between various communities through a process known as **cultural maintenance**. Through the creation of a public discourse, the members of a community learn about each other and think critically about their social mores and cultural values.

Media and Mass Communication

Development of Radio Communication

At one point in American history, radio communication was the most important means of mass communication. The first commercial radio station began broadcasting in 1920. At first, radio was not very popular, because most people could not afford home receivers. As these devices began to become more common in American homes, however, programming expanded and the radio became a source of information and entertainment. In 1941, the first FM station began broadcasting, allowing signals to be transmitted over long distances with a very small amount of static. Although radio communication has been somewhat superseded by television and the internet, it is still an invaluable source of information and entertainment for millions of people

Relationship of Radio to Other Forms of Mass Media

When it was first introduced, radio was the most important form of mass communication. Unlike telegraphs, radios could deliver complex messages about events as they happened. Also, radio allowed for dramatic use of the human voice and special sound effects. In general, radio is a more personal medium than telegraph communication. Eventually, however, the ability of television to transmit images and sound allowed this medium to supersede radio as the primary form of mass communication. Nevertheless, radio remains the predominant medium for the transmission of music and continues to be an important vehicle for the transmission of news.

Development of Radio Networks

One of the most important periods in the history of radio communication was the development of radio networks. Radio networks first developed as a way to offset the costs of maintaining radio towers and transmission equipment. Radio networks began to sell commercials to businesses that wanted to advertise. These businesses would pay the radio station for the right to air their advertisements. Various radio stations joined together in networks and gave one another permission to air each other's shows. In this way, radio stations around the country standardized programming and made radio a viable business. Each station was able to produce a smaller amount of better programming.

Development of Motion Pictures

The first motion pictures were developed by Thomas Edison and his associates in 1893. After a few years of tinkering, motion pictures were introduced to the general public and were immediately popular. Many stores offered "nickelodeons," in which patrons could watch a brief presentation for a nickel. Around 1910, a small film industry began to develop in Hollywood, California. In 1912, the first full-size theaters were introduced. In the mid-1920s, sound was added to motion pictures, which had previously been silent or accompanied by live music. By 1929, all new films had sound.

Significance of Motion Pictures

Motion pictures have played an important role in the economic and social life of the United States. Perhaps the first example of the effect of the movies was during the Great Depression, when motion pictures continued to portray images of success and wealth in spite of the widespread poverty beyond the theater. It was at this point that people began to note the escapism inherent in the movie-watching experience. Since then, movies have proven to be a powerful medium for exploring real events, including tragic ones. Two good examples of this are the newsreels of battle footage from World War II and the many powerful movies that have been made on the subject of the Vietnam War.

Development of Television Communication

Television is such an entrenched part of daily American life that some might forget that it has really only been part of the culture for the past sixty years. Although the first television broadcasts took place in 1939, it was only after World War II that television truly burst onto the American scene. At first, televisions were extremely expensive and signals were only broadcast in black and white. Also, when televisions were first introduced, radio communication was still the most popular medium. Over time, however, televisions became smaller and less expensive and better quality programming became available. After approximately a decade, television supplanted radio as the most popular form of mass communication in the United States.

News Coverage

Because of its ability to deliver visual images and sound, television has proven to be an excellent medium for transmitting news. Many people get the majority of their information from television broadcasts. Television transmission has allowed people to get global news and learn about life in even the farthest reaches of the world, which they might otherwise never be able to see or visit. At the same time, many television news programs seek to provide in-depth analysis and evaluation of local, state, federal, and global issues. Television has proven to be an excellent medium for interviews and documentaries as well.

Entertainment

For most people, television is primarily a source of entertainment. Comedies, sports, dramas, game shows, and reality programs are among the most popular forms of television entertainment. Perhaps the most venerable form of television entertainment is the soap opera, so named because the first programs targeted housewives and were sponsored by soap companies. Some television programs air at a regular time for years on end, while others, such as miniseries, are only on the air for a limited time. Television executives determine which entertainment shows they will continue broadcasting by evaluating Nielsen ratings, which measure how many viewers are tuning in to each program.

Relationship Between Television and Business

Over time, television has become a big business. Television stations make most of their money by airing commercials. Although television stations must pay for their transmission equipment, their primary expenditure is for the development of programming. Television networks, similar to radio networks, developed as a way to share the costs of program development. Broadcast television, which is available simply with the use of an antenna, is free to the general public. Cable television, on the other hand, must be purchased by subscription. The advent of cable television in the 1950s allowed television stations to fund special-interest programming for a limited audience.

Media's Role in Informing the Public

The mass media plays a central role in informing the general public about local and global events. When most people think about information disseminated through the media, they think about news programming. But there are a number of other venues through which information is transmitted to the public. For instance, nature documentaries and talk shows inform the general public on issues that are perhaps less immediately pertinent to their lives. The federal government uses channels of communication such as radio and television to broadcast emergency messages and to promote governmental policies. Magazines and newspapers can also disseminate detailed information on behalf of government agencies.

Media's Role in Changing Attitudes and Behavior

Although the precise power of the media is a matter of controversy, it is beyond question that the major media outlets have an ability to persuade the general public. To take the most obvious example, advertisements on television clearly have a positive effect on sales. Many of the ways in which the media can influence attitudes and behavior are more subtle, however. For instance, the media can influence popular opinion simply by providing information about a particular subject. One indication of the media's influence on behavior is shown simply in the fact that people commonly choose to spend time watching television or listening to the radio rather than doing other things.

Media's Role in Entertaining the Public

In public surveys, people cite entertainment as the number one reason for engaging with mass media. This data is produced by Nielsen ratings, which indicate that people watch sports, comedy, and drama programming much more frequently than news. Moreover, the line between information and entertainment is often blurred. For instance, many documentaries that purport to be informative are also quite entertaining. Indeed, the inherently entertaining nature of mass media communication makes such media a powerful tool for engaging an audience in educational and informative programming. Many people acquire a broad knowledge of the world through television and radio without ever realizing they are engaged in a process of education.

Development of the Internet and Its Effect on Communication

Although the internet has been around for approximately 20 years, it did not truly become part of the mainstream media until the mid-1990s. Today it is ubiquitous within American culture and is an integral part of the way people communicate with one another. Instantaneous forms of communication such as email, instant messaging, blogging, and video blogging and conferencing have all become available to people who formerly would have had no access to them. The result is that it is now possible to communicate with people around the globe at virtually any time. The internet has brought formerly isolated geographic areas into contact with other parts of the world and has provided forums for members of every special-interest group in existence. At the same time, many critics charge that the instantaneous communication afforded by the internet has impoverished communication on the local and community level.

MEDIA

Mass communication is defined as the one-way transmission of messages to a large, diverse audience. Radio, television, and the internet are the typical vehicles for mass communication. Some people include print media as a component of mass communication, although others declare that mass media requires almost instantaneous transmission. One of the signature qualities of mass media communication is that it can be reproduced and replayed in exactly the same way more than once. In other words, since it has the capability of being recorded, it can be played more than once and for more than one audience.

USE OF A MEDIA DIARY

Many people would be shocked to realize just how much time they spend engaged with mass media. Spending a half-hour here, forty-five minutes there in total can add up to a huge chunk of time. One way to gain control over the time spent engaged with mass media is to maintain a media diary. A **media diary** is simply a daily catalog of the amount of time devoted to different forms of media. For instance, a student might want to keep a media diary listing the amount of time spent listening to the radio, watching television, or surfing the internet. It might also be a good idea to include activities such as watching movies and playing video games. Students should record how much time they spend in each one of these activities and then calculate it as a percentage of their total free time.

USE OF A MEDIA EVALUATION FORM

Another way to keep track of individual media intake is through the use of a media evaluation form. Unlike a media diary, which simply indicates how much time was spent with various media, a **media evaluation form** keeps track of the quality and content of the media that is consumed. For instance, a media evaluation form will include a list of the various television programs the individual watched during the week, along with a brief summary and evaluation of the programs. Many people are shocked to discover how much time they spend every week engaged with programming they do not particularly enjoy. The use of the media evaluation form is a great way to streamline media intake because it encourages an individual to devote time only to content he or she most enjoys.

MEDIA'S ABILITY TO SPUR PUBLIC CONVERSATION

One of the key roles of the mass media is to inspire and shape public dialogue. For instance, the news media's coverage of a political issue can set up debate. Many people have alleged over the years that the news media in the United States has a particular political bias. Some people claim it has a liberal bias, while others claim it is a conservative bias. Perhaps the safest criticism one can make of the news media is that it has an inherent interest in conflict, because controversy and disagreement is more interesting to viewers. Most critics of the mass media agree that it is influenced in large part by the desire to sell advertising space.

MEDIA'S ABILITY TO FRAME DISCUSSION

One of the media's greatest responsibilities is to frame public discussion in a fair and objective way. In other words, the media is charged with reporting the news in a way that gives ample space to all reasonable points of view and does not ignore pertinent facts on either side. The role of the media in influencing discussion in a society has led some critics to refer to news outlets as "information gatekeepers." It is important that there be vocal critics of the news media, to identify and remedy problems of objectivity to a certain degree, all citizens are responsible for casting a skeptical eye on the news media and for making sure these media enable free and fair discussion.

IMPORTANCE OF APPLYING CRITICAL ANALYSIS SKILLS TO THE MEDIA

When the news media is free and unfettered, it is essential for all citizens to maintain a skeptical attitude and apply critical analysis skills to informative programming. Television viewers should keep in mind that the way a subject is photographed can influence the way it is perceived. For instance, individuals who are photographed in shadow tend to seem more dangerous or malevolent. Most people are good at critically appraising commercials but do not necessarily apply the same skills to avowedly informative programming. Viewers should remember that a persuasive element exists in every communication, no matter how impartial, and so should remain alert to signs of bias.

General Feedback is Offered to the Media

The providers of mass media communication receive general feedback from a number of different sources. Television companies, for instance, are constantly organizing focus groups to view and offer feedback on new television shows and commercials. Sometimes networks will arrange for a focus group to be composed entirely of members of a particular demographic, as for example women or African-Americans. Perhaps the most famous example of general feedback for the mass media is the Nielsen ratings, which are used to determine how many people watch a particular television program. The providers of mass communication use all of this general feedback to refine and tailor their messages to the audience.

Personal Feedback is Offered to the Media

The media receives a great deal of personal feedback from individuals in the general public. Any time a person writes or calls a television or radio station to convey his or her response to a program, he or she is giving personal feedback. Many television and radio programs explicitly call for audience participation, which is to say they ask for personal feedback to use as content in their programming. In a way, consumers provide personal feedback to the media in their choice of purchases, since these consumer decisions indicate which television and radio advertisements are effective. Individual voices actually do play a great role in affecting the quality of the content of media presentations.

Programming Process for Radio and Television

Radio and television programming are primarily a matter of economics. Networks want to schedule their most expensive and most popular programming at the times when the most people are likely to see or hear it. For radio this means during the morning and afternoon, when people are likely to be in their cars, whereas for television this means the early evening hours. New television dramas and comedies are usually introduced twice a year. Networks usually produce ten to fifteen new episodes in each television season. A show may have two seasons in a year and during the remaining weeks reruns will be broadcast. Traditionally, news programs are broadcast in the early morning, at noon, around dinnertime, and in the late evening.

How Media Outlets are Funded

In large part, television and radio networks are funded by commercials. The Nielsen ratings indicate how many viewers watch a particular television program. The more viewers a program receives, the more expensive is the advertising space during the program. Every year, the Super Bowl marks the most expensive four hours of programming on American television, with some 30-second advertising slots going for more than one million dollars. There are alternatives to advertising-funded television and radio, such as public television and radio stations, which are primarily funded by viewer donations and contributions from grant organizations. Also, some small public access television stations are funded by their local government.

Use of Commercials in Mass Communication

Nearly all programming on radio and broadcast television is funded by commercials. Cable and satellite television receive part of their funding from distributors but are in large part also funded by advertising. Commercials are generally more expensive when they run during programs with a large viewership. Businesses also like to position their advertising during programs that attract viewers who are likely to buy their products. So, for instance, one is likely to see a lot of truck commercials during football games, since presumably a large number of males are watching. Similarly, commercials during the weekdays are often for products preferred by senior citizens and housewives, who are more likely to be watching television at this time.

Advances in Mass Communication Have Changed the Legislative Process

In the past fifty years, the legislative process has been subtly modified by advances in communication technology. Television first made it possible for the president to speak face to face, as it were, with the American public. This meant he could push his legislative agenda without having to spend as much time currying favor among members of Congress. Perhaps the most important change has been the introduction of C-Span, a network that televises all the proceedings in the US Senate and House of Representatives. This has made members of Congress even more conscious of their appearance and has led to much more grandstanding and many more public displays on the floor of the legislature. Also, the acceleration of the news cycle has put perhaps unfair pressure on Congress to move quickly on legislative decisions.

Internet's Effect on Politics

The Internet has influenced politics in unpredictable ways. For one thing, it has made it possible for citizens to acquire political information from sources other than the traditional mainstream media. In the past, many people have complained about the prejudices of the news media, but now people are easily able to get news from sources that share their same personal ideologies. Many people complain, however, that this "hyper-partisanship" of many Internet news sources has polarized the country. Another area in which the internet has radically changed politics is in campaign financing. Candidates can now solicit donations over the internet, which has led to amazing increases in the amount of money available to popular candidates.

Communication Media Affects the Political Campaign Process

Advances in communication technology have drastically altered the political process. Before the advent of television, political candidates could only reach large audiences on the radio or by delivering addresses to enormous crowds. The development of broadcast television made it possible for presidential debates to be transmitted to the entire country. At the same time, candidates began to pay much more attention to the visual elements of presentation. With the introduction of the first 24-hour cable news networks, it became more and more important for ambitious politicians to supply ready-made news events. This has spawned the omnipresent, continuous cycle of political news and campaign coverage. Many critics complain that the incessant need for fresh news by the cable networks has devalued political discourse in the United States, even as these networks provide information to many more people than were reached in the past.

Radio Drama

Vocal Techniques Used in Radio Drama

Some of the best oral interpretation of famous stories and plays has been done over the radio. For oral interpretation to work on the radio, however, the performers must have excellent vocal control. For one thing, they need to be able to indicate excitement or nervousness with their rate of speech. An excited speaker tends to talk more quickly. Radio drama performers also have to indicate their emotional state by varying the volume of their voice. For instance, in many radio dramas a speaker will almost whisper during the most dramatic parts, because the audience will then be forced to listen more intently to what he or she is saying.

Preparing a Radio Drama

A great deal of effort goes into the preparation of most radio dramas. Not only do the performers need to become familiar with their roles and practice the performance, but the producers need to decide on the appropriate sound effects to accompany the performance. Like television programs and movies, radio dramas have directors, who are responsible for organizing the actors and overseeing the general interpretation of the text. Typically, a director will go through the text before auditions are even held, so he or she can get a good idea of the particular themes that should be emphasized in the performance.

Rehearsing a Radio Drama

It is just as important to rehearse a radio drama as it is to rehearse a scene in a movie, a television program, or a play. The director of a radio drama usually organizes a rehearsal right after the parts have been cast, so the group can run through the entire script together and get a general idea of the direction in which they are heading. During this rehearsal, members of the cast make notes on their scripts. In subsequent rehearsals, the director will probably interrupt the cast in order to offer suggestions and make corrections. It is typical to do a final rehearsal a short time before the premiere presentation.

Sound Effects in a Radio Drama

Radio dramas have famously been enlivened by the use of sound effects. Sound effects serve a number of purposes in the presentation of a radio drama. For one thing, they can be used to differentiate between scenes. Often, a bit of background noise helps to establish a new scene in the minds of an audience. For instance, a scene might begin with the sound of shuffling feet and low conversation, to indicate that the action is taking place in a hallway or on the street. Sound effects also add depth to a radio drama. Instead of just listening to the human voice, the audience hears a variety of noises that advance the action, from ringing telephones to slamming doors. Because radio only transmits through the medium of sound, radio drama producers have become extremely creative with the incorporation of sound effects.

Video Production Terms

Basic terminology used in video and film production includes the following:

Angle—the viewpoint from which the camera shoots the action.

Establishing shot—a shot from a long distance, used to establish the setting in the mind of the viewer; often a shot of the building in which the action takes place.

Close-up—a shot in which the camera only focuses on one person; extremely close shots are referred to as tight close-ups and extreme close-ups.

Dolly—a platform on wheels that allows a camera to remain stable while moving; used primarily in action scenes or when there is a change in perspective during a shot.

Medium shot—a camera perspective in which an individual is framed to the waist; a medium shot contains enough width for two people; sometimes used to frame people as they walk or run.

Long shot—a camera perspective in which several people can be included from head to foot; a long shot is often used to establish a conversational group at the beginning of a scene.

Wide angle—a camera perspective that has an extremely broad horizontal distance.

Reverse angle—a camera perspective in which the object being shot is seen from a perspective that is the opposite of the previous shot.

Pan—a filming technique in which the camera is turned horizontally on an axis; often used when the subject is in motion, as for instance when a character is walking.

Tilt—a camera technique in which the camera is moved up and down vertically on an axis; sometimes used to shift the frame from an individual's feet to the individual's head.

Cut—sometimes called a take; a transition from one scene to another.

Zoom—to move closer to or farther away from the subject with the camera.

Fade—a gradual dissolution of the scene; most often, movies and television shows use a fade to black.

Dissolve—a gradual transition between scenes, in which the first scene is slowly replaced by the second scene.

Wipe—a transition between scenes in which one moves in as the other moves out, with no overlap.

Over the shoulder shot—a classic camera perspective in which one individual is seen from the perspective of a point over the shoulder of another person.

Preparation of a Camera Shot Sheet

One of the most important tasks of a television or film director is to prepare a camera shot sheet. A **camera shot sheet** is a detailed set of instructions that the various camera operators must follow during filming. For each shot, the director should list what is to be framed, the type of lens to be used, the length of taping to be expected, and the sound requirements. All this information needs to be condensed into a format small enough for all the camera operators to carry around during shooting. It is very important that the sequence of shots be accurate, so the camera operators can spend their time preparing for their next shot.

Roles of Producer and Director in a Television Production

The **producer** of a television program has a variety of different roles. Perhaps most generally, the producer can be called the overall manager of the production. He or she arranges the financial backing, hires the crew, and assigns a director to the project. Once the production is underway, the producer acts as a liaison between the financial backers and the director. The producer may also have a role in assisting publicity. A television production's **director** is hired by the producer to interpret the script, cast the parts, and to manage the crew that will film the program. The director is responsible for creating an interpretation that is acceptable to the producer.

Associate Director, Floor Manager, and Production Assistant in a Production

An **associate director** has several tasks on the set of a television production. For one thing, the associate director is usually in charge of directing the background action. That is, he or she makes sure future shots are being set up while the director concentrates on what is being filmed at present. The associate director also tries to keep the director organized and on schedule. The associate director is often responsible for managing the logistics of production as well. The **floor manager**, meanwhile, is responsible for organizing the facilities that will be used in the production and for maintaining the operation schedule. A **production assistant** typically takes care of the finer details of production, from the making of cue cards to set design.

Microphones, Switchers, and Mixers in a Television Production

A variety of specialized equipment is required for television production. For one thing, television requires the use of hidden microphones. The most common microphone used on a television set is one suspended from a long horizontal pole, called a **boom mic**. The boom mic allows the microphone to be suspended above the performer but out of sight of the camera. Television production also requires the use of a **switcher**, which is a mixing panel that allows scenes to be placed end to end on a videotape. Finally, television production requires the use of a **mixer**, which is an electronic board on which various sources of sound and video can be spliced together.

Phases of Television Production

Television production includes four basic phases: preproduction planning, rehearsal, productions, and postproduction. During **preproduction planning**, the director familiarizes himself or herself with the script, and a production assistant arranges for the facility and the production equipment. The cast and crew are also hired at this stage. During the **rehearsal phase**, the actors and director figure out their roles and do the blocking. During the **production phase**, the program is filmed. Finally, during the all-important **postproduction period**, the program is edited and mixed. Also during this period, corrections are made, art and music are added, and any necessary dubbing is performed.

Use of a Personal Media Inventory

A personal media inventory is a record of one's media intake over a given period of time. A comprehensive personal media inventory would include categories for television, radio, movies, Internet, recorded music, and any other form of mass media. Most people are very surprised when they realize how much time they actually spend engaged with media. In particular, many people are shocked to realize just how much television they watch each week. One way to gain control over the amount of time one spends with mass media is to catalog this activity in a personal media inventory.

Chapter Quiz

Ready to see how well you retained what you just read? Scan the QR code to go directly to the chapter quiz interface for this study guide. If you're using a computer, simply visit the online resources page at **mometrix.com/resources719/osatspeechdd116** and click the Chapter Quizzes link.

Drama

Directing and Producing Theatrical Productions

Production Meeting

A production meeting is often held after the play is selected. It can occur before and/or after the actors are selected. The actors can be a part of the meeting or not depending on the director. This meeting allows the director to meet with the theatre staff and technicians to determine how the production will be laid out. The director relays his vision to the set designers, being careful to do so in a manner that will allow the designers the freedom to interpret and create the layout themselves. It is important for the director to provide a focus for the group while allowing each member to contribute in their unique way. The director can elaborate upon his vision and clarify what his exact needs are for the production. The group provides feedback on what they can or cannot do based on the director's expectations.

Heretical Approach to Directing

According to the heretical approach to directing, the director's job is to interpret the script to create a dramatic production that will be enjoyed by an audience. The director must work to make a script exciting to the audience. This approach requires that directors interpret the script, maintaining its overall meaning while exercising creative freedom to alter an ending or omit certain scenes. This approach can be seen in classical works that are translated to opera. English-born doctor Thomas Bowdler used this approach to rewrite the works of Shakespeare, omitting what he saw as offensive or unsuitable parts. He called his book The Family Shakespeare, as he believed he had transformed Shakespeare's work so that a father could read it to his children without fear of corrupting them. Directors may use this approach, though it is most often associated with a prudish censorship that does not lend itself to the theatre.

History of Directing

In ancient Greece the modern director's role was performed by a **choregus**. The choregus was the leader of the chorus and it was his job to direct and coordinate songs and movements. In ancient Roman theatre, productions were organized by a wealthy patron who provided the financing necessary for a performance. In medieval times, the role most closely related to that of the modern director was called the "master of secrets." The master of secrets was responsible for special effects and because of the detail and coordination required to perform these effects successfully and safely, he was essentially responsible for telling actors where to stand. In the period when actors had to register in order to perform, the director role was carried out by the keeper of the register. The register was an official copy of a script that was performed by a specific theatre company. The keeper of the register was usually a guild, or group of craftsmen, who were responsible for maintaining the integrity of the script by handing it down to each successive generation.

Modern Role of Director

Directors perform both artistic and managerial roles. The modern theatre director must interpret a script, cast actors, design the production, conduct rehearsals and coordinate a vast number of other tasks and elements. Oftentimes, interpreting a script requires the director's use of creative license. Directors must master human relations, as they work with actors, set designers and lighting crews to bring a script to life. Directors must be capable of making quick decisions while being able to adapt to change. Directors often act as business managers, publicity directors or even costume designers and they are skilled at working with the resources they have available to unify the various elements that comprise a dramatic production.

Coaching Actors

Due to the work of Konstantin Stanislavsky, it is now common for directors to collaborate with actors in order to create a successful performance. Directors can be encouraged to guide actors but should also be cautioned not to over-direct actors. This could lead to dependency, so it is usually best for the director to consult with the actor rather than instruct the actor. The director can be an advisor or a source of inspiration and encouragement for an actor. The actor and director each must recognize the other's creative talents and work together to incorporate their visions into a unified performance that leaves both parties, and the audience, feeling satisfied. The way in which the director cooperates with the actor can take many forms. Sometimes the director will assume one role and maintain it or perhaps fluctuate among different roles. Examples of these roles include the authoritarian, the visionary and the therapist.

Managerial Responsibilities

One of the many aspects of the director's role is that of manager. The director must serve both in an artistic capacity when interpreting a script and in a managerial capacity when organizing and coordinating the details of a performance. The director must handle scheduling, casting and rehearsals as well as conduct read-throughs in which the director and actors read the script and discuss their vision for the characters and design of the play. The director leads rehearsals, which can occur with all actors present to rehearse the entire play or with only a few actors rehearsing a portion of the play. The director leads run-throughs, technical rehearsals and dress rehearsals and may even conduct previews which involve executing a performance outside of the intended venue in order to discover any areas of the performance that need to be worked out before opening. The director's job usually ends after opening night, at which point the stage manager takes over.

Considerations When Selecting a Script for Study or Performance

When selecting a show for class use, whether it is to be read in class for instruction or evaluated for performance potential, teachers must consider several factors. First and foremost, it is imperative that teachers read the entirety of any script which they intend to bring before students. While pre-reading, they can evaluate whether or not the content meets community standards. A good way to evaluate this is to consider whether or not their administrator would be likely to approve a performance of this work. The teacher must also consider the age of their students, not only for whether certain themes are age-appropriate, but also whether the issues in the play would be valuable or important to the age group they are teaching. Related to this, teachers should seek out scripts that reflect the cultural atmosphere of their school and local community. While theatre can be an excellent tool for broadening horizons, it is also important to promote representation of the culture students are rooted in. A final consideration is how the student body would perceive and relate to the script if it was performed for them. Considering whether the students would be challenged, inspired, offended, educated, or entertained by the show is a good first step.

Researching a Script or Playwright Prior to Selection

Prior to selecting a show for class study or production, teachers should do their research to ensure the script is the right fit for their students and community. An important aspect of this that can easily be overlooked is the background of the playwright. Since teachers will need to present the background information to the students, and eventually teach students to research the author's background themselves, they need to be familiar with the author's life so that they can answer any questions the students have and guide the conversation where necessary. It is also important to consider the historical time period and political climate, both in which the script was written and in which the action of the script is set. Depending on the age of students and demographics of your school, period pieces which discuss or involve civil rights may need careful discussion and consideration. Another aspect that must be evaluated carefully is whether or not there is potential for issues with dialogue or casting. While permission from the author or publisher to modify dialogue by striking lines or cutting scenes can be requested, it is not always granted. Identifying any potential issues early and keeping in mind that they may not be resolved by simply striking problematic lines is key.

Coordinating Efficient Rehearsal Schedules

When scheduling rehearsals, teachers should consult any calendars they can access for school and community events, as well as athletic schedules. While conflicts are certain to occur, it is in the best interest of the students to be as flexible as possible. Teachers should consider creating a policy outlining a reasonable attendance expectation which the students can review prior to auditioning. If teachers choose to implement such a policy, a good practice is requiring students to fill out a conflict sheet on which they can list any upcoming vacations, community events, family functions, etc. that they will need to be out for during the course of the show. Anything on this sheet must be counted as an "excused" absence. Teachers may choose to set the rehearsal schedule prior to auditions, or they may choose to set it after casting to accommodate the schedules of the students that have been cast. All rehearsal schedules must comply with any state and district limits on student time.

Considerations When Scheduling Theatrical Performances

Teachers are frequently responsible for scheduling theatrical performances, whether that means choosing a date themselves or coordinating with a district event scheduler. In either case, the teacher needs to take multiple things into account, including the district calendar, athletic schedules, community events, and time of year. While there is no way to find a perfect date which has no conflicts, it's important to try to remember that behind each event on the calendar is a group of people trying to do just what you're doing. Collaboration and grace are key when scheduling, particularly when dealing with so many schedules and needs.

Determining the Budget for a Theatrical Performance

In many districts, teachers will be given a budget for the school year which will fund all activities for the theatre program. In some districts, there may be a separate budget for classroom supplies, but this varies and should be discussed early on. Most theatre programs will participate in some type of fundraising throughout the year to supplement the annual district budget. Regardless of what the budget is, the teacher must evaluate the year and plan in advance in order to properly allocate spending. Some contracts have show requirements, which must also be taken into account. For example, if a teacher is working in a district which has a $6,000 budget for the theatre program, and requires a minimum of two shows per school year, the teacher could reasonably consider dividing the budget in half to have $3,000 per show. Another option would be to do a smaller show and a larger show, and divide up the money accordingly.

Promoting Theatrical Performances

Promotion of performances is one of the most important, yet frequently unplanned and overlooked aspects of planning a show. A cast can have a wonderful show, but without selling tickets, no one will know. It is exceedingly important to get people in the door to see shows both for fundraising and for recruitment. Ticket sales are often one of the primary ways to raise funds for the program, so a low-performing event can affect the budget for the rest of the year. When students and their families attend shows that are excellent, it is more likely that they will want to become involved in the theatre program. There are so many things to plan and take care of when directing a show that promotion is often overlooked to the detriment of a program.

Managing Skills Employed When Directing a Production

Being a theatre teacher requires a lot of different skills, many of which are managerial in nature. It is important for teachers to be able to manage a budget, keep a rehearsal schedule, help students deal with interpersonal conflicts in the cast and crew, delegate tasks when appropriate, oversee teams of students responsible for various tasks, and ensure the safety of each and every student in their cast and crew. Many of the same skills necessary for good classroom management are necessary for directing a performance, including fair and consistent procedures and policies, clear communication with both students and parents, self-awareness and strong emotional regulation, and empathy.

Knowledge of Legal Issues

Teachers must be aware of the royalties and copyright information legalities. When a teacher purchases the rights to perform a show, they typically sign a contract with the publisher of the script which includes terms of use and royalty information. The legal ramifications of breaking this contract vary by publisher and show, and must be read very carefully. If a teacher breaches the terms of the contract, they risk disqualification in any contest the show is entered in, tarnishing the reputation of their school, financial ramifications, and quite possibly, their position as the theatre teacher.

Emotional Well-Being in Technical Theatre

Preparing a production is an intense and time-consuming process that can prevent cast and crew from "having a life" outside of theatre. As such, it is important that there be an effort to help protect the emotional and mental wellbeing. Social-emotional learning and self-care techniques should be addressed by theatre teachers. This will provide students with tools they need to be aware of any changes in their feelings and how to address them. Theatre provides a platform for teaching about emotions and what they look and feel like. This helps students understand their own emotions as well as build empathy and understanding for others. It is important to help students find and maintain a balance in their lives between their education, hobbies, and resting. Teachers should familiarize themselves with the resources that are available to students that will help maintain their well-being, such as school counseling services. All school staff members should be trained to recognize changes in student behaviors and refer them to the proper channels for assistance; theatre teachers are no exception. For intense roles, students may need assistance learning to **de-role**, the process of getting oneself out of character. This can be as simple as removing a costume or playing a game, but can be more intensive such as exercise, meditating, or talking it out with a trusted individual.

Potential for Student Development

Teachers should evaluate performance pieces with an eye towards how students might be able to grow and learn more about the craft of theatre. An ideal experience with the theatre program would teach students about themselves, the world, and those around them. However, the potential for students to learn about topics that are not age-appropriate is extremely high in the theatre world. Many directors succumb to the temptation to give their students material that is dramatic or interesting, but which contains themes that students might not be ready to be exposed to yet. Particularly in middle school, students are already facing extreme emotions, and teachers should take great caution before selecting any scripts which contain sensitive topics and themes.

Influences on the Selection of Works for Performance

Cultural Diversity of a Student Body

Teachers must consider the cultural diversity of their potential cast when seeking out a show. It is very important to present opportunities for all students who might be interested, and sometimes the concept of "color-blind casting" isn't enough to encourage students to audition. A teacher might clearly tell students that they will not be considering race as an audition element, but choose a script that feels limiting. For example, an African American student might not feel comfortable auditioning for a historically white role like Fanny Brice in Funny Girl. Even though a teacher has communicated they will be utilizing color-blind casting, if the script they select doesn't align with the cultural diversity of the student body, students might not feel that there is a place for them in the program. Students may feel more uncomfortable challenging a role's historical precedence with famous works, especially those that have movie adaptations.

Cultural Diversity Presented in the Script

When selecting a performance piece, teachers should consider whether or not their student body can accurately and appropriately depict the cultural diversity presented in the source material. For example, a program with an extremely small Hispanic or Latino population might not be the right fit for a show such as West Side Story. While a show such as this would likely be a great learning opportunity, the teacher would need to cautiously consider whether they would be able to respectfully depict the racial tension in the show without making their Hispanic or Latino students feel more marginalized. On the other hand, Hispanic students might enjoy the opportunity to play characters from their own heritage, so this show might be an excellent choice for a school with a group of Hispanic or Latino students that love performing. Shows that contain cultural diversity can be excellent choices, but teachers must consider all factors carefully, and seek guidance from administrators, before making final decisions.

Characteristics of a Potential Audience

When selecting a performance piece, teachers must consider the potential audience that will be watching the show. In a school setting, the most likely scenario is that the audience will be full of students' family members.

This might be parents, grandparents, or younger siblings, so a range of ages needs to be taken into account. The general atmosphere of the community also needs to be considered. For example, if a school is in a more conservative community, shows with liberal elements should be approached cautiously (if at all). Fellow teachers and administrators, as well as school board members, might also be members of the potential audience. While these factors should not completely dictate the show selection, they should be considered.

THE PERFORMANCE SPACE AND NUMBER OF PARTICIPANTS

Before selecting a show, teachers must consider the space they will be performing in as well as the number of participants they might have. Most teachers will be able to look around their performance space prior to choosing a show. They should take note of the size of the stage, the amount of backstage space, storage space, amount of dressing rooms and restrooms, and number of seats in the audience. Teachers should also have a general idea of how many students are interested in participating. The number of students auditioning should influence the size of the show the teacher plans. For example, if 20 students are interested in auditioning, the teacher should consider shows with casts of 10-12 people. (There will inevitably be students that change their minds, auditions that go poorly, and students that drop out unexpectedly.)

Acting Methods and Performance

ELEMENTS OF ACTING

Relaxation, concentration, imagination, and observation:

There are several schools of thought about the qualities that one must either naturally possess or work to acquire in order to be an actor. The elements of relaxation, concentration, imagination and observation are most common among these qualities. An actor must maintain control of voice and body while performing and this ability is compromised by nervousness. Actors must learn to force their minds and bodies into a state of relaxation. Concentration allows the actor to focus attention on the desired outcome. Actors must use their voices and bodies in a way that conveys the essence of the character. An actor who is properly concentrating on the role will think about what they are doing rather than how they are doing it. Actors must also be mindful of the full range of human emotion. They must observe the manifestations of emotions in themselves and others and use these memories while performing. The actor should also be able to imagine the joys and sufferings of their characters, conveying that through performance.

PREPARING FOR PERFORMANCE

PSYCHOLOGICALLY AND EMOTIONALLY

The concept of the "magic if" is often an effective tool used by actors. The magic if theory requires that actors imagine they are in the character's situation. These scenarios can be played out in two ways. Actors can be themselves but act as if they were in the same situation as characters or they can act as if they are the characters. In the first method, actors react to the situation personally. Once they have mastered their own personal reactions, actors can then analyze their reactions and examine how these compare to what the character would do in that situation. By combining the two reactions actors can often give the most believable performance. It is also helpful to draw upon sense memory and emotional memory to be able to depict a realistic emotion or reaction during a performance.

ALEXANDER TECHNIQUE

The Alexander Technique was developed by Shakespearean orator and actor Frederick Matthias Alexander. The technique arose from Alexander's desire to overcome his chronic laryngitis. Alexander discovered that he held unnecessary muscular tension while performing which caused his vocal problems. His technique requires that actors become aware of the tension they hold in their necks while performing. By releasing the neck tension, the head relaxes and allows the spine to remain long and uncompressed. This simple physical alignment results in an overall healthy condition of the body. The technique attempts to rid the body of tension and stress through the alteration of one's daily physical movements. Tension blocks an actor's ability to effectively portray the characters and stories in a performance. Studying the **Alexander Technique** can help an actor to reduce the amount of tension in their bodies and better understand how energy should be allocated to certain tasks in order to most efficiently accomplish one's goals in both acting and daily life.

James-Lange Theory of Emotion

The **James-Lange theory** was developed by psychologist William James and physiologist Carl Lange. The theory states that emotions are a result of physiological response to external stimuli. Our emotions, according to this theory, are based on our interpretations of physical sensation. For example, if we are at the beach and see a shark while swimming, our body becomes tense and our heart races. We interpret these physical reactions as fear. The theory suggests that emotion is not the cause of a physical response, but the result. This can be incorporated into acting techniques by having students describe or act out physical symptoms while other students guess the corresponding emotion. Nervous actors may also be taught to physically force themselves to relax, which, according to this theory, would result in a more calm emotional state. The theory can also be used to predict emotional reactions after observing one's physical behavior.

Cannon-Bard Theory of Emotion

The **Cannon-Bard theory** was developed by psychologists Walter Cannon and Philip Bard. Their theory states that emotion results in a physiological response, suggesting that our emotional reaction to external stimuli in turn leads to a physiological reaction. For example, feeling fearful may cause our heart to race and our body to tremble. This theory is in direct opposition of the James-Lange theory, which suggests that emotion is the result of physiological reaction and not the cause. The Cannon-Bard theory states that one must feel an emotion before the body can physiologically react. This theory can be incorporated into acting techniques by having students participate in scenarios that may make them fearful, anxious, angry or excited and then having them describe the physiological symptoms which accompanied each emotion.

Delsarte System of Expression

Francois Delsarte is best known for his system of expression involving the holding of specific poses to convey emotion or attitudes. The method was used in the first acting school founded in the United States. Delsarte began his career as a disgruntled student at the Paris Conservatory. Unsatisfied with the conservatory's acting classes, Delsarte began to independently study human movement and behavior. He also studied anatomical medicine, voice, breath and body language. All of his observations were conducted with the aim of understanding the role played by these various components as tools of instinctual and emotional expression. Delsarte's work was introduced to the US by his protégé, Steele Mackaye. Delsarte's system consists of nine principles of gesture, the relationship of inner experience and physical manifestation and the symbolism of various lines and their connection to human awareness.

Meisner Technique

The goal of the Meisner technique has often been described as getting actors to "live truthfully under imaginary circumstances." The technique emphasizes carrying out an action truthfully on stage and letting emotion and subtext build based on the truth of the action and on the other characters around them, rather than simply playing an action or emotion. One of the most well known exercises of the **Meisner Technique** is called **Repetition**. In Repetition, one person spontaneously makes a comment based on their partner's behavior, and that phrase would be repeated back and forth between the two in the same manner until it changed on its own. The objective is always to react truthfully and not merely change because it felt like change was called for.

Acting Terms

- **Articulation**: the ability to clearly pronounce words while acting or performing.
- **Blocking**: the development of the movements of actors on stage in relation to other actors and scenery/props.
- **Catharsis**: the purging of an emotion, such as fear or grief, which can occur while performing on stage.

- **Concentration**: the ability of an actor to be "in character" through use of dialogue, attitude, voice, costume, expressions and mannerisms.
- **Cold reading**: reading a script for the first time.
- **Context**: the conditions or climate in which a play was written or meant to be performed.
- **Cue**: signal that serves as an indicator of another action that is about to occur.
- **Denouement** occurs when the final conflict in a production is resolved.
- **Diction** is the choice of words that actors use to express themselves.
- **Downstage** is the physical location on the stage that is closest to the audience.
- **Emotional memory** is a tool used by actors in which they use their own specific memories of events in which they reacted emotionally to understand the emotions of the character they are portraying.
- A **dramaturg** is a specialist in theatre who may be called upon to advise actors, directors and producers in certain aspects of theatrical productions.
- **Exposition** occurs when one must provide information regarding the facts of the plot, usually to the audience either before or during a performance.
- **Level** is the height of an actor's head in a performance while carrying out certain actions.

Role-Playing

In **role-playing**, participants adopt and act out the roles of characters, or parts, that may have personalities, motivations, and backgrounds different from their own. Role-playing is like being in an improvisational drama or free-form theater in which the participants are the actors and the audience. People use the phrase "role-playing" in at least three distinct ways:

1. To refer to the playing of roles generally such as in a theater, or educational setting.
2. To refer to a wide range of games including computer role-playing games, play-by-mail games and more.
3. To refer specifically to role-playing games.

Children's Games

Children's games that involve role-play generally require no specific props and have no rules other than to stay in character. They are normally fun and can sometimes also serve the purpose of allowing children to explore adult roles and relationships. Play can reveal a lot about a child's psychological state, perception of gender roles, home life and interpretation of the world around them. Examples of common games include:

- *Cowboys & Indians*: This game remains popular around the world, even though the films, television series, and books that might have been thought to give rise to it have largely fallen from prominence. This gives an insight into the child's perception of good and evil.
- *Cops & Robbers*: Similar to Cowboys & Indians, seen by some as the politically correct version.
- *House*: The main aim is to explore familial relationships. Children can act like a family and explore other family arrangements with each other. It also deals with gender roles.
- *Shopkeeper and Customer*: This is interpretation of basic social interaction and can also be an insight into the child's parent's income status.

Improvisational Theatre Tradition

Another role-playing tradition is the improvisational theatre tradition. This goes back in some sense to the Commedia dell'Arte tradition of 16th century. Modern improvisational theatre began in the classroom with the "theatre games" of Viola Spolin and Keith Johnstone in the 1950s. Viola Spolin, who was one of the founders the famous comedy troupe Second City, insisted that her exercises were games, and that they involved role-playing, as early as 1946. She thought of these exercises as training actors and comics rather than as being primarily aimed at being fun in their own right.

HISTORICAL RE-ENACTMENT

Role-playing in the form of historical re-enactment has been practiced by adults for millennia as well. The ancient Romans, the Han Chinese and medieval Europeans all enjoyed occasionally organizing events in which everyone pretended to be from an earlier age, and entertainment appears to have been the primary purpose of these activities. Within the 20th century, historical reenactment was often pursued as a hobby.

PUPPETS

A **puppet** is a representational object manipulated by a puppeteer. It is usually but not always a depiction of a human character and is used in a play or a presentation. The puppet undergoes a process of transformation through being animated and is normally manipulated by one (or sometimes more than one) puppeteer. Some puppets can be moved electronically. Puppets are made of a wide range of materials, depending upon the effect required and the amount of usage intended, and can be extremely complex or very simple in their construction. In contemporary visual or puppet theatre, puppets are often called "performing objects." There are many different varieties of puppets. Puppeteer Anita Sinclair states, "Through puppetry we accept the outrageous, the absurd or even the impossible, and will permit puppets to say and do things no human could. We allow a puppet to talk to us when no one else can get us to speak. We allow a puppet to smile at us even when we have not been introduced. We also allow a puppet to touch us when a person would lose an arm for the same offence." Puppeteer David Logan states, "Puppetry is a highly effective and dynamically creative means of exploring the richness of interpersonal communication. By its very nature, puppetry concentrates on the puppet rather than the puppeteer. This provides a safety zone for the puppeteer and allows for exploration of unlimited themes through a safe and non-threatening environment for communication."

MASKED PERFORMANCE

Throughout the world masks are used for their expressive power as a feature of masked performance. They are a familiar and vivid element in many folk and traditional pageants, ceremonies, rituals and festivals, many of which are of an ancient origin. The mask is often a part of costume that adorns the whole body and represents a tradition important to a particular society of people. Used almost universally, masks maintain their power and mystery both for their wearers and their audience, retaining an important place in the religious and social life of the community. The continued popularity of wearing masks at carnivals, and for children at parties and for festivals such as Halloween are reminders of the enduring power of pretense and play. The mask is also used in theatrical performance. In many cultural traditions, the masked performer is a central concept and is highly valued. In the western tradition it is sometimes considered a stylistic device, which can be traced back to the Greeks and Romans. Ancestors of the modern clown can be traced to the masked characters of the Commedia dell'Arte. In contemporary western theatre the mask is often used alongside puppetry to create a theatre that is essentially visual rather than verbal. Many of its practitioners have been visual artists.

MASKS

A **mask** is an artefact normally worn on the face, typically for protection, concealment, performance or amusement. Masks have been used since antiquity for both ceremonial and practical purposes. They are usually, but not always, worn on the face, although they may also be positioned for effect elsewhere in relation to the wearer's own head.

The word mask came via French masque and either Italian maschera or Spanish máscara. The 5000-year-old Sumerian mask of Warka, believed to be the oldest surviving mask, was looted from the Iraqi National Museum in Baghdad and recovered in 2003.

CLOWNS

Clowns are comic performers, stereotypically characterized by their colored wigs, stylistic makeup, outlandish costumes and unusually large footwear. Clowning, in its most basic form, can be described as one form of drama without a fourth wall. In other words, a clown acknowledges his audience. The clown's humor today is often visual and includes many elements of physical comedy or slapstick humor.

History of Clowning

Clowning is a form of entertainment that has appeared in some manner in virtually every culture. In most cultures the clown is a ritual character associated with festivals or rites of passage and is often very different from the most popular western form. In Europe, up until as late as the 19th century the clown was a typical everyday character and often appeared in carnivals. The performance is symbolic of liminality. Being outside the rules of regular society, the clown is able to subvert the normal order. This basic premise is contemporarily used by many activists to point out social absurdity. A popular early form of clown was the fool, a role that can be traced back as far as ancient Egypt and appears as the first card in the Tarot deck. Most fools suffered from some physical or mental deformity, and were given to the local landlord as a charge because their families were unable to look after them. The surrounding communities often feared them. They were the butt of jokes and their masters had the power to inflict violence upon them, even taking their lives. However, being perceived 'idiots,' they were often the only people in court who enjoyed free speech, and during the 16th century, especially in France, actors began to train as fools often in order to have the ability to make satirical comment. There is evidence of the 'wise fool,' similar in function to the jester, in many other cultures.

Clowns of this era and eras previous to it were also associated with jugglers, who were seen as pariahs of society alongside actors, prostitutes and lepers, and thus (at least in Europe) wore stripes, or motley - cloth associated with marginalized people such as the condemned, with strong associations with the devil. Jugglers often used clowning techniques, and the later court jesters often danced, performed acrobatics and juggled. During the 16th century the Commedia dell'arte also became a huge influence on perceptions of the clown in Europe, and influence which passed through pantomime, into vaudeville and on to the touring circuses of the 19th and 20th centuries. The Commedia took influences from the grotesque masked clowns of carnivals and mystery plays and began in market places as a way to sell vegetables. It became incredibly popular throughout Europe amongst both the general public and the courts. The stock characters of the commedia originally included the Zanni - peasant clowns, Pantalone, the old Miser, Il Dottore - The Banal Doctor, and then grew from there to incorporate the Lovers, Arlecchino, Pedrolino, and Brighella, who have survived into the twentieth century in one form or another.

Mime

A **mime** is an actor who communicates entirely by gesture and facial expression. He mimics or imitates (a person or manner), especially for satirical effect. ("The actor mimicked the President very accurately.") He may also act out with gestures and bodily movements only, using no words. ("The acting students mimed eating an apple.") A mime gives a performance using gestures and body movements without words.

Terms Related to Show Preparation, Actors, and Performances

- The **acting edition** refers to the script that contains notes for actors or technicians and may be written by the playwright or the premiere production staff.
- **Ad lib** occurs when an actor must improvise lines or actions to compensate for forgetting their own or for another actor's lapse in memory.
- **Aria**: solo performance in an opera that conveys the emotional state of the main character.
- An **aside** occurs when an actor speaks directly to the audience, though the other characters are not privy to the information being shared.
- **Avista**: scene changes that are done in view of the audience.
- **Bastard prompt**: used in situations where the prompt corner must be stage right instead of stage left.
- **Beginners** term shouted by stage management to signify it is time for the actors who appear in the first scene to come onto the stage.
- **Bit part**: a very small role in a performance.
- **Book**: may refer to a prompt book or to the unsung parts of a musical.
- **Bump**: sudden flash of light often used as a cue.
- **Call**: a request that an actor come to stage to prepare for entrance into a scene.

- **Calling the show**: giving verbal cues to lighting-, sound- and fly- operators, as well as stage crew throughout a performance.
- **Catharsis**: occurs at the emotional climax of the play when the characters and the audience can achieve emotional cleansing.
- **Cheat**: an actor's movement without the audience's knowledge.
- **Clearance**: message to stage management from house manager to let them know that the house is ready for the performance to begin.
- **Come down**: refers to the closing time of a show.
- **Crossover**: the path an actor takes from one side of the stage to the other.
- **Curtain speech**: refers to a speech given by a director or theatre owner before a performance begins.
- **Denouement**: the moments in a performance when the point of the plot is revealed or explained.
- **Dialect coach**: specialist brought in to assist actors with specific accents necessary for conversations within the production.
- **Exposition**: background information on the characters or the plot of the play, usually occurring at the beginning of the play.
- **Fourth wall**: the imaginary wall that separates the audience and actors.
- **Half**: a term that stage management shouts to actors backstage when the show will begin in thirty minutes.
- **Interval**: a 15-20 minute break between sections of a performance.
- **Intonation**: the emphasis of certain words during any oral recitation.
- **On the book**: term used to refer to an actor who must use a script during a scene.
- **Places**: a term called out by directors when it is time for actors to stand in their appropriate positions to begin a scene.
- **Preproduction**: refers to the time before a production in which the planning is done.
- **Preview**: performances that occur prior to opening night.
- **Principals**: refers to the main actors in a production.
- **Prompter**: theatre's staff member who follows the script as the play is performed, standing ready to remind an actor of a line in the event they forget during a performance.
- **Quarter**: a term that stage management shouts to actors backstage when the show will start in fifteen minutes.
- **Quick change**: costume change that must happen so quickly that it must be done near the side of the stage instead of completely backstage.
- **Repertoire**: theatrical company organization in which two or more productions are alternated throughout the performing season.
- **Reprise**: term used in musicals to refer to the repetition of a song or dance at a later point in the show.
- **Run**: refers to the number of times a production is scheduled to show.
- **Segue**: used in musicals to refer to the act or scene that immediately follows another.
- **Show report**: report provided by stage management detailing any problems from the previous performance; actors and technical staff receive copies so that problems can be addressed.
- **Snap**: refers to a cue that has no fade time; usually a lighting or sound cue.
- **Soliloquy**: refers to an oration by an actor on stage when they are speaking to themselves.
- **Stagger-through**: the first run-through of a performance.
- **TBC**: acronym that stands for to be confirmed; usually seen in a cast list when an actor has not been chosen for a part or if a venue or date has not yet been selected.
- **Transformation**: refers to an immediate scene change that involves the use of gauze and lighting to hide or show certain areas of the stage.
- **Typecast**: term used to refer to an actor who is repeatedly cast in a similar role.
- **Visual cue**: a cue based on the action on stage rather than given by a stage manager.
- **Walk-on**: acting role that requires the actor be physically present on stage but not speak.

Literary Elements in Drama

Styles of Drama

Classicism

Classicism is a theatrical style developed by French playwrights in the 17th century. In general, classicism places emphasis on society, reason and enlightenment. Classicism as a theatrical style incorporates the rules and traditions of ancient Greek and Roman theatre, embodying Aristotle's theories regarding the unity of time, place and action.

Neo-Classicism

Neoclassicism is a product of the 18th century. Neoclassicism, as a theatrical style, is characterized by extravagant costumes and elaborate scenery with stories that involve a high degree of melodrama. Neoclassic theatre has clearly defined genres of either tragedy or comedy.

Elizabethan

Elizabethan theatre is characterized by a high number of characters, several subplots that eventually merge and a varied mixture of emotion.

Restoration

Restoration drama, also known as the comedy of manners, is characterized by witty dialogue with themes of virtue and honor. Restoration theatre also featured plots involving the sexual behavior of sophisticated society.

Romanticism

Romanticism was the dominant style from 1750 to 1800. Romanticism is characterized by mankind's unfaltering trust in the kindness of nature. Reason was regarded as secondary to instinct and logic was forsaken for emotion. Romantic ideals encouraged the idea that a simple life was the most desirable kind. Romanticism allowed for the glorification of past civilizations, especially that of the Greeks. It also boasted the merit of the natural man in a primitive setting such as Native Americans. Romantic ideals encouraged the elimination of social classes and the heightened sense of detail. Romanticism fused comic and tragic styles into a unified form of drama that favored the individual actor above the type actor. Romanticism also favored abstraction and idealism. Romantic dramas had a tendency to use special effects because the style focused on visual appeal.

Realism

The ideology of realism was based on science and technology, suggesting that science could solve the problems of humanity. Realism stressed that truth was that which could be felt by the five senses and was characterized by contemporary settings and periods. The themes of realist drama were common to everyday people.

Naturalism

Naturalism, a branch of realism, was developed as a result of the work of Charles Darwin. Darwin's theories on evolution materialized into a form of drama with a prevailing pessimistic attitude in which there was no climax.

Expressionist

The goal of expressionist theatre was to express raw emotion, not to teach, entertain or duplicate reality. Expressionism is characterized by highly exaggerated movements and voice techniques to express the emotion of the characters. Expressionism also tends to dramatize the struggles and spiritual nature of protagonists as well as the struggles between differing social classes.

Absurdist

Absurdist drama is characterized by a lack of realistic characters, an ambiguous concept of time and a vague attempt to define the setting.

Types of Plays

Chronicle Plays

Chronicle plays are historical dramas based on English history written primarily during the Elizabethan and Jacobean periods. The source of many of these plays was Holinshed's "Chronicles of England, Scotland, and Ireland", thus the title "Chronicle Plays".

Mystery Plays

Mystery Plays are dramatic works based on the Bible. These dramas were usually produced by local trade guilds for the pleasure of their villages. They were presented in cycles that sometimes dramatized the entire New and Old Testaments. Mystery plays were performed in England, France, Spain, and Italy, among other countries. Passion plays are specialized mystery plays based on the passion of Christ.

Heroic Dramas

Heroic Dramas featured heroes of epic deeds. Usually written in blank verse or heroic couplets, these plays reached the apex of their popularity during the Restoration period.

Interludes

Interlude refers to a very short form of drama sometimes performed between courses of a banquet but also the term came to refer to any kind of musical or dramatic entertainment. These were usually performed for private parties and fell out of favor with the opening of public venues. Their popularity peaked in 16th century England.

Nos

No is a form of traditional Japanese theatre that use music, dance, and poetry. They make no claim to be realistic, rather creating a serene and peaceful mood through spectacle and imagery. No are based on eastern religions, reflecting themes from Hinduism and Buddhism. The plays have a fixed repertory that has been constant since the 1500's. William Butler Yeats adapted No for western audiences in a series of short plays. They remain popular with drama critics and certain classes of Japanese.

Problem Plays

Problem plays focus on social problems and movements. Alexander Dumas, son of the great French novelist, wrote a series of short plays attacking the ills of society. The early 19th century was the heyday of problem plays. Henrik Ibsen is perhaps the most celebrated playwright of problem plays, particularly with his treatment of women's rights in "The Doll House". Lillian Hellman and Arthur Miller have both written popular problem plays in the 20th century.

The term "problem plays" is used in a different context by Shakespearean scholars. These critics use the term for plays that have caused interpretation problems for audiences. Plays such as "All's Well That Ends Well", "Troilus and Cressida", and "Measure for Measure" lend themselves to various interpretations and pose literary problems for students of the bard.

Farce

A farce is a dramatic comedy that is full of action, escapades of characters always on the brink of disaster, and full of stereotypical characters filling stock roles. The farce is one of the oldest forms of comedy, found in folk plays, Greek drama, the Renaissance and modern theatre. The 'Bedroom farce' is a special type of comedy based on the foibles of attempted seductions. It continues to be popular in modern theatre, notably in the work of Alan Ayckbourn. The theater of the absurd uses farce to represent the essential meaninglessness and chaos of life. Specialized forms of this are tragic farce, which combines farce with tragedy. Farce is perhaps best known by the public through silent films, where Charlie Chaplin, the Keystone Cops and many other slapstick comedians made film an excellent example of farce enjoyed by a wide audience.

Aristotle's Six Elements of Drama

Aristotle identified six elements that define drama:

- Plot refers to the story elements of a play, including the arrangement of the events that take place in the story.
- Character refers to the physical, mental or emotional qualities demonstrated by actors allowing the audience to see them as unique individuals.
- Diction refers to the language employed by the playwright.
- Idea or Thought is defined as the theme that the author is attempting to convey to the audience.
- Spectacle refers to the visual elements of a play. These include make-up, costumes and sets.
- Sound or Song refers to the actual music used in a play as well as all other auditory devices, which can include the rhythm of spoken lines and sound effects. Diction refers to the language of the play. The language is a crucial element, as it reveals both overt and subtle information about characters and situations in a play.

These six elements are, according to Aristotle, what every drama has in common. Modern critics often also refer to all of the elements of plot, character, and dialog as one single element, also called plot.

Action

Modern critics have elaborated upon these elements. Aristotle's original element of action is comprised of eight sub-elements: exposition, problem, point of attack, foreshadowing, complications, crises, climax, and denouement. Exposition provides the audience with information about the time period, setting, characters, relationships and events of the play. The problem is the event that sets the plot in motion. The point of attack is the way the author presents the problem. The author may have the problem occur before or after the main character is introduced. Foreshadowing refers to the clues planted by the writer that will result in a believable finish. Complication is the event that occurs after the problem is introduced. The complication is the obstacle that could prevent the character from achieving a goal. The crisis is the point where the character must make a crucial decision or undergo a significant event. The height of the crisis is the climax, which represents the peak of the entire plot. The story finally concludes with the denouement.

Key Aspects of Drama

Theme

Ideas or concepts given sustained attention in a drama highlight the major themes of the work. Often the title of the play reflects themes to be presented.

Argument

Some works are really expositions of arguments and points that the author wants to make. Arguments and themes are given dramatic force through the form in which they are expressed. This could be action, speech, or narration.

Patterns of Imagery

These include the use of symbols and keywords. These are recurring motifs that form themes and plot development together. Some plays focus on a particular image. Symbols are subtle devices used by authors for a variety of reasons, and they are usually a key to the major themes of the drama. Symbols may change as the play progresses, and these changes are important in plotting and action. Some key words are used as symbols and are repeated and emphasized to enrich the material. These keywords may be tied to one character or shared by many.

Progression of a Dramatic Plot

When studying dramatic works, significant events in the story should be recognized. Major shifts or reversals in the plot, and subsequent action should be followed carefully. Aristotle's "Poetics" described a typical progression pattern of a plot as follows:

1. Exposition
2. Complication
3. Reversal
4. Recognition
5. Resolution

This progression is still valid today as we study and analyze plots. The plot may follow the pattern of comedy (ending with a celebration), or tragedy (ending with death). The plot may be explained through dialogue, stage action, and off-stage events or by a chorus. While plots of well known plays are easily understood and analyzed, more esoteric drama requires more careful attention to the plot's complexities.

Advancing the Plot

Authors use many devices to maintain interest and advance the plot. Among these are building tension between characters, creating difficult situations that cannot easily be resolved, and highlighting conflict and romance. Often authors choose not to reveal some information that increases tension. Action is the physical events in a play. Action can be important or have little dramatic impact. Some plays depend on spectacles rather than dialogue to emphasize plot and characters. Staging is an important element in the action of a drama. The play may be written for a particular acting space, necessary for the action employed. The theatre the play was written to be performed in often dictates the scope of action in the work. A work requiring lavish spectacles is usually not written for small theatres. Adaptations may be made in specific productions to allow more or less" action space".

Knowledge of Characters

In order to understand a dramatic work, detailed knowledge of major characters is essential. Details of their past, motivations for their actions, fatal flaws, romantic relationships, antagonistic characters, and historical context all weave a tapestry of characters that fill out a drama's skeleton. It is vital to distinguish between major characters, who are central to the drama and minor ones who are only functional. The extent to which each character is developed is a good clue in identifying major and minor personae. Details of the relationships between characters often are an excellent guide to plot development and resolution. Who loves whom, who hates whom, who are allied, who are enemies, and the implications of these tangled webs form the structure of plot and drama. Of the many possible relationships in a play, only a few will be crucial. These should be identified and followed closely.

Review Video: Determining Relationships in a Story
Visit mometrix.com/academy and enter code: 929925

Speech and Dialogue

Analysis of speech and dialogue is important in the critical study of drama. Some playwrights use speech to develop their characters. Speeches may be long or short, and written in as normal prose or blank verse. Some characters have a unique way of speaking which illuminates aspects of the drama. Emphasis and tone are both important, as well. Does the author make clear the tone in which lines are to be spoken, or is this open to interpretation? Sometimes there are various possibilities in tone with regard to delivering lines.

Asides and Soliloquies

Asides and **soliloquies** can be important in plot and character development. Asides indicate that not all characters are privy to the lines. This may be a method of advancing or explaining the plot in a subtle manner. Soliloquies are opportunities for character development, plot enhancement, and to give insight to characters' motives, feelings, and emotions. Careful study of these elements provides a reader with an abundance of clues to the major themes and plot of the work.

Apostrophe and Soliloquy

Apostrophe occurs when a character addresses an abstract idea or a persona not present in the scene. This differs from a soliloquy where a character seems to be speaking to himself or thinking out loud. The soliloquy was used extensively in English Renaissance drama and made popular by Shakespeare in his dramatic works. The soliloquy has evolved into interior monologues in fiction where the musings of a character are used to develop depth and advance plots. Apostrophe and soliloquy are often confused, and it should be remembered that a soliloquy occurs when there is only one character on the stage, while in apostrophe there may be other characters in the scene but not addressed.

Antistrophe

Antistrophe is a device in Greek drama where the chorus responds to a previous stanza of verse. Antistrophe is rarely seen today outside of the production of classical Greek drama.

Agony

Agony is the Greek word for struggle or conflict. As used in classical Greek drama, it indicates a portion of the play in which two characters engage in a heated argument or debate. Each of the characters is supported in their arguments by a part of the Greek chorus. The agony is a device used extensively in both comedies and tragedies. It is often the part of Greek drama when climaxes of the plot unfold. The opposing characters usually represent conflicting themes or ideas in the drama. In tragedies the agony is sometimes followed by the death or exile of the protagonist.

In modern literature the term is used in literary criticism to denote a competitive battle. Harold Bloom used the term as an element in literary history in terms of the conflict between a major poet and his or her predecessor whom the poet feels he must displace.

Chorus

Utilized in Greek drama, the **chorus** is a group of actors who furnish a commentary on the play as it unfolds. The chorus in Greek drama probably evolved from the choral tradition of musical productions. Traditionally, the chorus speaks for society rather than any character in the play. This means the chorus is the objective observer of the dramatic action. Shakespeare occasionally used the chorus in some of his plays. Henry V and Romeo and Juliet are examples of this. In musical dramas, the term refers to a group of singers and dancers who play an important part of the production. Modern drama usually does not employ a chorus, although it was used in T.S. Eliot's play "Murder in the Cathedral" in 1935. The chorus in modern musical theatre often acts a collective actor that adds to the spectacle of the production.

Brainstorming

Brainstorming is a technique used frequently in business, industry, science, and engineering. It is accomplished by tossing out ideas, usually with several other people, in order to find a fresh approach or a creative way to approach a subject. This can be accomplished by an individual by simply free-associating about a topic. Sitting with paper and pen, every thought about the subject is written down in a word or phrase. This is done without analytical thinking, just recording what arises in the mind about the topic. The list is then read over carefully several times. The writer looks for patterns, repetitions, clusters of ideas, or a recurring theme. Although brainstorming can be done individually, it works best when several people are involved. Three to five people is ideal. This allows an exchange of ideas, points of view, and often results in fresh ideas or approaches.

Freewriting

Freewriting is a form of brainstorming in a structured way. The method involves exploring a topic by writing about it for a certain period of time without stopping. A writer sets a time limit and begins writing in complete sentences everything that comes to mind about the topic. Writing continues without interruption until the set period expires. When time expires, read carefully everything that has been written down. Much of it may make little or no sense, but insights and observations may emerge that the free writer did not know existed in his mind. Writing has a unique quality about it of jogging loose ideas, and seeing a word or idea appear may trigger others. Freewriting usually results in a fuller expression of ideas than brainstorming, because thoughts and associations are written in a more comprehensive manner. Both techniques can be used to complement one another and can yield much different results.

POETRY

FIGURATIVE LANGUAGE

Poetry is a genre in which language is used in all its variations and embellishments to convey a sense, mood, or feeling the poet deems important. Poetry uses elaborate linguistic constructions to explain the world in creative ways. Poetry manipulates language itself to convey impressions in new and innovative constructions. It makes extensive use of figurative devices such as conceits, similes, metaphors and many more to express things in fresh ways. These devices will be treated separately later. Together, poets use **figurative language** to suggest rather than give direct meanings. This language provides a creative experience for the reader who is asked to understand meaning in unconventional terms. Poets relish the opportunities to express themselves in creative and unusual words. Figurative language provides both poet and reader an opportunity for unique expression and understanding. Emotions, feelings, and moods are invoked by the skillful use of figurative language.

HYPERBOLE

Hyperbole is a figure of speech that uses extreme exaggeration for dramatic effect. It usually functions to compare and is used quite often in romantic works. Love poetry is an example of a subgenre that fosters the use of hyperbole. Hyperbole may also be used in a farcical manner for comic effect.

PERSONIFICATION

Personification is another figure of speech, which attributes human qualities to an inanimate object or abstract entity. Personification helps us to use our self-knowledge and extrapolate it to understand abstract concepts, forces of nature, and common events. Personification is sometimes achieved by similes or analogies to strengthen the imagery.

FORESHADOWING

Foreshadowing uses hints in a narrative to let the audience anticipate future events in the plot. Foreshadowing can be indicated by a number of literary devices and figures of speech, as well as through dialogue between characters. In Ibsen's play “Hedda Gabler”, Hedda plays with a gun early in the play, which foreshadows her eventual suicide. In Shakespeare’s “Macbeth”, the three witches in the opening scene foreshadow horrific events to come. Examples abound in all forms of literature but are perhaps most evident in drama.

ALLUSIONS

An **allusion** is a reference within a text to some person, place, or event outside the text. Allusions that refer to events more or less contemporary with the text are called topical allusions. Those referring to specific persons are called personal allusions. An example of personal allusion is William Butler Yeats’ reference to "golden thighed Pythagoras" in his poem "Among School Children". Allusions may be used to summarize an important idea or point out a contrast between contemporary life and a heroic past. An example of this would be James Joyce's classical parallels in "Ulysses" in which heroic deeds in the "Odyssey" are implicitly compared to the banal aspects of everyday life in Dublin. Allusions may also be used to summarize an important idea such as the concluding line from "King Kong", "It was beauty killed the beast". A writer may use allusions as literary devices to achieve a number of dramatic effects as noted above.

Style of Literature

In literature, **style** is a particular manner of using language to narrate a story, develop a dramatic mood, or evoke a mood. Style can also refer to a period of literary history or to an individual writer.

Tone

Tone refers to the attitude expressed about the subject through the author. This expression is communicated by language, character development, plotting, and the creation of attitudes about the subject. Mood is sometimes mistaken for tone, but the two have important differences. Mood is generally understood to be the feeling the work provokes in the audience. Although this can sometimes be identical to tone, they are often quite different.

Diction

Diction is the choice of language in a literary work. Diction may be formal, colloquial, or slang. The use of diction to set a tone for the work is meant to induce a mood in the audience. Slang is used commonly in modern fiction while formal and colloquial diction are used for specific effects.

Characters

A **protagonist** is the central character in a play or story. The character opposing the protagonist is called the **antagonist**. Either may be the hero or villain of a drama or work of fiction. In modern literature the protagonist-antagonist struggle is often represented as an internal conflict in one individual. Freudian thought has had a great influence on this inward battle of psychological forces in a person. The **hero** or **heroine** is also the major figure in a literary work. The term may be used instead of protagonist. Finally, the villain is the major evil character in a literary work. Usually the **villain** opposes the protagonist but sometimes is the protagonist of a work. The roles of heroes and villains are exaggerated in melodrama and often seen in early films. The conflict in these cases usually involves a "**fair damsel**". Modern literature usually reflects a more **mixed character**, with both qualities present in a character.

Plot Development

Climax

A **climax** occurs when a state of tension in a literary work reaches its peak, usually with a resolution of some kind. There may be many or only one climax in a work, depending on the plotting and length of the story. A climax is usually preceded by an increasing level of tension, usually between the protagonist and antagonist. The climax may take the form of action, speech, or symbolism.

Anticlimax

An **anticlimax** occurs in fiction or drama when a critical point in the work is resolved and the dramatic tension recedes. The term can be used negatively if it refers to a weakness in a drama or story. Sometimes an anticlimax is used to enhance a scene or serve as a respite from a period of action.

Closure

Closure is the modification of the structure of a work, which makes absence of further development unlikely. It creates the expectation of nothing and leaves the reader or audience satisfied that the plot development is over. Closure often has a dramatic force of its own and sometimes is the final climax.

Review Video: How to Make a Story Map
Visit mometrix.com/academy and enter code: 261719

Syllogism

Deductive reasoning is constructed in a three-step method called a **syllogism**. The three steps are the major premise, the minor premise, and the conclusion. The major premise is a generalization, and the minor premise is a specific case. The conclusion is deduced from applying the generalization to the specific case. Deductive arguments fail if either the major or minor premise is not true, or if the conclusion does not logically follow from the premises. This means a deductive argument must stand on valid, verifiable premises, and the conclusion is a logical result of the premises.

Straw Man Fallacy

The "**straw man**" fallacy consists of an oversimplification or distortion of opposing views. This fallacy is one of the most obvious and easily uncovered since it relies on gross distortions. The name comes from a side setting up a position so weak (the straw man) that is easily refuted.

Actor vs. Dramatist

The dramatist must make sure that the venue for which he is writing will be physically able to handle the demands of his play. The dramatist must also be mindful of the audience for which he is writing as well as the abilities of the actors who will be portraying the characters he creates. The ability of the actor is crucial to the creation of a character because an actor can impose his or her own personality onto a character created by a dramatist. Some dramatists tend to write about characters in the abstract, creating characters from their imagination. Some dramatists create characters based on actual people. Ancient dramatists created characters for the actor who would play the role and both Shakespeare's and Moliere's works were influenced by the actors for whom they were writing. The actor whom the dramatist has in mind when creating a character has a great impact on the creation of that character.

Deus ex Machine

The term **deus ex machine** is Latin for "God out of a machine." The term originated in Greek tragedy where an actor playing the role of God was lowered onto the stage by some mechanical device. In modern usage, the term refers to a character or event that is suddenly introduced into a work of fiction in order to help resolve some problem or dilemma.

History and Impact of Theatre

Egyptian Passion Plays

One of the earliest preserved documents attesting to the existence of dramatic productions is a stone tablet from 2000 B.C. The tablet contains a description of the roles played by the Egyptian king Ikhernofret. The ancient productions are believed to resemble today's passion plays and served as a means to communicate the suffering and successes of a particular deity. Like modern passion plays, the ancient forms showed the trials faced by the god and ended with the resurrection of the god. Egyptian passion plays generally centered around the central god figure of Osiris, whose legend claims that he was murdered by his brother, but later resurrected. Osiris is often seen as the god who rules over the underworld. Records indicate that passion plays depicting the life of Osiris occurred annually in the cities of Abydos and Heliopolis.

Origin of Comedy

According to Aristotle, comedy was first introduced in a performance or festival called komos. Komos was an ancient Greek ritual in which a group of drunken males danced and sang, often in a procession, while carrying a large phallus. The phallic symbol was a tribute to the god Phales, believed to be the companion of Bacchus, the god of wine. Greek celebrations often ended with a group of young males parading in the city streets with torches in hand. Members of the group, called comoedus, were led in song by a flute- or lyre-player. The activity was known as a comus or komos. Aristotle further claimed that these events could be traced back to the Greek cities of Megaris and Sicyon. Aristotle supported this theory on the origins of comedy by stating that the first comic poet, Susarion, was an inhabitant of a town very near Megaris.

Origin of Tragedy

According to Aristotle, tragedy can be traced to the Greek songs called **dithyrambs**, which were sung in honor of the fertility god Dionysus. Greek men would dance while wearing costumes of goatskins in order to impersonate satyrs, as these were the constant companions of Dionysus. The song sung by these men was called a **tragoedia**, which means "goat-song" in Greek. This ritual was expanded upon by the addition of a central male figure to which the songs were addressed. The central male figure would answer questions sung to him by the surrounding circle males or chorus. The word chorus is derived from the Greek word "choros," which meant to dance in a circle. There are many differing views on the exact origin of the tragedy, but the above describes the basic consensus among scholars.

William Ridgeway's Theory

In 1904, the interpretation of Aristotle's origins of tragedy came into question. Scholars began to question Aristotle's theory as well as modern man's interpretation of this theory. William Ridgeway, a writer and scholar, published a book in which he presented the theory that tragedy originated not from the worship of the god Dionysus but from the worship of the dead. This completely changed the geographical origins of Aristotle's theory because the worship of the dead was much more widespread. Ridgeway believed that the cult of Dionysus was introduced to the city of Sicyon by the statesman Cleisthenes. Ridgeway further explained that Dionysus was worshipped as a hero among the Greeks because he was a mortal man who became a saint and was elevated to god-like status. Ridgeway supported his theory by offering as evidence the fact that Dionysus, like most dead kings of the time, had an oracle within his temple. Based on this knowledge, the worship of Dionysus is actually the worship of the dead, making both Aristotle and Ridgeway's theories correct.

Elements of Tragedy

A **tragedy** is a play in which a heroic character, through unfortunate circumstances, experiences a downfall. The unfortunate circumstances are usually orchestrated by the gods as a punishment for the sin of hubris, the sin of pride. It is common for the hero to have a desire to attain some type of power that would liken them to a god. The constraints of mortality would not allow a human to achieve a goal or attain a power that is reserved for gods. The hero in a tragedy is usually depicted as a likeable but flawed character who begins the tragedy as an ignorant being but ends the tragedy as an enlightened being. The events that unfold are such that they change the hero's life and manner of thinking. The hero is not required to die to learn his lesson but must go through a major change or enlightenment as the tragedy progresses.

Characteristics of Greek Comedy

Old Greek Comedy

The year of 450 B.C. marks the approximate start of **Old Comedy**, which evolved from the celebrations of the god Dionysus. Old Comedy was best known for its crude language and lack of restriction. Dramatists of Old Comedy were allowed to exercise poetic license to its fullest extent. It was common for the actors to verbally attack, ridicule and defame a well-known person who was generally disliked by the populace of Greece. Old Comedy served both as a source of entertainment and as a front for political campaigns. In order to best understand plays written in the time of Old Comedy, modern readers should take time to study the political climate of the time period in which the work was written. Although Old Comedy differed from Greek tragedies, the two also shared some attributes, such as the vital role of the chorus. Unlike the tragic plays of that time, Old Comedy did not use myths and legends as a basis for plot.

Middle Greek Comedy

Middle Comedy was the dominant form of Greek comedy from the end of the fifth century to the middle of the fourth century B.C. Middle Comedy differed from its predecessor in that it lacked the chorus. This was the first time the importance of the chorus was diminished in theatre. Prior to Middle Comedy, Old Comedy and tragedy had emphasized the role of the chorus. Unlike Old Comedy, Middle Comedy ceased to impersonate public characters on stage, diminishing the use of theatre as a political outlet. The focus of Middle Comedy shifted to fictional characters rather than current or historical figures. Middle Comedy introduced the comic figure of the sharp-tongued cook, present in many Greek plays.

NEW GREEK COMEDY

New Comedy was the genre that ruled the Greek stage from the late fourth century through 260 B.C. New Comedy was largely focused on the idea of unrequited or unattainable love and introduced the character of the mercenary soldier returning home from war. This form had no characters likened to public figures or heroes. Rather, the characters of New Comedy were common people who faced everyday problems. This new genre completely eliminated the chorus and was received well by audiences because the nature of its plays involved universal themes. The use of these common themes allowed for New Comedy to translate well in other geographic regions and it subsequently spread to Rome, Italy and to England. This ancient form of New Comedy was the foundation for the comic forms used in theatre and television today.

ANCIENT ATHENIAN DRAMA

Athenian drama was seen as not only a source of entertainment but also as a religious celebration. The religious connection was a result of the fact that Athenian plays were performed only twice a year, usually during the two Dionysian festivals. Since the entertainment of the masses was considered a governmental duty, theatrical productions of ancient Athens were managed by the state. The state chose playwrights and actors while the wealthy upper-class citizens footed the bill. Plays were performed from morning to night during several days of the festivals. Generally, the performances were contests in which the winning poet was given a prize by the state. Almost every Athenian citizen would attend these productions and the twenty-thousand plus capacity of the theatre ensured that everyone could attend. The poets and playwrights chosen by the state received the great privilege of being heard by the entirety of Athens and it for this reason that these ancient artists had such a great impact on the manner in which we now view those times.

ORIGINS OF SATIRE

While most ancient forms of theatre are credited to the Greeks, **satire** was the invention of the Romans. The Roman satire was a tool used to criticize the current social situation. Roman satire took one of two forms: **Menippean** or **verse**. Menippean satire was named for its originator, Greek cynic Mennipus and is characterized by a rhapsodic blending of prose and verse that ridiculed various social characters. Seneca's work entitled The Apocolocyntosis is an example of the Menippean satire. Verse satire, created by Lucilius but most readily seen in the works of Horace, was generally composed in epic meter. The Roman satire bore a similarity to the Greek form of Old Comedy in that both were a means of attacking the injustices perpetuated by the political climate of the time.

SATYR PLAYS OF THE EARLY GREEKS

Pratinus is recognized as the first writer of the Greek **satyr play**. Satyrs were the half-man, half-goat companions of the god Dionysus. In the early Greek plays, a group of males wearing goat costumes danced and sang in an act of worship directed towards the god Dionysus. These groups of goat-skinned dancers were impersonating satyrs and evolved into what became known as the chorus in many Greek tragedies. The chorus of satyrs, generally prone to merriment, were not appropriate accompaniment for the more serious Greek tragedies, so their role was increasingly diminished over time. In order to preserve the fun-natured spirit of the satyr chorus, Pratinus began to compose short plays in which this group took center stage. Athenian theatre became organized into tetralogies, compilations of three tragedies followed by one satiric piece. The purpose of including the satyr form was to allow the audience to recover from the serious nature of the tragedy by enjoying the more light-hearted jests of the satyr chorus.

PRESERVATION OF GREEK PLAYS

It was the responsibility of the Athenian archons, or magistrates, to maintain records of Greek productions. They recorded names of the upper-class citizens who financed the productions, the poets, actors, plays and contest winners. These records were later published by Aristotle. Athenians had an insatiable appetite for theatre, as their normal viewings were limited to only a few days of the year. In order to satisfy the need for theatre during the off-season, many of the great plays of that time were rewritten by people known as adapters. To preserve the integrity of the original work, the law required that the distribution of any copy of an original work had to be recorded by a public secretary. The library at Alexandria holds copies of various tragic and satyr plays. The most common of the ancient Greek plays seen today are those that were preserved for use in educational institutions of the Middle Ages, including the works of Aeschylus, Sophocles, Euripides and Aristophanes.

Contributions to Theatre

Aeschylus, Sophocles and Euripides

Aeschylus, Sophocles and Euripides are considered the most famous Greek tragedians. Aeschylus is most noted for his trilogy called The Oresteia, which is comprised of Agamemnon, The Libation Bearers, and The Eumenides. Aeschylus became known as the father of Greek tragedy, since he pre-dated both Sophocles and Euripides. According to Aristotle, Aeschylus was responsible for changing the ancient form of the tragedy by adding a second actor, which diminished the participation of the chorus and focused on the dialogue. Sophocles, known for his work Oedipus the King, heightened the tragic form by adding a third actor and downsizing the chorus to fewer than fifteen members. Euripides is known for several plays, including The Bacchae and Medea.

Position of Actor

Profession

In the plays of ancient Greece, there were two distinct roles: an actor and chorus members. Chorus members were selected by a group called the **choregus**, while actors were chosen by the state. The title of "actor" only applied to the person in the play with the most prominent dialogue. Early Greek plays featured only one actor with the number increasing to three in the later years. While only a limited number were called actors, several characters were present in plays, most of whom were silent or spoke only a few words. Before Aeschylus, the profession of actor was not distinct from that of poet because poets generally performed as actors. This distinction came about when Aeschylus introduced the second actor, meaning someone other than the poet was required to play a role in the production. In the early Athenian contests, only the poets received awards for their playwriting skills, but by the fifth century, awards were given to actors for their talents, thus turning acting into a distinct profession.

Social Position

In ancient Greece, the status of the actor was elevated over time. In the fifth century B.C., acting became a profession and as such was viewed with great admiration and respect. Roman actors, however, had a much more contemptible social status. Playwriting was not a sought-after trade; rather, it was bestowed upon one by heredity. Actors were often slaves or foreign captives who were made to perform in exchange for their freedom. Many Roman rulers passed laws forbidding certain high-ranking officials from entering theatres or consorting with those who participated in the theatre. Women rarely appeared in Roman productions and those who did so were limited to roles as mimes.

Origins of Roman Theatre

Roman theatre can easily be traced to Greek roots, as the Romans borrowed much of their theatre from Greek poets, even using Greek actors in Roman productions. It is believed that Rome had no intrinsic growth of poetry; rather, it was transplanted into Roman culture during a time when the Roman population sought to cultivate exotic luxuries. Livius Andronicus is credited with being the first Roman to imitate the theatre of the Greeks and is therefore credited with bringing theatre to Rome. The forms that were most easily converted from Greek to Roman were that of New Comedy and tragedy. Prior to Andronicus, the earliest spoken Roman productions were those of the Italian-import known as the Atellan Fables. The Greek form of theatre, in its transfer to Roman culture, was altered to better suit its Roman audience. The chorus, which historically sat in the orchestra area of the theatre, was removed, leaving the orchestra occupied by high-ranking spectators. Comedies were more easily received in Roman theatre than were tragedies.

EXPERIENCE OF ATTENDING A ROMAN PLAY

Roman theatre usually consisted of a daytime production that lasted for approximately two hours, plays being most often performed immediately before or after the noon meal. Comedy was the dominant form of Roman theatre, using masks, wigs, costumes and makeup. Women were forbidden from participation in these plays, leaving the role of any female characters to be played by young boys. The earliest Roman venues consisted of very basic amphitheatres where the audience reclined on the ground and actors had very few resources at their disposal. As theatre evolved, the Roman stage was composed of a common street with several houses in the background and audiences were entertained by flute players during scene changes. Pompey the Great built the first Roman theatre auditorium in the year 55 B.C., where audiences were most entertained by outrageous and crude spectacles.

ROMAN PLAYWRIGHTS

TITUS MACCIUS PLAUTUS AND PUBLIUS TERENIUS AFER

Both Plautus and Afer wrote comic plays. Their work, in fact, is the only surviving comic drama of the ancient Roman theatre. Plautus' work was very popular in his lifetime. His most notable works include Pot of Gold, The Menaechmi and Braggart Warrior. Like all Roman theatre, Plautus' comedy was based on the Greek New Comedies. He added allusions familiar to Roman culture as well as Latin dialog and poetic meters. Afer, who was better known as "Terence," was a freed Roman slave. The six plays he wrote that survive today are Andria, Hecyra, Heautontimoroumenos, Eunuchus, Phormio, and Adelphi. His plays used more complex plots, intriguing characters and even double-plots. The language used by Terence was more elegant than that of Plautus' plays, though Terence did not achieve the same popularity that Plautus did.

ROMAN TRAGEDY

Romans favored comedy above tragedy as a form of theatre, thus few tragic works have been preserved. The writings of Seneca provide the most notable remnants of the Roman tragedy. Additionally, Marcus Pacuvius and Lucius Accius are both noted for their imitations of Greek tragedy. The failure of the evolution of tragedy as a theatrical form in the hands of the Romans is in part due to their inability to reconcile the elements of song, dance and dialogue. The Romans seemed only able to successfully produce either a song and dance or a dialogue. The song and dance form evolved into a comedy that later lent itself to the pantomimus, or modern-day mime. Dialogue was used to enact tragic productions, usually involving one actor reciting tales to a small audience.

DECLINE OF ROMAN DRAMA

The Roman theatre offered little entertainment for citizens, as their daily lives were already filled with shocking drama. It was common for Romans to see crucifixions, chained slaves paraded through streets and men killed by beasts in arena shows. The Roman culture had little tolerance socially or politically for the offerings of the theatre. They were more concerned with the matters of law than with the matters of the heart. The theatre productions borrowed from the Greeks were of a light-hearted and witty nature, lost on the Roman population, most of whom were unable to comprehend what they considered such trifles. The Roman Empire continued its expansion, requiring that the ruling class be distributed among newly acquired territories, which led to an overall decrease in the number of upper-class citizens in Rome. The remaining citizens, who were undereducated, were unable to understand the classical Latin language that was common in the theatre and were more intrigued by arena shows and circus performers than theatrics. The religious conversion of Roman emperor Constantine led to the outlaw of drama by Christian churches.

INDIAN DRAMA

Indian drama was born from an ancient tradition in which social and religious poetry was read at celebrations and feasts. According to Indian lore, theatre has mythical origins. The Indian culture believed there were three ages of man, each growing more distant from the will of the gods. According to this philosophy, humans began warring with each other, so the gods split the race into two sexes: men and women. The goal of the split was to create love; however, it only created desire for worldly things. Once the heart was drawn to outward desire, man lost his ability to be introspective. Pitying man's insatiable desires, the god Indra solicited the head god to create a spectacle so that humans could sate their appetite. The head god came up with the idea of Natya Veda or the Veda of the Theatre. Drama is the fifth Veda, a combination of the four earlier Vedas, which are dance, song, mimicry and passion.

India's Indigenous Drama

India's drama is unique in that its development was unaffected by foreign influence. Early European scholars held the view that Indian drama was originally an imitation of Greek drama but modern scholars know this to be untrue. The father of Indian drama, Bhrata, wrote many plays, thirteen of which exist today. The earliest one is dated 400 A.D. Indian plays had a unique structure in which they opened with a prayer followed by a narration of what was to come in the play. The narration would blend into the dialogue, giving way to the full performance. The majority of the plays' lines were in the form of prose in which beauty, morality and wisdom were described and reflected upon. Acts of violence and displays of affection were not part of Indian productions, though the plays did use stock characters such as the sneaky servant, the hero and the jester. Magic was the subject of many performances, having a character changed into an animal and requiring the intervention of the gods. The play would end with another prayer.

Medieval Plays

Minstrels traveled from town to town in medieval days offering some source of entertainment. The minstrel often dressed in a festive costume as he wandered between towns on the back of a mule. Minstrels, accompanied by their harps, would sing about the saints, heroes and scripture at gatherings and feasts. Enthusiasts would often award the minstrel with gifts and tokens and the most talented minstrels were hired for permanent service by ruling kings and bishops. Minstrels served an important role, paving the way for the reintroduction of drama in the Middle Ages after Greek drama had been outlawed by the Christian church. As the popularity of minstrels increased, Paris became the headquarters of minstrelsy, allowing the minstrels to band together into groups that could command rights and privileges exclusive to their craft.

Dramatic Literature in the Middle Ages

With the spread of Christianity, drama was outlawed as a vile and blasphemous spectacle. Rome experienced a fall from grace as the city of Constantinople became the new capital of civilization, during which time drama was mostly extinct. However, theatrics began to experience a rebirth after the human appetite for drama had lain dormant for years. Acrobats and traveling minstrels visited towns and performed for audiences and jesters and singers were called upon to entertain at the feasts of rulers. The dramatic plays written by famous Greek poets were looked upon as texts rather than scripts. People of the Middle Ages read the works of the ancient poets but did not feel the need to bring them to life in the form of theatrical production which the authors had intended. Dramatic literature of the Middle Ages existed primarily in the form of the ancient scripts with no new dramatic literature matching the form created by the ancient Greeks.

Rise of Drama

The drama of the Middle Ages had its origins in religion, born of the Christian church. Whereas the church had outlawed ancient theatre as blasphemous, the new forms of drama were created by the church as a means of spreading its beliefs. In order to best relay the dialogues that occurred in the stories relating to Jesus's life, priests would each read the lines spoken by one character in the story. Priests began acting out their lines to capture the interest of the congregation. These performances were common during Easter and the tradition soon extended to Christmas mass, where the Nativity story was retold through a theatrical production. The productions, however, began to grow into more elaborate and exaggerated tales that eventually bore little of the original intent. Priests could no longer exclusively handle the multitude of roles in a performance and were forced to invite laymen to participate. Eventually, the responsibility of these performances came to rest solely in the hands of laymen, who formed guilds and various organizations to handle each aspect of the productions.

English Cycles

The religious drama of the Middle Ages began as performances created by priests reenacting the stories of Jesus. The popularity of the productions grew to such an extent that the priests could no longer handle the various roles and the walls of the church could not accommodate the eager audiences. The productions were originally a unit portraying a certain episode in the life of Jesus or a saint. These units were eventually linked together to form a cohesive narrative called a Cycle. The Cycles could be broken into three main groups: Creation of man and the Old Testament, the Mystery of Atonement and the History of the Living Church. Old Testament plays tell of Adam and Eve in the garden, the corruption of mankind and the great flood. Atonement tells of the birth, life and sufferings of Jesus. The final Cycle tells of the lives of the saints, ministry of the apostles and of the Miracle of the Sacrament.

Origins of Interludes, Moralities and Farces

Interludes, moralities and farces were all forms of drama that made an appearance in the Middle Ages. During this time, the classical definitions of comedy and tragedy did not apply. All that was required for a production to be a tragedy was the staging of a fight. The morality play was a religious performance that used allegory, featuring characters named after certain qualities that could be seen in men: Greed, Pride, Avarice and Patience. Interludes and farces were the more secular performances of the Middle Ages. They featured a variety of performers including pantomimes, strolling players and professional actors. Many of the performers had the ability to act, sing, juggle, perform acrobatics and do magic. Farces were most noted for comic situations that used characters to which the audience could relate. Interludes were exactly what the name implies and were performed between acts of longer plays. Interludes, due to their brevity, were also commonly shown to entertain guests during celebrations and banquets.

Japanese Drama

Noh plays, created by Kwanami Kiotsugu, were the dominant form of drama in 14th-century Japan. Noh plays, featuring only male actors, incorporated the use of masks for the parts of women or gods. This form of theatre is characterized by its rigid structure and unchanging tradition. The play always began with a traveler who reveals his own name and the destinations to which he will travel in the play. A chorus describes the scenery and the thoughts of the traveler as he wanders the stage. Each place the traveler visits is inhabited by the Spirit of the Place, a ghost that must tell a story of suffering. The ancient legend of the site is revealed through a combination of dialogue among actors and recitations from the chorus. The play ends as the traveler prays for the ghost to find peace and then a song is sung to honor the gods.

Kabuki

Kabuki theatre began in Japan in the late 16th century. In the Japanese Edo Era, there was a strictly observed distinction between the warrior class and the common people. It was during this era that kabuki theatre began to grow in popularity. Kabuki theatre addresses the injustices of the people faced with the harsh laws of the feudal system. Kabuki served as a means of expression for the merchant class, whose wealth surpassed that of commoners, but whose status was not part of the warrior class. Kabuki began as a production in which the majority of players were female; however, due to concerns that the actresses were garnering undue attention, the government banned females from playing in kabuki performances in 1629. In kabuki theatre, female roles are played by males called onnagata. Kabuki is a unique form of theatre that combines several other types of Japanese theatre, taking inspiration from the Noh plays, puppet theatre (bunraku) and the realist productions of the 19th century.

Morality Plays

Near the beginning of the 15th century, the miracle plays of the Middle Ages gave way to plays of a different nature: morality plays. The miracle plays, started at the hands of priests, were reenactments of episodes in the life of Jesus. As these plays grew in popularity, priests and churches could no longer accommodate the various roles or the space needed for such large-scale productions. Left to the guilds, the miracle plays began to evolve into plays that focused not on the life of Jesus, but on the lives of everyday people. These plays used allegory to teach a moral lesson. Characters in morality plays had names such as Good Counsel, Pride and Avarice and the role of the Devil was popularized. While these plays strayed from using religious figures as characters, the message maintained a religious tone: good men were religious men.

Masques and Court Comedies

The theatre of the 16th century was divided into several groups, each suited to a particular class of people. Court Comedies were productions that were to be performed for the queen. Court Comedy was a variation on the popular pastoral drama form, many written by pastoral dramatist John Lyly. They were designed to sometimes subtly and other times overtly compliment Queen Elizabeth and the members of her court. Lyly's most notable work was the play Endimion, based upon the Greek myth of the shepherd named Endymion. Court Masques were introduced during the reign of Henry VIII in 1512. Players in masques were members of the king's court or even the royal family. Elaborate spectacles featuring music, costumes, scenery, mechanical effects and characters of mythological or allegorical origin, masques were limited to the private viewing by royalty as the performances were too costly to show in public theatres.

Origins of Elizabethan Theatre

The story of Robin Hood was popularized in Tudor England by the companies of roving players. Productions were held in barns and inns as public theatre was poorly regarded by English government of the time. The government even attempted to stop the strolling players from performing in 1572 with the passage of laws forbidding the practice. There was concern that the performances were apt to incite rebellion among the population and that the players were escorting diseases such as the plague from town to town. Only actors hired by noblemen were allowed to perform and from 1572 to 1574 only four noblemen obtained license to begin theatre companies. As in Roman theatre, women were forbidden from participation and female roles were played by young boys. The popularity of the performances grew to such an extent that James Burbage, in 1576, built a theatre in London to accommodate the large audiences.

William Shakespeare's Role

William Shakespeare is the most notable playwright of Elizabethan drama. Shakespeare's Henry VI was performed in 1592, followed by Hamlet, Romeo and Juliet, The Merchant of Venice, King Lear, Julius Caesar and Macbeth. Tudor audiences favored Shakespeare's plays involving the corrupt former kings of England and Elizabethan drama was both a source of entertainment and a podium for political propaganda. Shakespeare's work was well-received by the masses because it appealed to all classes and all levels of education. His work drew upon both current and classical theories of the organization of the universe and man's place within it. Shakespeare's work was greatly influenced by the events of his time but it also maintained a universality that can be appreciated even today. Christianity was no longer the singular source of religion; the authority of Rome was in question and capitalism was on the rise. The replacement of classic ideas with more modern knowledge and thought made audiences all the more receptive to the works of Shakespeare.

Regulations Imposed Upon Elizabethan Actors

In Elizabethan England, it was common for nobility to employ troupes of performers. These troupes began rapidly and some falsely claimed to be in the services of this or that lord. Members of false troupes were often beggars and vagabonds from whom nobility preferred to be distanced. In order to regulate the activity of false troupes, credentials were granted to credible performers and the aristocracy that maintained them. Elizabeth granted a royal patent, the first of its kind, to James Burbage and his four partners allowing them to perform anywhere in England. The only restriction was that political and religious subject matter could not be performed on stage, which led to objections by groups who had previously encouraged productions so long as they carried a religious message. In 1578 a total of six companies had a license to perform. In Elizabethan times, it was also the common practice for plays to be written by several authors with the actual owner being the company who performed the piece.

Impact of Reformation on German Drama

The Reformation was a catalyst of change all across Europe between 1517 and 1648. The movement began as an attempt to reform the Catholic church; however, it only managed to further divide the Christian sects. While the intentions of the Reformation were religious in nature, its ideas infiltrated all areas of society, including the theatre. Martin Luther, a German monk who later became a Protestant and a major supporter of Reformation, supported theatre and believed that certain books of the Bible had been written as plays. He viewed theatre as a means for spreading religious truth. Luther approved of Christmas plays depicting the birth of Jesus but he banned Passion plays, as he did not agree with the portrayal of Jesus's suffering. During this time, every part of the Bible became eligible for depiction through drama. Clown-plays also began during this time. The clown-play, or Sottie, featured a costumed actor who told jokes to lighten the often-somber mood of many plays. Sotties often occurred between acts of religious plays.

Origins of Drama in Spain

The Spanish culture was known for its ballads, which translate well into a dramatic performance. The ballads of Spain contained legends that were introduced to the area from various locations. Spain's battle with the Moors had ended, but the culture of the Moors had left an imprint upon the Spanish. Travelers from countries north of Spain brought tales of chivalry, knightly quests and heroic tournaments. These stories, along with oriental influences, all made their way into the already popular Spanish ballads. The ballads became more and more elaborate, requiring multiple singers and detailed costumes and scenery. The addition of these elements transformed the ballad into full-blown dramatic productions. The works of both Lope de Vega and Calderon de Barca characterize Spanish drama at its height.

Origins of Russian Drama

Drama made its way into Russia by way of Poland in the 12th century. The plays were known as Religious Dialogues or Histories. The performances were exclusive to monasteries until 1603 when they began to be performed in universities. The university performances were done in Polish or Latin, the earliest of which was a Latin piece entitled Adam, dated 1507, followed by a Polish piece entitled The Life of the Savior from His Entry into Jerusalem, which was dated 1533. While the origin of Russian drama is rooted in religious performances, Russia had a unique form of theatre called the Vertep. Vertep is a puppet theatre in which puppeteers control the dolls using strings attached to various parts of the doll. Vertep plays were used to depict religious stories. The word "Vertep" means "the secret place" and refers to the cave in which the Russian Orthodox Church believes Christ was born. Puppet characters include the Virgin Mary, Joseph, Jesus and various other figures central to the birth and life of Christ. Vertep plays eventually began to incorporate stories of a more secular nature.

Claque in French Theatres

The **claque** was an organized group of people hired to applaud during theatrical performances. The idea is believed to have originated when the emperor Nero required that five thousand soldiers chant his praise after a performance. Sixteenth-century poet, Jean Daurat, used this ancient practice as the foundation for the formation of the claque. "Claque" is derived from the French term "claquer," meaning to clap one's hands. Daurat's idea to ensure applause for performances was to give free tickets to any patrons who agreed to show their approval of the show. Eventually this practice became so popular that there developed a professional organization for claquers. In 1820 a man by the name of Sauton formed a business that supplied claquers to playwrights. It was the responsibility of the theatre manager to request the number of claquers necessary for a performance. The duties of the claquers reached beyond simple clapping. They could laugh at jokes, fake tears, encourage encores and generally ensure the audience remained happy.

Commedia Dell'arte

Commedia dell'arte, referring to improvisational drama, has its roots in Italy during the 16th and 17th centuries. These plays featured a scenario in which the characters were named and made aware of their relation to one another, the basic plot was outlined and the outcome was predetermined. The scenario, or canvas, was the skeleton of the play and it was up to the actors to provide the flesh. The subject of this theatre form seemed to focus on the intrigues of love and clever schemes. There were several stock character types, usually identified by masks, including a sneaky servant, a group of old men, a lady's maid, a doctor, a captain or adventurer, a jester and a hunchback. Each character had a stock of phrases and gestures to be used during a performance in the event that they could think of nothing original to fill in the blank spaces.

Creation of Opera

Opera, as a theatrical form, found its footing in 17th-century Italy. Musical science was a much sought-after field of study during this time in Italy. The Inquisition had limited the creative outlets in which previous artisans had found release. Music, however, remained one of the few forms of expression that the Inquisition allowed to exist. Poetry and literature began to decline and soon became secondary to the operatic form. Previous forms of drama, as they had been based on the Greek form, featured the dialogue of actors with a choral accompaniment in the background. In 1597 Italian poet Ottavio Rinuccini joined musicians Peri, Corsi and Caccini to create a piece in which this standard was reversed. The primary method of delivery became singing rather than dialogue and it became increasingly common for poets to write pieces specifically meant to be sung rather than spoken.

Review Video: Musicals vs Plays
Visit mometrix.com/academy and enter code: 537548

Bavarian Passion Play

In the year 1634, the citizens of the Bavarian city Ober-Ammergau began a ritual performance of a passion play depicting the life and death of Jesus. The year before, a disease swept through southern Bavaria killing many of the inhabitants, though the valley of Ammer remained free of the illness. Authorities would not let anyone into or out of the city for fear of contracting the deadly disease. However, a resident wishing to return to the Ammer valley after working in a neighboring town managed to secretly gain entrance into the city. He brought the deadly disease with him, leading to his own death and to the deaths of one fourth of the city's population. The remaining citizens made a pledge to God that if He protected them from being wiped out by the plague they would perform a Passion Play every ten years depicting the life and death of Jesus Christ. The town's legend states that from that moment the infected citizens were cured and the town remained free of the disease.

British Theatre

Attack by Puritans

Elizabethan drama became a popular attraction for many citizens, but its value soon came into question by Puritanical minds. Beginning in 1622, the popularity of theatre declined rapidly, and by 1642, laws demanded that theatres be closed. Lawmakers believed that theatre was an unfit indulgence for the times and that the minds of citizens should be focused upon the political strife occurring within the country. A 1647 law threatened to imprison and punish anyone who attempted to violate the no-theatre laws, followed by another law declaring all actors vagabonds and requiring the demolition of any theatre-related equipment and buildings. During this time, actors who were found in violation of the laws were fined, whipped, stripped of clothing and imprisoned. It was not until the Restoration that theatre regained its footing in England.

Comedy of Manners

Comedy of manners is a theatrical form credited to William Wycherley, George Etherege and William Congreve of 17th-century England, though Oscar Wilde rejuvenated the form in the 1890s. The comedy of manners is characterized by the distance between a society's selfish individual motives and simultaneous concern of projecting the image of being polite, well-mannered, educated citizens. This form of comedy became what is now known as Restoration Comedy. The style is characterized by its mocking of society and social norms and often targets marriage and love as the subjects of its mockery.

Restoration Theatre

Restoration theatre is also known as the comedy of manners. For almost twenty years prior to the return of the Stuart dynasty in England, theatre was outlawed. Charles II, ruling king of England in 1660, greatly influenced by his earlier years in Paris, allowed two companies of players to begin performing while he ruled England. William Davenant was in charge of the Duke's Company while Thomas Killigrew ran the King's Company. During this time, women began to appear on stage for the first time. The most notable playwrights of Restoration comedy include William Wycherly, George Etherege and William Congreve. Popular themes of Restoration comedy included the comical nature of love and marriage.

Origins of Pantomime

The **pantomime** maintained a very indistinctive role in productions until English actor Joseph Grimaldi reinvented the pantomime clown role in Harlequin. Clowns, especially pantomimes, were a common character in many forms of theatre, and were generally portrayed as the servant of a more important character. Grimaldi had a talent for visual tricks and general buffoonery and brought clowns to life through his elaborate mechanical tricks. Actor John Rich, in 1717, played the role of Harlequin in the pantomime Harlequin Executed. Harlequin was originally a speaking part, but people like John Rich only used gesture, movement and facial expression to convey the same sentiments that had previously been expressed only through words.

Origins of American Theatre

American theatre is believed to have originated early in the 18th century. The state of Virginia is recognized as the place in which American theatre first originated based on the 1716 construction of a theatre in Williamsburg. The New England provinces housed some of the earliest public theatres on record, despite their reputation for abhorrence of the theatre. The North as a whole seemed to view theatrical performances with much more contempt than their neighbors to the South. Few records exist relating to early American plays as a result of the multitude of laws passed prohibiting the performance or advertisement of such productions. Even with laws forbidding theatre, records of theatrical performances indicate that plays existed as early as 1702 in America.

George Farquhar's Comedy the Recruiting Officer

The Recruiting Officer holds a place in American history as the earliest play presented in New York of which a record exists. The play took place at the New Theatre in New York on December 6, 1732. The New Theatre was in a building that was owned by the city's acting governor, Rip Van Dam. The cast was composed of a group of actors who are believed to have come to America from London for the purpose of acting. The play itself, written by Irish-born George Farquhar, was written in London at a time when the town's recruiting officers were busy signing citizens into the military. The play had an overall witty tone and the dialogue was often bordering on indecent and raunchy by modern standards.

Origins of Vaudeville

The creator of **vaudeville**, Tony Pastor, was a professional circus clown. Vaudeville is a type of variety show involving various types of acts, usually unrelated to each other. They included singers, dancers, acrobats, comedians, animal acts, impersonators and magicians. These shows were originally exclusive to bars and dance halls until Tony Pastor altered the style to make it suitable for the stage. In order to achieve the level of success that Pastor wanted, he knew that he had to make the shows appeal to highly reputed citizens. Pastor rejected the lewd acts that were typical of vaudeville shows and banned drinking and smoking in the theatre where the shows were held. Edward Albee II and B.F. Keith also played a large part in shaping the vaudeville theatre.

Origins of Realism in Italian Theatre

Realism made its debut in Italy following the fifty-year stint of Romanticism that began in 1852. Realism rejected the sentimental notion of the Romantics for a more practical view on life. Realists sought to examine the inner motives of the human being, desiring to use art as a means of depicting real life, as opposed to the

Romantics, who used art to express what they wanted life to be like. Realists rejected the Romantic idea that life was rational and emotionally fulfilling. Realism was an attempt to objectively portray life through various forms of art. While this modern way of thinking was drawing organized opposition in France, Germany and England, Italy had no mass of opposition. Certain small groups and outspoken individuals criticized realism, but there was no organized movement to protest it in Italy as there was in other countries.

PROLETCULT

Proletcult was the term given to the Russian movement of 1917, which aimed to create a form of art that was devoid of bourgeois influence. The intent of Proletcult Theatre was to create productions in which political propaganda was not the sole content and purpose. The Proletcult Theatre served to remind Russia's working class that they were subservient to an arrogant and often tyrannous upper-class. This form of theatre was also called theatre of attractions because it did not use plot-driven scripts, but instead employed random dynamic spectacles to shock the audience or solicit some other form of emotion.

THEATRE OF THE ABSURD

Theatre of the Absurd, also called New Theatre and anti-theatre, is a phrase brought into existence by drama critic Martin Esslin. Esslin wrote a book bearing this title in 1962 addressing the type of play in which the human condition is decried as meaningless. The view of man's meaninglessness in the universe was a philosophy born of the Frenchman Albert Camus. Camus claimed that man had to resign himself to the fact that the universe defied logical explanation and could only be seen as absurd in its behavior. Esslin identified Eugene Ionesco, Samuel Beckett, Jean Genet, Arthur Adamov and Harold Pinter as the five defining playwrights of the absurdist movement. While this form of theatre was only recently assigned its own title, absurdist elements can be noticed in works as far back as those of Aristophanes. Absurdist elements can be identified in most plays predating the definition of Theatre of the Absurd, including Medieval morality plays and Elizabethan dramas. World War II, it is thought, readied the minds of playgoers for the themes presented in the Theatre of the Absurd.

CHINESE DRAMA

Chinese drama is rooted in and still holds true to religious tradition, relying heavily on the principles, superstitions and symbols of Taoism, Confucianism and Buddhism. The use of various combinations of these religious beliefs allow for Chinese dramatists to create extravagant productions often set in unearthly realms. While both Buddhism and Taoism provide a rich supply of symbolism, Confucianism is a much more intangible belief that centers on the worship of ancestors. Confucianist belief is most often represented in the musical theatre of the Chinese and Buddhist beliefs are often seen represented in acts of buffoonery towards gods and demons. The involvement of Chinese religion in theatre can be simplified in the following way: Confucianism places emphasis on morality, humanity, and worship of ancestors; Buddhism involves the idea of suffering, the changing future, and worship of images; Taoism includes the idea of balance, evils in the present, and worship of spirits.

SYMBOLISM

China is rich in national symbolism and this is reflected in its theatrical productions. Chinese drama views scenery as superfluous to a production, so it is implied through the words and actions of the actors. Lighting, also, is not an integral part of Chinese theatre. What the Chinese theatre lacks in scenery it makes up for in costumes, which are recreated accurately in the finest detail. The symbolism used in Chinese theatre is ancient and knowledge of its meaning has been handed down for generations, linking the past with the present. One such symbol is the yin-yang, which represents duality. Others are the dragon, a symbol of masculinity and heaven, and foxes, which symbolize deceit and trickery. Chinese drama also utilizes the sacred symbols known as the Hundred Antiques. These include the pearl, which prevents flood and fire; the coin, which signifies wealth; and jade, which brings justice. The Twelve Ornaments are also essential to Chinese theatre. These include images involving the sun, moon, dragon, birds and mountains.

History of Cleopatra

Since the time when the famous Queen of Egypt lived, her likeness has appeared in the dramatic productions of many artists. Samuel Daniel, in 1594, wrote a play entitled Cleopatra. In 1608, Elizabethan dramatist William Shakespeare wrote Antony and Cleopatra. John Fletcher and Francis Beaumont in their co-authored work, The False One, describe a Cleopatra much like the one found in Shakespeare's tale. In 1626, Thomas May wrote a play called The Tragedy of Cleopatra, Queen of Egypt. John Dryden's adaptation of Shakespeare's Antony and Cleopatra was entitled All for Love, featuring Cleopatra as a main character. American drama used Cleopatra as a central character in H. Rider Haggard's 1890 drama, Cleopatra. In 1899, famed comic dramatist George Bernard Shaw wrote a five-act play entitled Caesar and Cleopatra.

Superstitions Involving Theatre

Theatrical participants ranging from managers to actors, even today, hold some of the same superstitions that originated in the early years of theatre. One such superstitious belief is that blue scenery robs actors of wealth or lead to death. Blue scenery, in early European theatre, was allowed only if silver ornaments were hung, as silver was believed to ward off evil. Another superstition warns that Sunday rehearsals ensure disaster for actors and patrons. This arose from the death of New York's Grand Opera House manager after he called for a Sunday rehearsal. Another belief is that on the opening night of a new play, the first person admitted cannot be the holder of a free ticket or the play will fail. The black cat is seen as a sign of good fortune in theatres, while peacock feathers are renowned as bad luck. The luck in carrying a rabbit's foot led early actor Edmund Kean to dig up the remains of a deceased actor and procure one of his toe bones, to which Kean later attributed his great success.

Evolution of Stage Lighting

In its earliest days, theatre lighting was limited to the effects that could be harnessed from the sun, moon and stars. Early theatre was presented during daylight hours and the light that was cast upon the stage was controlled by nature. It can be assumed that theatre stages may have been built with this in mind. It is possible the stages were built in such a way as to cast shadows in the necessary places while positioning the most intense rays of light in others. Italian theatre began making use of candles for lighting effects in the 16th century: English theatre, in the 17th century. Oil lamps, in the 18th century, became the lighting method of choice. Gas lighting became available in the 19th century and the first theatre to use it was the Chestnut Street Theatre in Philadelphia. The first theatre to utilize electricity, discovered in 1879, was London's Savoy Theatre. In America, Boston's Bijou Theatre was the first to install electric lighting.

Time Line of Illumination Techniques

Specific illumination, which became the preferred lighting method in the mid-19th century, involves a controlled shaft of light that can focus and highlight any part of the stage. The first form of specific illumination was the limelight, also called a calcium light, and was invented by Thomas Drummond. Arc lamps, powered by a battery, did not become a practical source of lighting until the invention of the generator. The invention of the incandescent spotlight soon replaced the arc light in theatres. The baby lens, invented by Louis Hartmann, was followed by Thomas Edison's invention of a concentrated filament for use in a spotlight. By the 1920s, spotlights were the predominant form of lighting.

Lighting Designers

Adolphe Appia

The writing of Adolphe Appia is said to have given rise to modern lighting theory. Appia described three types of lighting in one of his plays: diffused light, creative light and painted light. He also identified four lighting cues: dazzling sunlight, the blood-red light of sunset, twilight and hazy darkness.

NORMAN BEL GEDDES

Norman Bel Geddes, while best known for his impressive and large theatrical designs, also contributed to modern lighting techniques. Bel Geddes built a model theatre with an electric lighting system. He used this model to experiment with light sources and positions until he discovered the optimal combinations.

ROBERT EDMOND JONES

Robert Edmond Jones, often referred to as the father of American scene design, used minimal scenery but dramatic lighting effects. One of his most memorable pieces was his staging of Macbeth. The entire performance took place on a bare stage with three giant moveable witch masks gazing down upon the performance. Jones used only single spotlights to isolate the acting areas.

ABE FEDER

Abe Feder, who studied at what is now Carnegie-Mellon University, was the first to coin the title "lighting designer." During his career, Feder was the lighting designer for over 300 Broadway shows. Feder was also known for his architectural lighting design, having created the lighting for the Empire State building, the RCA/GE building in Rockefeller Center and the United Nations building.

JEAN ROSENTHAL

Jean Rosenthal is best known for her lighting design in musicals from the 1950s and 1960s. She is credited as the inventor of dance lighting.

PEGGY CLARK

Peggy Clark was the first female to hold the position of president in the United Scenic Artist organization. She assisted in scene design and was the lighting designer for several Broadway plays.

CONTRIBUTIONS OF LOPE DE VEGA

Lope de Vega was a Madrid-born dramatist whose work is viewed as some of the best drama to come out of 16th- and 17th -century Spain. De Vega's work was characterized by his desire to place emphasis upon the individual. It is believed that de Vega's works were so popular that dramatists such as Voltaire, Shakespeare, Moliere and Marlowe all borrowed from de Vega's vast selection of writings. Lope de Vega's work consisted of four distinct styles: chivalrous drama, historical heroic drama, social life drama and sacred plays. It is believed that de Vega wrote near 2,200 plays in his lifetime, of which 481 exist today. Lope de Vega created Spanish drama from the Spanish tradition, folklore and stories that were native to his country. He ignored the classical traditions of the ancient Greeks and created some of the first plays belonging to the genre of romantic drama.

CONTRIBUTIONS OF CALDERON DE LA BARCA

Calderon de la Barca is best known for his ability to write both comic and tragic dramas. De la Barca, though he could write comedy, was most skilled with tragic drama. Much like Lope de Vega, de la Barca ignored the classical tradition of writing and instead drew material from the stories and culture of his native land. Of the hundreds of plays that have been credited to de la Barca only 181 have been proven authentic. His work often featured supernatural themes, grim humor and innovative plots. Much of de la Barca's work was influenced by his devout Catholicism just as much of his work was limited by his refusal to accept modern thinking. He was deeply medieval in his beliefs and resisted modern ideas, yet he still managed to produce some of the best romantic dramas of 17th-century Spain.

JEAN BAPTISTE POQUELIN DE MOLIERE

In many circles Moliere, whose birth name was Jean Baptiste Poquelin, is considered one of the greatest comic dramatists of all time. The name Moliere was taken by the young Poquelin as a stage name but it soon became so popular that his original surname effectively ceased to exist. He was known for both writing and acting in many French satires that still exist today. Moliere's play titled Tartuffe is considered one of his most successful works. Tartuffe was first performed for Louis XIV but was attacked by 17th century censors, who managed to suppress the play for three years after its debut. Moliere trained in France and traveled with a company of actors for over twelve years developing his craft. Among his most notable works are Don Juan, The Misanthrope and The Learned Ladies. Moliere died during a stage performance after a coughing fit caused a blood vessel to burst.

Contributions of Voltaire

Francois-Marie Arouet was a famed French playwright during the Enlightenment. He was more commonly known by the name Voltaire, which he assumed following his first successful production in 1718. Voltaire, classically educated by Jesuit priests, was known for his rebellion against intolerance, which landed him in jail on multiple occasions. Voltaire was exiled from France for his radical views at the time and he sought refuge in England. He traveled to several places, including Brussels and Holland. One of Voltaire's earliest works, written when he was only 19, is Oedipe. The success of this play was followed by Brutus, Zaire and Eriphile. Voltaire is best noted for his use of exotic influence in his works. He used plot material from foreign lands including China and South America. Voltaire's works extended to works of poetry, prose and letter writing.

William Hallam

William Hallam was a theatre actor-manager hailing from London. Hallam, recognizing America as rife with possibility for theatre arts, decided to create a company of players that he could send there. Hallam charged Robert Upton with traveling to America and preparing theatres for his vision; however, Upton took the money Hallam gave him and joined another company of players in America, completely neglecting the mission for which he was sent. Despite losing the aid of Robert Upton, Hallam decided to continue as planned. William Hallam, while not the first to introduce drama to America, did much for establishing its permanence. He put together a company of players who had the talent to execute a variety of theatrical genres, thus allowing the company to offer a multitude of productions.

Lewis Hallam

Lewis Hallam came to America in 1753 with the acting company sent over by his brother William Hallam. Lewis and his wife were both members of this theatre company, which presented a signed testament of the members' ability and character from Governor Dinwiddie, the British advocate for colonial expansion in America. Despite the support of Dinwiddie, colonial magistrates refused to issue a license to Lewis Hallam for theatrical performances in New York. Hallam rousted public interest through petitions and was soon granted license to perform. He produced twenty-one plays during a six-month stay in New York, including comedies, tragedies and farces. Once the company had solidified itself in New York, the members decided to pursue similar fame in Philadelphia. Hallam faced the same reluctance from authorities in Philadelphia but soon managed to overcome them. Hallam remained in Philadelphia for two months before the company retired to the West Indies. It is here that Lewis Hallam passed away after a long illness. Hallam is credited as part of the original company that solidified the place of American theatre.

George II, Duke of Saxe-Meiningen

The Duke of Saxe-Meiningen has been dubbed the first modern director. His works influenced theatrical pioneers including actor/manager Andre Antoine Konstantin Stanislavski. George II was known for designing his own sets, training his actors and conducting every rehearsal. The Duke paid special attention to details and planned each moment of each scene. He preferred to have stage props such as chairs, chimneys and doors that were real rather than drawn or created. The Duke created his own design rules, exemplified by his utilization of steps and levels to divide the stage into separate areas. . He refused to set anything in the middle of the stage, believing that a pleasing visual composition was one in which the middle of the picture was not centered on the middle of the stage. He also used various natural materials such as tree branches to hide technical equipment above the stage. In order to craft the most effective production, the Duke felt it was necessary to observe all movements on stage from visual and acoustic perspectives of various audience positions.

Henrik Ibsen

Norwegian native Henrik Ibsen is best known for bringing the French play to its height of perfection. Ibsen was not only a modern dramatist, but also a theatre manager and philosopher. Henrik Ibsen's work was prone to reflect his changing ideals. One work would proclaim the value of an ideal while in another work he would decry the selfsame value as worthless. He addressed this difference of opinion in his work titled An Enemy of the People, stating that most truths are obsolete after twenty years. His work further exposed what he saw as the social prejudices of his time. He extolled upon the value of the individual and each person's right to choose their own path in life. Ibsen believed that the true destiny of each man and the ultimate source of happiness was being true to one's self. Ibsen's ideas were not well-received during his lifetime and he was attacked by other playwrights for his seemingly ridiculous ideas.

Lewis Carroll

Lewis Carroll is the pen name of Charles Lutwidge Dodgson, author of "Alice's Adventures in Wonderland" (1865), and its sequel "Through The Looking Glass" (1871). His literary reputation rests on these two children's books, although he wrote several other novels including "The Hunting of the Shark" (1876), "A Tangled Tale" (1885), and "Sylvie and Bruno" (1889). Carroll also wrote several significant works on logic and mathematics. "Alice" was inspired by his favorite child-friend, Alice Liddell, and her two sisters to whom he related the story. Carroll was born in England in 1832 and became a mathematics teacher and resident Scholar of Christ Church College, Oxford. He assumed his pen name to protect his academic reputation that might be affected by authoring children's books. "Alice" brought him instant celebrity and served as an entreé to Victorian society. Carroll remained at Oxford until his death in 1898.

Louisa May Alcott

Louisa May Alcott is one of America's beloved children's writer, novelist, and short-story writer. Alcott began her publishing career writing popular "dime novels" under pseudonyms to make a living. The publication of "Little Women" in 1868, and its huge popularity, allowed her to pursue serious fiction thereafter. "Little Women" is a fond narrative of family life based partially on her own family. It is a romantic, yet realistic novel with strong and memorable characters. Alcott's later novels include "Little Men" (1871) and "Rose in Bloom" (1876), both written for young readers. Her best adult fiction includes "Moods" (1864), a novel of married life, and "Work" (1874), a story based on her financial problems. Alcott was born in Boston in 1832 and reared in nearby Concord. Her father was the famous Transcendentalist thinker, Bronson Alcott. She died in 1888.

Mark Twain

Mark Twain, the pen name of Samuel Langhorne Clemens, was a true American voice in literature. Humorist, novelist, and travel writer, he is best known for "Tom Sawyer" (1876), and "The Adventures of Huckleberry Finn" (1884), beloved novels with memorable characters and undertones of social concern. "Life on the Mississippi " (1883) was an autobiographical account of his days on a riverboat. Twain's acid humor, and stories of a fading rural America, made him one of the most popular figures of his day. Born in 1835 in Hannibal, Missouri, Twain who was self-educated, became a journalist and sometimes printer. His literary success made him a popular lecturer in America and Europe. His travels abroad provided Twain with the material for the satirical "A Connecticut Yankee in King Arthur's Court " (1889), and "The Innocents Abroad" (1869). His later life was marred by tragedy including the death of his wife and two daughters, as well as financial difficulty. He died in America in 1910.

Thomas Hardy

Hardy was an English novelist, playwright, and short-story writer. His dark works, often drawn from his own experience, include his first novel "Far from the Maddening Crowd" (1874), a tale of a strong woman and her three lovers. Hardy followed this modest success with four powerful novels, "Jude the Obscure" (1895), "The Return of the Native" (1878), "Tess of the D'Urbervilles" (1891), and "The Mayor of Casterbridge" (1896). All these volumes showcased Hardy's skills as storyteller and creator of strong characters. Hardy's poetry is also considered to be some of the best of his time. Hardy was born in Dorchester in Southwest England in 1840.

Hardy was trained as an architect, which he gave up for writing when he achieved success. With death of his wife, Hardy was guilt ridden and his grief fueled the writing of his greatest poetry, "Poems of 1912-13". Hardy married again and lived until 1928.

Contributions of Richard D'Oyly Carte

Richard D'Oyly Carte is recognized as the manager of the Royalty Theatre in London, as well as the creator of English comic-opera. D'Oyly booked a short opera to be performed at the Royalty Theatre. In order to make the event longer in length, he hired W.S. Gilbert and Arthur Sullivan to write a one-act comic opera, which they entitled Trial by Jury. The performance was a huge success and D'Oyly booked many of Gilbert and Sullivan's productions in the various theatres he managed. Examples of comic-operas include The Sorcerer, Patience and The Pirates of Penzance. Carte also owned and directed multiple theatre companies in both England and America. Among the many theatre houses he owned in London were the Opera Comique, the Savoy Theatre, and the English Opera House, later to become the Palace Theatre. D'Oyly Carte was also a musical composer, creating such works as Dr. Ambrosius: His Secret and Marie.

Robert Louis Stevenson

Robert Louis Stevenson was a Scottish essayist, novelist, poet, and short-story writer. After writing for weeklies for a few years, his "Treasure Island" (1883) brought him acclaim and wealth. Stevenson followed this success with "Kidnapped" (1886), "The Strange Case of Dr. Jekyll and Mr. Hyde" (1886), and "The Master of Ballantrae" (1889), all critical and financial successes. Stevenson also wrote a book of verse for children, "A Child's Garden of Verses"(1885). His swashbuckling tales and colorful language engaged the fancy of the public, and he retired a wealthy man. Stevenson was born in Edinburgh in 1850 and was educated in law. His life was tainted by chronic tuberculosis, and he sought cures and more healthy climates all over the world. Stevenson finally found the relief he sought in Samoa, where he settled and lived the last years of his life. He died there in 1894, at the young age of 44.

David Belasco

American-born David Belasco was a playwright, director and producer who got his start in theatre in San Francisco, where he was born. He worked as script copier and callboy in various theatres until his playwright skills were noticed. He then moved to New York and became a stage manager for the Madison Square Theatre before becoming an independent producer in 1859. His most notable works are Madame Butterfly and The Girl of the Golden West. Belasco wrote, directed or produced most of the plays shown on Broadway between 1884 and 1930. He also furthered naturalism in the theatre by using unconventional methods, such as placing scents in air ducts in the theatre to heighten the reality of a scene. He used working washing machines and dryers in his productions and his actors would cook real food if the script called for scenes involving eating. Belasco's attention to detail also gave rise to some advanced lighting techniques, which he used to create a mood or evoke a certain setting.

Contributions of George Bernard Shaw

Irish-born socialist George Bernard Shaw authored over sixty plays in his lifetime, most of which was comedy but it always contained some form of social or political propaganda. Shaw claimed that the primary reason of high-writing was to sway the masses to his way of thinking. Shaw was considered a freethinker of the 20th century. He spoke out for women's rights and demanded equality of income. When he was awarded the Nobel Prize in 1925 for literature, he accepted the award but refused the money associated with it. Shaw's work was greatly influenced by Norwegian playwright Henrik Ibsen. In addition to being a dramatist, Shaw was a literary critic and an accomplished public speaker, especially as a spokesman for socialism.

Sir Arthur Conan Doyle

Conan Doyle's contribution to literature was the enigmatic detective, Sherlock Holmes. Conan Doyle based his character on a former professor at the University of Edinburgh. Holmes first appeared in 1887 in " A Study in Scarlet", and more stories of the master of deductive reasoning appeared in magazines of the day. These stories were collected and published as "The Adventures of Sherlock Holmes" in 1892. Most memorable among the Holmes novels include "The Hound of the Baskervilles" (1902), " The Valley of Fear" (1915), and "The Sign of Four" (1890). Holmes also wrote a number of popular historical romances. Conan Doyle was born in London in 1859 and educated at Edinburgh. He trained as a physician and practiced medicine in Southsea from 1882-90. The success of his writing allowed him to largely retire from medicine.

Adolphe Appia

Adolphe Appia shaped modern day stagecraft through his early theories involving staging, lighting and the use of space. He believed that space was a dynamic element that could be utilized to convey a much more realistic feel for audiences. Appia began studying opera and soon decided that it did not offer the fluidity and staging that properly accentuated the human presence. He theorized that stage space would be better incorporated into a performance if it contained steps, ramps, platforms and drapes, all of which could be unified with actors through the use of lighting. Appia studied various operatic scenes in differing light and staging scenarios in order to find the best combinations. He published books on his theories, most notable of which are The Staging of Wagner's Musical Dramas, Music and Stage Setting and The Work of Living Art.

Contributions of Konstantin Stanislavsky

Russian-born Konstantin Stanislavsky is one of the most influential figures of the 20th century with regard to the acting process. He began acting at the age of 14 and as he got older moved to producing and directing. Stanislavsky's approach to acting was created over a forty-year period. He invented a method called the Stanislavsky System, which was at the forefront of modern psychological and emotional aspects of acting. His system became known as the Method. The fundamental principle of the Method is that it is the actor's primary responsibility to be believed. Method acting uses emotional memory. This approach was a novel idea in the acting world because it required actors to use parts of their own life, memories and personality while acting, whereas previous methods required actors to be blank slates, always ready to assume a new character's identity.

Contributions of Gordon Craig

Gordon Craig is credited with being one of the most influential faces of modern theatre. Craig's ideas on theatre can be seen in his 1904 book The Art of the Theatre. While many of Craig's peers believed that stage-directors should be merely interpreters, Craig saw the stage-director as a creator. It is a commonly held notion that the dramatist, director and actor align in a hierarchal form in which the actor is told what to do by the director, who is interpreting the words written by the dramatist. Craig believed that the role of the director superseded that of both the actor and the dramatist. He believed that theatre needed to be unified under the guidance of the director. One of Craig's most controversial philosophies is that theatre can function independently of literature. He felt that impulses of the director or even the actor were sufficient to create a performance and that a script was not essential.

Vsevolod Emilevich Meyerhold

Russian-born Vsevolod Emilevich Meyerhold performed the roles of actor, director and producer during his lifetime and was known for his socialist tendencies. He studied law for a short time, but soon abandoned law school for the Moscow Philharmonic Dramatic School, which was co-founded by Konstantin Stanislavski. Meyerhold went on to act in and direct several productions, each of which served as an opportunity for him to experiment with staging methods. He incorporated symbolism into most of his work because he believed it was a crucial part of any dramatic production. Stanislavski despised Meyerhold's work and wanted nothing to do with his work. One of Meyerhold's goals was to reinvent Commedia dell'arte in a more contemporary style. Meyerhold's acting technique was in direct opposition to Stanislavski's method. Meyerhold believed that emotion could be conveyed through use of practiced postures and gestures regardless of the actor's actual emotional state.

Freie Bühne

Freie Bühne is a German phrase meaning free theatre. The Freie Bühne was a German society in Berlin that sponsored performances that were banned or censored by commercial theatres. The origins of the society coincide with the visitation of Paris' Théâtre Libre to Berlin. Otto Brahm, theatre critic and proponent of naturalism, was part of the group that formed to create the society. One of the first works the society sponsored was Henrik Ibsen's Ghosts. Vor Sonnenaufgang, written by Gerhart Hauptmann, was the second play performed. This production was the first naturalistic play to be performed in Germany, relating a tale of a family's downfall at the hands of alcoholism, corruption and desire for wealth. The society ceased to exist in 1893 after only four years.

Antonin Artaud

Antonin Artaud was a French poet, playwright, actor and director. Artaud aspired to create a form of theatre where actors would serve as an extension of the audience's most repressed realities. Artaud, who was a follower of the surreal movement, unfortunately suffered from mental problems and was hospitalized repeatedly throughout his lifetime. Most noted for his concept of the theatre of cruelty described in his book, Theatre and its Double, he believed that theatre needed to awaken people to the truths that they struggled to suppress in their daily lives. He rejected the idea that theatre could only exist as a story involving a character who, when faced with a problem, could find resolution by the end of the play. The cruelty Artaud spoke of was not physical violence but a mental deliverance in which actors were presented as characters stripped of preconceived notions and outward appearances, the ultimate goal being to force audiences to see reality for what it was and not what others would have them believe it to be.

Eugène Ionesco

Romanian-native Eugene Ionesco is credited with creating the theatre of the absurd. Ionesco was born in 1909, but his family relocated to Paris, where he remained for sixteen years. In 1925, Ionesco returned to Romania with his father after his parents divorced. After a period of study, Ionesco wrote his first play in 1948. Ionesco's work rejected logical plots and standard character development. His plays were a comic portrayal of what he viewed as the absurdity of reality: man's existence as devoid of meaning in a universe ruled only by chance. Ionesco was attacked by critics for the lack of realism in his work and his rebuttal to these criticisms was that his writing was an effort to revitalize language and communication by saying things in a new way. People were shocked by Ionesco's views of drama and they either loved or hated it. In either case, talk of his work brought it increasing recognition. In 1962 Ionesco's niche in theatre history was defined by theatre critic Martin Esslin, who coined the term "theatre of the absurd" to describe Ionesco's work.

Contributions of Gao Xingjian

Chinese-born dramatist Gao Xingjian was educated in the People's Republic with a love of theatre nurtured by his actress mother. His love of theatre and freethinking resulted in his incarceration in a re-education camp for six years. Under threat of persecution from Communist leader Mao Zedong, Gao Xingjian wrote in secrecy, believing that literature was a link to human consciousness. His works were not published until 1980 and in 1981 his plays were performed at the Beijing People's Art Theatre. His plays were influenced by Samuel Beckett, Antonin Artaud and Bertolt Brecht, causing his work to be dubbed the "Chinese Theatre of the Absurd." Xingjian's play Bus Stop was based on Beckett's Waiting for Godot. Bus Stop was viewed as highly controversial and received much scrutiny from Communist Party authorities. Though the Chinese government could not accept the value of his work, Xingjian was awarded the Nobel Prize in Literature in 2000.

Major Contributors

- **Alfred Bunn** was an English theatrical manager who managed London's Drury Lane Theatre, Birmingham's Theatre Royal and London's Convent Garden. He also attempted to establish the opera in England.
- **James Burbage**, an English actor, erected the first theatre in London called The Theatre in Shorditch and started the Blackfriar's Theatre.
- **Christopher Marlowe** was famed for his blank verse. Marlow's plays include Tamburlaine, Doctor Faustus and The Jew of Malta He was an Elizabethan dramatist who preceded Shakespeare, a poet and a fictional writer.
- **William Congreve**, an English dramatist, was famed for his comic dramas.

- **Gao Xingjian** created what is known as the Chinese Theatre of the Absurd. Xingjian won a Nobel Prize for Literature in 2000.
- **John Heywood**, English dramatist, transformed morality plays from the Middle Ages into modern productions by changing the allegorical characters into real people.
- **John Lyly** brought the pastoral to England and created the form of Court Comedy.
- **Ben Johnson**, a London-born dramatist, was famed for works of comedy and satire.
- **Hans Sachs** was a German shoemaker, writer, singer and songwriter. He wrote over 208 plays during the 16th century.
- **Lope de Rueda** was a Spanish actor, manager and playwright who invented the Spanish version of the short farce called pasos.
- **Emile Zola** was a French writer who supported naturalism.
- **Honore de Balzac** was a French writer who is credited as the founding father of realism in European literature.
- **Henry Becque** was a 19th-centuryFrench playwright who incorporated both naturalism and realism into his work.
- **Aphra Behn** was the first female English playwright and a British spy.

Major Playwrights

- **Ionesco**: Rhinoceros, The Chairs, The Bald Soprano, The Lesson, The Killer, Exit the King, Hunger and Thirst and A Stroll in the Air.
- **Shaw**: Pygmalion, Caesar and Cleopatra, Androcles and the Lion, The Doctor's Dilemma, Candida and Major Barbara.
- **Marlowe**: Tamburlaine, Doctor Faustus, The Jew of Malta, Edward II and The Massacre at Paris.
- **Congreve**: The Way of the World, The Old Bachelor, Love for Love, The Double-Dealer and The Mourning Bride.
- **Xingjian**: Absolute Signal, Wilderness Man, Between Life and Death and Dialogue.
- **De Vega**: The Star of Seville, The Sheep Well, The Foolish Lady and Punishment Without Revenge.
- **De la Barca**: Devotion of the Cross, Life is a Dream and The World is a Fair.
- **Ben Johnson**: The Alchemist, Every Man out of His Humor, The Sad Shepherd, The Masque of Blackness.
- **Hans Sachs**: Lucretia, Virginia.
- **Lope de Rueda**: Eufemia, Medora, Armelina.
- **Giovanni Verga**: The She-Wolf, In the Porter's Lodge, The Wolf Hunt, The Fox Hunt, and Rustic Chivalry.
- **J. M. Barrie**: Peter Pan, Mary Rose, What Every Woman Knows, Quality Street, The Admirable Crichton.
- **Pierre Beaumarchais**: The Barber of Seville, The Marriage of Figaro.
- **Samuel Beckett**: Waiting for Godot, Endgame, and Happy Days.
- **Bertolt Brecht**: Baal, A Man's a Man, The Threepenny Opera, The Life of Galileo, Mother Courage, The Caucasian Chalk Circle, The Visions of Simone Machard.
- **Anton Chekhov**: The Seagull, Uncle Vanya, The Cherry Orchard, and The Three Sisters.
- **George Cohan**: Seven Keys to Baldplate, The Little Millionaire, Little Nelly Kelly, and Forty-five Minutes from Broadway.
- **Richard Brinsley Sheridan**: The Rivals, The Critic, A Trip to Scarborough, and The School for Scandal.
- **Friedrich von Schiller**: The Robbers, Don Carlos, Maria Stuart.
- **Johann Wolfgang von Goethe**: Faust, The Lover's Caprice, Clavigo, Egmont, Stella, Iphigenia in Tauris, Torquato Tasso.

Chapter Quiz

Ready to see how well you retained what you just read? Scan the QR code to go directly to the chapter quiz interface for this study guide. If you're using a computer, simply visit the online resources page at **mometrix.com/resources719/osatspeechdd116** and click the Chapter Quizzes link.

Pedagogical Content Knowledge

Diverse Student Populations

Understanding Students' Diverse Backgrounds and Needs

Self-Education

Educating oneself on students' diverse backgrounds and needs enhances one's overall understanding of their students and creates a culturally sensitive, accepting classroom environment tailored to students' individual needs. There are several avenues through which teachers should educate themselves in an effort to build an accepting and respectful classroom climate. Communication is key for learning about diversities; thus, it is important for teachers to foster and maintain positive communications with students' families to deepen understanding of cultures, beliefs, lifestyles, and needs that exist within their classrooms. This could include learning some language of students with different cultural backgrounds, attending family nights at school, or participating in social events within their students' communities to integrate themselves into the culture. Furthermore, teachers can learn more about their students' backgrounds and needs through gaining an understanding of student differences, incorporating these diversities into the curriculum, and encouraging students to participate in learning by sharing aspects of their lives with the class.

Teaching, Learning, and Classroom Climate Benefits

A deep understanding of students' diverse backgrounds and needs provides multiple benefits for teaching, learning, and overall classroom climate. Knowledge of students' diversities allows teachers to understand the individual needs and abilities of their students and tailor instruction accordingly to maximize student development and achievement. Additionally, it allows teachers to know which authentic materials to incorporate in lessons and instructions to best create an engaging, relevant, and respectful learning experience that fosters student interest in learning and promotes success. Furthermore, by enhancing understanding of students' diverse backgrounds and needs, teachers consequently begin to model an attitude of inclusivity, acceptance, and respect for differences, which is then reflected by students and achieves a positive, welcoming classroom climate that promotes diversity.

Implications for Teaching, Learning, and Assessment in Diverse Classrooms

In any classroom, a teacher will encounter a wide range of variances among individual students that inevitably will influence teaching, learning, and assessment. Diversities in ethnicity, gender, language background, and learning exceptionality will likely exist simultaneously in a single classroom. Educators must be prepared to teach to these diversities while concurrently teaching students the value and importance of diversity. The curriculum and classroom environment must be adjusted to meet individual student needs and create an **inclusive**, **respectful**, and **equitable** environment that welcomes differences and allows for success in learning. This begins with the teacher developing an understanding of the unique diversities that exist within their students and using this knowledge to **differentiate** curriculum, materials, activities, and assessments in such a way that students of all needs, interests, backgrounds, and abilities feel encouraged and included. Furthermore, the teacher must understand how to instill appropriate supports to accommodate the diverse needs of students and how to modify the classroom environment in such a way that is reflective of the diversity of the students.

Considerations for Teaching in Diverse Classrooms

Ethnically Diverse Classrooms

As society becomes increasingly diverse, teachers will certainly encounter classrooms with students of multiple ethnicities. Thus, to create an accepting and respectful classroom environment that allows for success in learning for all students, there are several factors to consider. Teachers must educate themselves on the various ethnicities within their classroom. This includes being mindful of the **social norms, values, beliefs,**

traditions, and **lifestyles** of different ethnic groups and learning to communicate with students and families in a respectful, culturally sensitive manner. Additionally, teachers must make a conscious effort to incorporate aspects of each ethnicity into the curriculum, activities, and classroom environment to create an inclusive atmosphere that teaches the acceptance, respect for, and celebration of differences. Teachers must be **culturally competent** and ensure that all materials are accurate, relevant, authentic, and portray the different ethnicities within the classroom in a respectful, unbiased manner. Furthermore, teachers must consider how their own ethnicity impacts their teaching style and interactions with students, how they may be perceived by other ethnic groups, and how to respond in a manner that fosters respect and inclusivity.

Gender-Diverse Classrooms

When approaching a gender-diverse classroom, teachers need to consider their perceptions and expectations of different genders as well as their interactions with different genders. Teachers should also consider how the classroom environment and materials portray gender differences. Teachers must work to eliminate possible stereotypical beliefs so that all students feel respected, accepted, and encouraged to participate. Furthermore, teachers must consider how their behavior acts as a model for how students perceive gender roles and should act in a way that eliminates gender divisiveness. Teachers should use gender-neutral language when addressing students and ensure that all students receive equal attention. Teachers must maintain equal academic and behavioral expectations between genders and be sure to equally praise and discipline students so that neither gender feels superior or inferior to another. Regarding curriculum and classroom materials, teachers must ensure that the classroom environment encourages equal participation in, access to, and choice of all activities and procedures. Activities and materials should provide equal opportunities and foster collaboration between genders. Furthermore, teachers must ensure that curriculum materials avoid gender stereotypes and highlight each gender equally in order to create an accepting and respectful learning environment that provides equal opportunities for students of all genders to develop their individual identities and abilities.

Linguistically Diverse Classrooms

In a **linguistically diverse** classroom, teachers must consider how to effectively demonstrate value for students' native languages while simultaneously supporting the development of necessary language skills to thrive in the school setting. By accepting and encouraging students to use their native languages, teachers can establish an inclusive learning environment that celebrates linguistic differences and encourages students to want to build upon their language skills. Through this, teachers create an equitable learning environment that allows for academic success. To develop English language skills, teachers must first consider each student's language ability, level of exposure to English prior to entering the classroom, and the level of language learning support each student has at home. Teachers can then implement effective instructional strategies and supports to modify curriculum in a way that addresses students' language needs. Teachers must also consider the implications of the classroom environment on language acquisition. By creating an atmosphere that encourages language acquisition through **literacy-rich resources** and **cooperative learning**, teachers promote the use of language skills and ultimately provide opportunities for success for all students.

Linguistic Supports and Instructional Strategies for English Language Proficiency

Incorporating a variety of linguistic aids and instructional strategies is beneficial in supporting ELL students of varying levels of English language proficiency. **Visual representations** to accompany instruction, such as posters, charts, pictures, slide shows, videos, tables, or anchor charts, are valuable in providing clarification and reference while promoting vocabulary acquisition. When delivering instruction, **body language** such as hand gestures, eye contact, and movement to mimic verbal directions and explanations can provide clarification to enhance understanding. These students may also require **translation devices** for clarification, an interpreter to help with understanding instructions and new concepts, alternate assignments with simplified language, or **individualized instruction** from an ESL teacher. Frequently checking for understanding and providing clarification as necessary throughout instruction are necessary to ensuring ELL students understand learning materials, instructions, and assessments. In addition, creating a print- and literacy-rich environment is valuable in promoting English language acquisition. This can be done by including word walls for new vocabulary, reading materials that vary in complexity, labels, and opportunities for speaking, reading, and writing within instruction.

Learning Disabilities and Other Exceptionalities

In a classroom where learning disabilities and exceptionalities are present, teachers must consider accommodations for students of various learning needs while fostering an atmosphere of respect and acceptance. Teachers must understand the individual learning needs of each student and differentiate instruction accordingly to create an equitable and inclusive learning atmosphere. For **learning disabled** students, teachers must consider accommodations that allow for inclusion in all areas of curriculum and instruction. Such considerations may include extended work time, individualized instruction, and cooperative learning activities to ensure that learning disabled students are provided the necessary supports to achieve academic success. For students with other exceptionalities, such as **gifted and talented** students, teachers need to consider ways to provide challenging and stimulating opportunities for expansion and enrichment of curriculum. Furthermore, teachers must be aware of their own interactions with students in order to demonstrate and encourage respect and acceptance among students. By providing supports for individual student success, teachers can effectively highlight students' strengths and teach students to accept and celebrate differences in learning abilities.

Educating Students about Diversity

Goals of Teaching Diversity in the Classroom

Teaching diversity in the classroom aims to establish a welcoming and inclusive classroom environment that encourages academic achievement and whole-child development. Diversity education works to develop students' understanding, acceptance, and respect for others' perspectives while instilling the concept that people are ultimately more alike than different and that diversity should be celebrated. Teaching the importance of differences creates a positive, inclusive classroom atmosphere in which all students feel respected, safe, and valued by their teacher and peers. Such an environment promotes academic achievement among students in that it encourages participation in learning and builds the self-esteem necessary for positive growth and development. Furthermore, teaching diversity has a significant role in **whole-child development** in that it instills the ability to understand and respect multiple frames of reference, thus increasing the child's ability to problem solve, cooperate with others, and develop a broader global perspective. Additionally, it allows for the development of cultural competency and ultimately creates accepting and respectful contributors to society.

Review Video: Multiculturalism/Celebrating All Cultures
Visit mometrix.com/academy and enter code: 708545

Recognizing and Eliminating Personal Biases

Personal biases are often subtle and unconscious, yet it is essential that teachers work to recognize and eliminate them to create an accepting and respectful classroom environment. Personal biases may negatively impact teaching style, interactions with students, student learning, and self-esteem. In eliminating personal bias, teachers ensure that they establish an inclusive classroom environment where each student is treated fairly. Furthermore, students' beliefs toward diversity are influenced by the attitudes and behaviors modeled by their teacher; therefore, eradicating personal bias is vital in positively influencing students to accept and respect differences. To eliminate personal bias, teachers must **reflect** on their own culture's attitudes toward diversity as well as how these attitudes influence their interactions toward other groups, and work to make positive changes. Teachers must **educate** themselves on the diversities among their students and work to deepen their understanding of different groups through **communicating** with families, **integrating** themselves into students' communities, and participating in **professional development** that focuses on **cultural competency** and the importance of teaching diversity. Through making positive changes against personal biases, teachers foster a classroom environment that promotes diversity and empowers all students to be successful.

Impact of Diverse Cultural Climate in the Classroom

Creating a diverse cultural climate in the classroom results in an empowering and engaging learning environment that facilitates academic success. An atmosphere that respects and accepts differences fosters a sense of inclusivity and welcoming among teachers and students, which allows students to feel comfortable with differences, safe in their own identities, and comfortable to engage in learning. This fosters a positive attitude toward learning that promotes academic achievement. Additionally, when students accept one another's differences in a diverse cultural climate, they are better able to work together and adopt creative problem-solving solutions through others' perspectives, which results in success in learning. Furthermore, a successfully diverse cultural climate reflects the diversity of the students within it, which ultimately creates a more engaging and relevant academic environment that sparks motivation and curiosity toward learning. Learning environments that reflect students' diversity create a sense of unity and belonging in the classroom and positively contribute to success in learning through building students' self-esteem and self-concept to empower them in believing they can achieve academic success.

Authentic Classroom Materials

Authentic classroom materials are artifacts from various cultures, events, or periods of time. These items enhance the relevancy of instruction by promoting students' real-world connection to learning and may also be used to incorporate students' backgrounds and experiences into the classroom to increase engagement. Such materials include magazines, newspapers, advertisements, restaurant menus, and recipes. In addition, resources such as video clips, films, television shows, documentaries, news segments, and music serve as authentic media sources to incorporate into instruction. Original works or documents, including art pieces, literature, poetry, maps, or historical records, are also valuable authentic resources for providing students with a real-world learning experience.

Locating and Implementing

Authentic classroom materials and resources are integral in creating a classroom environment that fosters engaging, relevant, and positive learning experiences. Teachers must work to develop an understanding of the diversities among their students and use this knowledge to locate and implement authentic classroom materials into daily instruction. In doing so, teachers create a positive learning environment that accepts and respects differences through incorporating **relevant** and **familiar** materials that make students from all backgrounds feel valued and included in instruction. When students can see aspects of their culture reflected in authentic learning materials, they can make **personal connections** between what they are learning and their own lives. This makes learning become more valuable, engaging, and relevant, thereby promoting success in learning.

Incorporating Diversity Education into the Classroom

Incorporating diversity into the classroom maximizes student opportunities for academic success through creating a welcoming, empowering, and inclusive atmosphere. Teachers can implement multiple strategies to incorporate **diversity education** into the curriculum both as its own unit and woven into content instruction once they develop an understanding of the diversities among their own students. Through **building relationships** with students, teachers can use their knowledge of students' lives to incorporate aspects of their backgrounds into the curriculum by creating specific **cultural lessons** on food, music, language, art, and history. Additionally, **cultural comparison** studies are an effective method of teaching students the value of diversity and highlighting the fact that people from different backgrounds often have more similarities than differences. Teachers can further implement diversity education by encouraging students to participate in learning through having them share elements of their culture and background with the class through activities such as show and tell or hosting family nights. Furthermore, integrating **cooperative learning** activities into instruction allows and encourages students from different backgrounds to work together and gain an understanding of the perspectives and backgrounds of others.

Incorporating Diversity in the Curriculum

Incorporating diversity into the curriculum is vital for teaching the value and importance of differences and for contributing to a respectful and accepting environment. Additionally, it is imperative that diversity education extend from the curriculum to the entire classroom environment to maximize student growth and opportunity to reach potential. When students learn in an atmosphere that celebrates diversity and identifies strengths in differences, they feel a sense of belonging and confidence that encourages them to engage in learning, thus maximizing the potential for academic success. Teachers can effectively integrate diversity into the classroom environment through making authentic cultural materials such as texts, music, and art readily accessible for students. Additionally, providing several opportunities for students to collaborate and socialize in a natural setting allows them to gain an understanding and respect for their peers' backgrounds. By encouraging students to share aspects of their own lives and backgrounds with the class through cultural activities, teachers facilitate a diverse climate that celebrates differences.

Culturally Responsive Teaching

Culturally responsive teaching is an instructional approach in which the teacher practices awareness, inclusivity, and sensitivity regarding the social and cultural diversities that are present within the classroom. With this awareness in mind, the culturally responsive teacher designs curriculum, instruction, activities, and assessments that are inclusive and reflective of students' social and cultural backgrounds and experiences. When planning instruction and learning experiences, teachers can demonstrate awareness of social and cultural norms through consciously educating themselves on the beliefs, values, and norms of their students. This is achieved through connecting with students and building positive relationships to learn about their individual backgrounds and locate authentic learning materials that are reflective of their experiences. Through communicating with students' parents, family members, and members of the community, teachers can practice and build awareness of the diverse social and cultural norms of their students to gain an understanding of how to design culturally responsive instruction. By educating themselves on the social and cultural norms of their students, teachers can effectively ensure that students' diversities are reflected in all areas of instruction in a culturally sensitive manner to create an empowering learning environment that engages all students.

Practices for Culturally Responsive Teaching	
1	Create an inclusive classroom environment.
2	Recognize personal biases and work to eliminate them.
3	Self-educate on the community and students' social and cultural backgrounds.
4	Use curriculum that reflects students' diversities using authentic materials.
5	Frequently communicate with students' families.
6	Build positive interpersonal relationships with students.
7	Be involved in the community.

Learning Goals and Objectives

Determining Instructional Goals and Objectives

Role of Assessment in Meeting Individual Student Learning Needs

Assessing students' prerequisite skills and knowledge is integral in gaining the understanding necessary to effectively determine instructional goals and objectives. This understanding provides the teacher with information about students' background knowledge, diverse experiences, and individual needs. With this information in mind, the teacher can establish goals and objectives based on state standards that are tailored to meet students' individual learning needs and ensure that learning targets are relevant, challenging, and attainable. In assessing background knowledge, teachers can develop high quality instruction that builds on students' prior experiences, thus fostering engagement in learning by allowing students to make personal connections in their learning. Additionally, assessing prerequisite skills and knowledge allows the teacher to identify gaps in learning, misunderstandings, or specific learning needs. This information allows the teacher to adjust and adapt instructional goals and objectives that align with students' abilities, learning styles, and knowledge, thus maximizing student learning potential by establishing student-centered instruction.

Assessment Strategies

Several assessment strategies can be utilized when determining the prerequisite knowledge and skills of students. Assessments may be either formal or informal and serve to provide valuable information to the teacher for effectively determining an instructional plan that is tailored to students' individual needs. Before introducing new content, teachers can administer a formal diagnostic test that contains the new material to assess prior knowledge and skill level. Teachers can then analyze the results to adjust goals and objectives as necessary. Additionally, knowledge and abilities can be evaluated by analyzing prior test scores or project portfolios to gauge student understanding of previously taught material. This allows the teacher to identify gaps in knowledge or make necessary clarifications to information. Some informal methods of assessment include conducting individual or whole-class formative assessments such as concept maps, polls, or observations to gain understanding of students' background knowledge on new material prior to teaching it. Teachers can also have students self-assess their prerequisite knowledge on new instruction through administering a test or questionnaire about content material. Often, when assessing prerequisite knowledge and skills, it is important that teachers keep assessments anonymous to ensure they receive accurate and unbiased data on student understanding and ability.

Role of Standards in Determining Instructional Goals and Objectives

State standards for achievement provide a guideline and reference point for specific benchmarks of student academic progress based on grade level. Additionally, they serve to ensure that teachers and students are held to the same expectations for teaching and learning, thus focusing instructional goals and objectives. Teachers must have a solid understanding of state standards, as they are responsible for referring to them as an outline for planning instruction, lessons, learning outcomes, and assessments and ensuring that students achieve these learning targets. State standards provide a structure for teachers to effectively plan and adjust instructional goals and objectives based on individual student learning needs and ensure that all students have the necessary support to reach these academic standards. State standards are also the reference point for establishing the pace of instruction, monitoring student progress, and determining if learning goals have been met before progressing through the curriculum.

Appropriate Learning Goals and Objectives

Setting appropriate learning goals and objectives is an integral component of quality, effective instruction that communicates high expectations, is developmentally appropriate, and is tailored to students' individual learning needs. Specific learning targets allow the teacher to effectively determine the path of instruction based on students' skills and abilities in a manner that is challenging and attainable while supporting students in achieving state academic standards. Through focusing the method of instruction on specific targets, teachers can better determine which lesson materials, activities, and assessments will best support students' learning needs to achieve success in learning. Additionally, appropriate learning goals and objectives are necessary for student academic success because they communicate clear expectations and the purpose of learning. When students understand why they are learning a given concept and what they are expected to achieve, they are encouraged to be engaged and focused in learning. Clear learning goals and objectives are also important for monitoring student progress, as they allow teachers to concretely measure student achievement and provide specific, meaningful feedback that allows for student growth.

Elements of Appropriate Learning Goals and Objectives

When determining learning outcomes, the teacher must consider the elements of appropriate learning goals and objectives. Effective **learning goals** communicate long-term learning targets, such as at the end of a unit or chapter, whereas **objectives** should dictate what students are expected to learn at the end of a daily lesson or activity. Proper learning goals and objectives are derived from state academic standards and simultaneously reflect individual student learning needs. They are age- and grade-level-appropriate, challenging, and aimed toward higher-order thinking while still attainable to students according to their developmental level and learning differences. Appropriate learning goals and objectives clearly and succinctly communicate measurable expectations and define a clear purpose for instruction to make learning relevant. Additionally, they consider students' current skills and abilities in order to set targets that build upon background knowledge and allow students to make personal connections in their learning.

Determining Effectiveness of Learning Goals and Objectives

Learning goals and objectives provide a necessary foundation for successful students. Proper learning targets clearly and succinctly communicate expectations, engagement, and achievement. The effectiveness of goals and objectives can be determined by their level of clarity, relevance, and significance of desired outcomes to students, thus allowing for focused instruction and learning. Goals and objectives are most successful when they are relevant to both curriculum material and students' individual experiences, as this fosters engagement through allowing students to forge personal connections and apply new concepts to their own experiences. Moreover, appropriate goals and objectives convey significance to overall learning. When students understand why what they are learning is important, they are more likely to be engaged and focused on instruction, and ultimately, achieve success in learning.

Framing Learning Goals and Objectives to Promote Student Understanding

The language of learning objectives and goals must be **age-appropriate, clear**, and **succinct** for students to comprehend them. Learning goals must represent broader learning outcomes, whereas learning objectives outline the steps for doing so. This includes utilizing verbs that align with the level of understanding that teachers intend for their students to achieve. For example, when introducing a concept, learning objectives may include verbs such as *identify*, *match*, or *define*. As students develop mastery, the language of objectives should incorporate **higher-order thinking** verbs, such as *analyze*, *interpret*, or *predict*. Learning objectives and goals should also be measurable in order to communicate to students exactly what they are expected to achieve by the end of the lesson or unit. For example, a learning objective written as, "students will be able to discuss the economic impact of World War II," provides students with a specific and tangible goal to work toward. Academic goals and objectives should include the **purpose** for learning, such as to prepare for an assessment or complete part of a project, and should be connected to state or district standards.

Review Video: Learning Objectives
Visit mometrix.com/academy and enter code: 528458

Determining If Learning Goals and Objectives Are Responsive to Student Needs

In order for instruction and learning to be successful, goals and objectives must be responsive to the developmental levels and individual needs of the students. Teachers must determine the responsiveness of learning targets by their age-appropriateness, consideration of students' skills and abilities, and reflection of their needs, interests, cultures, and backgrounds. Age-appropriate goals and objectives promote student achievement by providing realistic yet rigorous expectations based on developmental level that facilitate academic success. In order to design instruction and activities that are challenging but not overwhelming, expectations must match students' individual skill levels and abilities. Finding the right difficulty for students can ensure that students feel empowered in their learning. Responsive learning goals and objectives also consider students' individual needs and interests, thus allowing for instruction that is relevant and engaging. Additionally, learning targets should be sensitive to and incorporate elements of students' cultures and backgrounds. This fosters engagement and success in learning through allowing students to make personal connections between instruction and their own experiences.

Evaluating Appropriateness of Learning Goals and Objectives

When evaluating the appropriateness of learning goals and objectives, teachers should first consider their relevance and specificity to the academic standards from which they are deriving learning targets as well as how well they facilitate the design of effective instruction. Learning goals should express the desired outcomes of long-term learning, whereas objectives should measure daily achievement as students work toward the learning goal and the specified state standard. Teachers should evaluate whether the goals and objectives precisely communicate what the students are expected to achieve to effectively design instruction that supports students in achieving learning targets. Furthermore, they must ensure that learning targets are tailored to students' individual learning needs to design challenging and realistic instruction. Additionally, teachers should consider the purpose of the learning goals and objectives to determine whether they communicate clear intentions for learning to students. Teachers must then decide which activities, instructional strategies, materials, and resources are most effective for supporting the achievement of learning targets and how they will design assessments to determine student achievement.

Role of Campus and District Goals in Student Academic Readiness

Aligning instructional learning goals and objectives with campus and district goals is imperative for student academic readiness. These standards indicate benchmarks of achievement that students are expected to reach at a given grade level and act as a framework for the design of goals and objectives that help facilitate this achievement. This allows for the focusing of instruction and learning as well as providing a measurable framework for assessing student progress. Additionally, it ensures that all students are held to the same academic expectations and that all students are given the same opportunities for learning. Creating learning targets based upon campus and district goals ensures that students are successfully able to advance to the next grade level with the same academic preparedness relative to their peers.

Designing Goals and Objectives to Address Different Skills and Ability Levels

While learning targets must be aligned with state academic standards, they simultaneously must be tailored to address students' unique skills and abilities. By differentiating instructional goals and objectives, teachers ensure that the instructional strategies, activities, and materials that they implement are effectively varied to meet students' individual learning needs. Additionally, they ensure that instructional expectations challenge students based on their skill and ability while supporting all students in meeting academic benchmarks. The language of objectives and goals should be layered to include varying levels of rigor to accommodate students' differing abilities as they work toward achieving intended learning outcomes. Learning targets should include scaffolding in order to ensure students have necessary supports and allow opportunities for expansion or enrichment as necessary. They should include differentiation in skills students are expected to attain based on their background knowledge and ability as well as variances in approaches to completing tasks and demonstrating understanding. In differentiating objectives and goals, teachers ensure that all students are challenged and supported as they work to achieve grade-level academic standards.

Instructional Planning

Designing Lesson Plans and Units to Align with Instructional Goals

The effective sequencing of units and lesson plans is key to developing coherent, comprehensible instruction that aligns with instructional goals and fosters success in learning. Teachers must first determine the instructional goals that students will be expected to achieve based on state academic standards as a framework and students' individual needs, knowledge, and abilities. Teachers must then logically arrange specific units of instruction aimed toward achieving the determined instructional goals. Each unit should build upon knowledge from the prior unit. Within each unit, teachers must determine what students must achieve as they work toward instructional goals and determine objectives that facilitate success based on individual need and ability. Once objectives are defined, teachers must design lesson plans in a logical sequence that will facilitate students in reaching these objectives and increasingly build upon knowledge as students work toward achieving the learning goal. When planning lessons, teachers must decide which activities, procedures, and materials are necessary for successfully completing lesson objectives while ensuring that individual learning needs are met. The teacher must also decide what will be assessed at the end of each lesson and unit to determine student success in achieving instructional goals.

Review Video: Creating Effective Lesson Plans
Visit mometrix.com/academy and enter code: 100377

Creating Developmentally Appropriate Learning Experiences and Assessments

Multiple factors must be considered when designing developmentally appropriate learning experiences and assessments that effectively facilitate student growth and achievement. Teachers must consider the general cognitive, physical, social, and emotional developmental levels of students as well as individual differences in background, skill, knowledge, and learning needs. With this understanding, teachers must then evaluate whether learning experiences are simultaneously appropriate to students' developmental levels and individual needs. This includes ensuring that learning activities and teaching strategies are varied in approach, are tailored to students' interests, and that they incorporate student choice in learning. Learning experiences must build upon students' background knowledge and experiences and provide challenging yet attainable learning opportunities based on individual skills and abilities. Additionally, teachers must consider whether learning experiences promote student participation and engagement as well as cooperative learning to ensure development across domains. Just as with learning experiences, the developmental appropriateness of assessments must also be evaluated. The teacher must consider whether assessments allow for choice in how students demonstrate their learning so as to address individual learning needs. Furthermore, it is important that teachers consider the purpose of each assessment regarding the feedback they are seeking and how it can help determine further instruction.

Role of Learning Theory in Instructional Process and Student Learning

Multiple learning theories exist to explain how people acquire knowledge, abilities, and skills. Each theory proposes its own approach for best practices in teaching and learning, and their effectiveness varies depending on the context of learning and individual student needs. These theories serve as frameworks for the instructional process and facilitating student learning. Teachers must understand the principles of various learning philosophies as well as their students' unique learning needs to effectively design and implement instruction from the perspective of the most applicable theory. Upon identifying desired learning outcomes, teachers can draw on applicable learning theories to make informed decisions about designing instruction, activities, and assessments that are most effective based on their students' learning styles, skills, and abilities.

The following are examples of some common learning theories that can be used as a framework in the instructional process:

- **Constructivism (Jean Piaget):** This theory proposes that students learn by interacting with the learning environment and connecting new information to their background knowledge to build understanding. This active process allows students to personalize their learning and construct their own perceptions of the world through the lens of their previous experiences.
- **Humanism (Abraham Maslow, Carl Rogers):** This theory proposes that learning should take a person-centered approach, with a focus on the individual's innate capacity for personal growth and self-actualization. It operates axiomatically from the principle that all humans have a natural desire to learn; therefore, a failure to learn is due to the learning situation or environment rather than a person's inability to learn. Teachers should act as facilitators and strive to create a safe, accepting learning environment, celebrate students' differences, and praise academic and personal achievement.
- **Connectivism (George Siemens, Stephen Downes):** This theory proposes that learning occurs by making a series of connections across pieces of information, ideas, concepts, and perspectives. Connectivism is rooted in the notion that learning occurs externally, and technology facilitates connections by giving learners access to several outlets for acquiring and processing new information.
- **Experiential Learning (David Kolb):** This theory proposes that students learn and retain information best through physical exploration and interaction with the learning environment. In the classroom, teachers can facilitate this student-led approach by providing students with varying relevant experiences and opportunities for hands-on learning, such as projects or learning centers.
- **Multiple Intelligences (Howard Gardner):** Gardner's theory proposes there are several versions of intelligence, and as such, the process of learning differs among individuals. Some learners may have a stronger intelligence in one domain but have difficulty in another and, therefore, learn best when instruction is presented through the lens of their dominant intelligence. Intelligences are categorized as logical-mathematical, verbal-linguistic, visual-spatial, bodily-kinesthetic, interpersonal, intrapersonal, musical, and naturalistic.

Connecting New Information and Ideas to Prior Knowledge

When students connect new information to prior knowledge, learning becomes relevant and engaging. Effective instruction encourages students to connect learning to background knowledge and experiences, which increases retainment, deepens understanding, and enhances the effectiveness of the overall learning experience. Fostering personal connections to learning is achieved through incorporating an array of strategies and technologies into instruction. Activities including KWL charts, anticipatory guides, graphic organizers, and brainstorming encourage students to consider what they know before learning new concepts, thus allowing them to build upon their prior knowledge and ability to make connections that strengthen learning. Cooperative learning strategies promote sharing and building prior knowledge with other students, thus increasing students' connections to new information. Numerous technologies exist to enhance the learning experience by fostering connections between prior knowledge and new information. Teachers can incorporate a wide range of apps and games across subject areas that build upon prior knowledge by providing activities with increasing levels of difficulty. Online polls, surveys, and word association websites allow students to demonstrate prior understanding of a topic to begin making connections. Self-reflection and closure opportunities at the end of instruction further strengthen learning by encouraging students to connect new material to prior knowledge and experiences.

Making Learning Meaningful and Relevant

Effective instruction occurs when learning is meaningful and relevant. When the purpose of learning is clear, students are engaged, motivated, and retain new information. Instruction must be student-centered, foster personal connections, and be applicable to real-life situations to create meaningful and relevant instruction. Teachers achieve this through an array of methods and technologies that are tailored to students' learning needs. Through forging positive relationships with students, teachers learn their unique interests, preferences, and experiences. Activities such as interest inventories, surveys, and community building develop a positive rapport between teachers and students. This allows teachers to make learning meaningful by creating learner-centered instruction that facilitates personal connections and builds upon prior knowledge. Field trips and community outreach programs are effective in enhancing relevancy through demonstrating the real-world applications of instruction. Additionally, technologies including virtual field trips and tours, videos, and documentaries assist in increasing students' understanding the purpose of learning by illustrating the real-world applications of instruction. Self-assessments make learning meaningful and relevant through encouraging student ownership and responsibility over learning as students seek areas for improvement. Moreover, closure activities serve to demonstrate overall purpose for learning through encouraging students to connect learning to the lesson's objective and their prior knowledge.

INTRADISCIPLINARY AND INTERDISCIPLINARY INSTRUCTION

Intradisciplinary and interdisciplinary instruction are both valuable strategies for teaching and learning. In **intradisciplinary** instruction, several elements of a single broad subject area are incorporated into the lesson. For example, in a science lesson, the teacher could incorporate elements of chemistry, biology, and physics into instruction. This method of instruction is beneficial in deepening students' understanding of the nuances of a particular subject area through demonstrating the various components that comprise the overarching discipline. **Interdisciplinary** instruction refers to the simultaneous integration of ideas, knowledge, and skills from several subject areas when approaching an idea, problem, or theme and applying principles of one subject area to another. For example, in an interdisciplinary unit on food, the teacher could incorporate elements of math by teaching students to measure ingredients, language arts by teaching them to read or write a recipe, science through examining chemical reactions of the cooking process, and social studies through having students explore the impact of food agriculture on economy and society. Interdisciplinary instruction is beneficial in deepening students' understanding across subject areas and developing real-world critical thinking skills by encouraging them to make connections between disciplines and teaching them to consider an idea or problem from multiple perspectives.

EXAMPLES OF INTRADISCIPLINARY INSTRUCTION

- **Language arts:** A single language arts lesson can incorporate components of reading, writing, grammar, and listening skills. For example, a lesson on a particular poem can include a close reading of the poet's use of grammar, symbolism, imagery, and other literary techniques as well as an audio recording of the poet reading aloud. At the end of the unit, students can be assigned to use what they learned to compose their own original poems.
- **Social studies:** Social studies units can incorporate elements of history, anthropology, archaeology, sociology, psychology, or any other field that involves the study of humans, civilizations, cultures, and historical events. For example, a unit on the Aztec people may include an examination of their religious beliefs, customs, architecture, and agricultural practices.
- **Science:** Intradisciplinary units in science can include several branches within the field, such as chemistry, biology, physics, earth science, botany, or geology. For example, a unit on volcanoes may incorporate lessons on plate tectonics, the Earth's layers, chemicals released during a volcanic eruption, islands formed from cooled volcanic rock, as well as plants that grow best near volcanoes.
- **Mathematics:** An intradisciplinary math lesson may simultaneously include several branches within the field, such as arithmetic, algebra, or geometry. For example, in a geometry lesson on the Pythagorean theorem, students must utilize algebraic equations and arithmetic to determine the length of the sides of a right triangle.

EXAMPLES OF INTERDISCIPLINARY INSTRUCTION

- **Language arts:** A unit based in language arts may also incorporate several other disciplines, such as social studies, art, or music. For example, a unit on William Shakespeare's *Romeo and Juliet* may include a reading of the play, an analysis of the use of literary techniques within it, and study of William Shakespeare's life and the society in which he lived, thereby incorporating social studies into the language arts lesson. Students can also act out the play to incorporate the arts and participate in a rhythmic study on iambic pentameter to incorporate music.

- **Social studies:** Units based in social studies can include lessons focused on multiple disciplines, including language arts, music, science, and math. For example, an interdisciplinary unit on Ancient Egypt may include a historical study of the culture, religion, architecture, and practices of the Ancient Egyptians while integrating other subject areas, such as a study of hieroglyphics to incorporate language arts and creating Egyptian masks to incorporate art. Students can also study the scientific advancements of the Ancient Egyptians and incorporate math to study how the ancient pyramids were constructed.
- **Science:** Scientific units can also incorporate elements of art, math, social studies, and language arts in order to become interdisciplinary. For example, a unit on Punnett squares focuses on biology and genetics but can also include several other subject areas. Math can be incorporated by integrating lessons on probability or students can be assigned to research their genetics, create a family tree, and write a report on their findings to incorporate language arts and social studies. Art can also be incorporated by having students create portraits of the potential outcomes from Punnett squares.
- **Mathematics:** Interdisciplinary units in mathematics can also include lessons focused on art, social studies, science, and music. For example, a geometry unit on measuring triangles may also incorporate songs to memorize equations, lessons on the pyramids of Ancient Egypt to incorporate social studies, as well as an art project in which students use only triangles to create an original piece.

Incorporating Cooperative Learning and Consideration from Multiple Viewpoints

In any classroom, teachers will encounter a wide range of diversities among students' backgrounds, cultures, interests, skills, and abilities. Thus, providing students with several opportunities for cooperative learning gives them access to others' perspectives and is highly valuable in teaching students to consider ideas from multiple viewpoints. As each student has different experiences and background knowledge, collaborative learning allows them to share their views on ideas with others. Additionally, in working together, students have the opportunity to work with others from different backgrounds that they may have otherwise never encountered and gain exposure to approaching ideas from multiple viewpoints. Cooperative learning opportunities allow students to understand and appreciate others' perspectives and teach them that there are multiple approaches to problem solving and ideas.

Learning Experiences That Develop Real-World Life Skills

The ultimate goal of education is to develop the whole child into a productive, contributing member of society; therefore, it is imperative to provide learning experiences that will develop life skills that are applicable and beneficial in the real world. In an increasingly fast-paced global society, students must be prepared to enter the professional and societal world as confident, independent, responsible, and adaptive individuals. They must have the leadership skills necessary to compete in the professional arena. Students must be able to work cooperatively with others, respect and value multiple perspectives, and be effective problem solvers and critical thinkers in order to be successful outside of the classroom. Teachers must also aim to help students develop the skills necessary to become lifelong learners to ensure continuous growth and development as they enter society; therefore, learning experiences that promote the development of real-world life skills in addition to academic skills are necessary in adequately preparing students for success.

Cross-Curricular Instruction for Exploring Content from Varied Perspectives

Cross-curricular instruction allows teachers to demonstrate that elements from one subject area can be applied to ideas or problems in another. Thus, this instructional strategy is highly valuable in developing students' abilities to explore content from varied perspectives. As this method incorporates several disciplines in approaching a topic, it deepens students' understanding that there are several perspectives that one can take when solving a problem and that elements of one subject area are relevant in another. In addition, cross-curricular instruction prepares students for the real world through developing critical thinking skills and allowing them to make connections between disciplines, thus allowing them to understand how to successfully approach ideas from varied perspectives.

Benefits of Multicultural Learning Experiences

Multicultural learning experiences demonstrate to students the array of diversities that exist both inside and outside of the classroom. Just as each culture has its own values, norms, and traditions, each has its own perspectives and approaches to ideas and problem solving. Incorporating multicultural experiences in the classroom exposes students to cultures and groups that they may have otherwise never encountered and teaches them to respect and value perspectives outside of their own. As students learn other cultures' beliefs, customs, and attitudes, they develop the understanding that each culture solves problems and considers ideas from multiple viewpoints and that each approach is valuable. As students learn other perspectives, they can apply this knowledge and build problem solving and critical thinking skills that will be beneficial in developing successful lifelong learning habits.

Incorporating Multiple Disciplines into a Thematic Unit

In **cross-curricular** (or **interdisciplinary**) instruction, multiple disciplines are incorporated into a thematic unit in order to deepen students' understanding through fostering connections and demonstrating multiple perspectives and methods of problem solving. Effective interdisciplinary instruction requires careful planning to ensure that all activities are relevant to the overall lesson theme and effectively support students in achieving desired learning outcomes. Teachers must first select a thematic unit based on state academic standards and then determine desired learning outcomes. Then, teachers must design lessons and activities for students to reach learning goals and objectives. When integrating multiple disciplines into a thematic unit, teachers must seek out materials, resources, and activities from various subject areas that are applicable to the main topic and reinforce lesson objectives. Teachers can then integrate these elements into lesson planning to create multifaceted instruction. Additionally, teachers can create activities that approach the overarching lesson theme from the perspective of different subject areas. The activities and materials should be coordinated and relate to one another in order to deepen students' understanding of the overall concept.

Effectively Allocating Time When Creating Lessons and Units

Effective time management is vital for successful teaching and learning. To ensure that all academic standards are covered within a school year, teachers must consider how to best allocate specific amounts of time for units and lessons that allow for review, enrichment, and reteaching. A unit plan for the school year is an effective strategy in allowing the teacher to visualize and plan the amount of content that must be covered. A unit plan can also be utilized on a smaller scale, as a framework for designing and allotting time for instructional goals, objectives, and lessons within each unit. By setting learning goals and daily objectives within individual units, teachers can determine the amount of time available for completing each unit. This ensures more effective lesson planning by allowing teachers to develop daily schedules with dedicated time for teaching and learning. When planning lessons, teachers must consider how much instructional time is necessary to cover each topic and the time students will need to complete lesson activities. Additionally, teachers must ensure that they allow time at the end of each lesson for reteaching if students have misconceptions, as extra time can be utilized for enrichment if reteaching is unnecessary.

Opportunities for Reflection

Opportunities for reflection within lesson plans enhance learning experiences through strengthening student understanding and influencing further instruction. When students are given the opportunity to reflect, they are able to connect their learning back to the original objective and better understand the overall purpose for learning, thus fostering engagement. Reflection deepens students' understanding by allowing them to connect new concepts to their own personal experiences, which ultimately helps in comprehension and retainment by making learning relevant. Reflecting on performance empowers students to become self-motivated lifelong learners by allowing them to analyze what they understood and did well. Reflection also encourages students to identify areas for improvement. Teachers can utilize students' reflections to influence and drive further instruction. Students' reflections allow teachers to identify areas in which students excelled and areas in which they need improvement. They can also aid teachers in tailoring future lesson plans to adapt to students' needs and interests.

Opportunities for Self-Assessment

Including self-assessments within lessons is a valuable formative assessment strategy that enriches student learning and provides insight to the teacher. Providing students with the opportunity to monitor their progress and assess their learning supports them in developing a wide range of skills that are beneficial both inside and outside of the classroom. Self-assessments create a sense of ownership and responsibility over learning, which foster self-motivation and engagement. They also serve to create a sense of independence and objectivity within students to effectively review their own work and identify areas of improvement, which is a vital skill needed to become a lifelong learner. When students evaluate their own performance, teachers are able to effectively assess student understanding, thus allowing them to identify areas of weakness or misconception for reteaching.

Opportunities for Closure Activities

Closure activities at the end of each lesson or topic are short activities that allow teachers to formatively assess student understanding of content covered within a lesson and identify areas of misconception for reteaching. Additionally, closure activities are valuable in measuring whether the intended lesson objective was achieved before moving to the next topic. For students, closures at the end of a lesson provide structure and organization to learning as well as emphasize the purpose for instruction by allowing them to connect what they learned back to the original objective. Moreover, in having students restate what they have learned in a closure activity, learning is strengthened by giving students the opportunity to internalize new information. In demonstrating their understanding, they can better make personal connections between their own learning, background knowledge, and experiences.

Instructional Techniques

Implementing Multiple Instructional Techniques to Maximize Student Learning

Incorporating multiple instructional techniques into the classroom maximizes student learning by enhancing intellectual involvement and overall engagement. When instructional material is presented through a variety of means, it facilitates an **active learning** environment in which students' interest is captured and they are motivated to participate in learning. Varying teaching strategies stimulates engagement and fosters achievement by encouraging students to actively participate in their own learning and implement critical thinking skills to consider information more deeply. Students' understanding is strengthened when content is presented in different ways through various instructional techniques by providing them with multiple frames of reference for making connections and internalizing new concepts. In addition, utilizing multiple instructional techniques allows the teacher to effectively **differentiate instruction** to access multiple learning styles and address individual student needs to ensure understanding and enhance the overall learning process.

Instructional Strategies to Differentiate Instruction

Implementing a variety of strategies for differentiation helps to ensure that instruction appeals to students' varying learning styles and needs. By incorporating **multiple modalities** into direct instruction, such as visual representations, written directions, video or audio clips, songs, graphs, or mnemonic devices, teachers can differentiate the presentation of new concepts and information. Using strategies to differentiate instructional activities is also beneficial in diversifying the learning experience. By providing opportunities for **independent, collaborative**, and **hands-on** learning, teachers can ensure that learning is accessible and engaging to all students. In addition, learning activities should allow for a degree of flexibility in order to appeal to students' varying needs and preferences. Activities such as task cards, educational technology resources, and learning stations provide this **flexibility** and allow for a student-directed experience in which students can choose to learn in the way that best suits their needs. Similarly, assigning open-ended projects as summative assessments allows for a degree of **student-choice**, thus differentiating the method in which students demonstrate their understanding.

Varying the Teacher and Student Roles in the Instructional Process

Varying the roles of the teacher and students as an instructional technique is beneficial in creating an engaging, dynamic classroom environment that maximizes learning. When different roles are implemented, instruction is diversified, thus stimulating student interest and engagement. In addition, certain teacher and student roles are most applicable and effective in specific learning situations. When teachers acknowledge this and understand when to adopt and assign particular roles, they can effectively deliver instruction in a way that deepens student understanding and fosters success in learning. In presenting new content, directions, or modeling new skills, for example, the roles of **lecturer** and student **observer** are effective. In hands-on learning situations, students can take on the role of **active participant** while the teacher acts as a **facilitator** to create a student-centered and engaging learning environment in which students are given ownership over their own learning. Such variation enhances intellectual involvement by promoting critical thinking and problem-solving skills through self-directed learning. Skillfully assigning different roles throughout the learning process also allows the teacher to effectively address students' individual learning needs and preferences to promote engagement and enhance the learning experience.

Fostering Intellectual Involvement and Engagement

Effective instruction includes a variety of strategies for fostering intellectual involvement and engagement to promote academic success. Presenting instruction using various approaches provides multiple avenues for learning new content, thus ensuring and strengthening student understanding to facilitate achievement. In addition, diversifying instructional strategies creates variety in the classroom that effectively stimulates students' interest and motivation to engage in learning. Strategies such as **cooperative learning**, **discussion**, and **self-directed opportunities** encourage active student participation that enhances intellectual involvement by allowing students to build on background knowledge, deepen understanding by exploring others' perspectives, and take ownership over their own learning. This ultimately increases student engagement and motivation for success in learning. Similarly, incorporating **inquiry**, **problem-solving**, and **project-based** strategies promotes curiosity in learning, creativity, and the development of critical thinking skills that stimulate intellectual participation and engagement to create a productive learning environment. Implementing **digital resources** and media throughout instruction is integral in enhancing academic success by making learning relevant, interesting, and differentiated to accommodate various learning needs. At the end of a lesson or activity, allowing students the opportunity to reflect is a valuable strategy in increasing intellectual involvement, retainment, and academic success by facilitating personal connections with learning to build understanding.

Actively Engaging Students by Incorporating Discussion into Instruction

Classroom discussion is a valuable instructional technique in engaging students throughout the learning process. When teachers skillfully pose higher-level questions in discussions, they establish an active learning environment in which students are encouraged and motivated to participate, thus enhancing overall engagement. Effective discussions prompt students to become **intellectually invested** in instruction by promoting the use of **critical** and **higher-order thinking** skills to consider information more deeply and devise creative solutions to problems. In addition, discussions stimulate engagement by providing students the opportunity to express their own thoughts and reasoning regarding a given topic to establish a sense of ownership over their learning. Furthermore, discussions foster a collaborative learning environment that actively engages students by prompting them to understand others' perspectives, consider alternative approaches, and build on one another's experiences to make deeper connections to learning.

Promoting Student Inquiry

The promotion of inquiry is a valuable instructional technique in enhancing student engagement and intellectual involvement. In an **inquiry-based** learning environment, students are encouraged to explore instructional material and devise their own conclusions or solutions to problems. This increases the effectiveness of the learning process by providing students with a sense of agency over their own learning. In addition, implementing this strategy fosters curiosity, self-motivation, and active participation, as it allows for hands-on, **student-led** learning that increases overall engagement. Incorporating inquiry into the classroom stimulates critical and higher-order thinking skills as students construct their own understanding by interacting with learning materials, analyzing their findings, and synthesizing their learning to create new conclusions, results, and responses. To effectively incorporate inquiry into the learning process, the teacher must provide several opportunities for self-directed learning, project-based learning, and student choice to stimulate curiosity. Questions must be open-ended, and students must be encouraged to hypothesize, predict, and experiment in their learning. The teacher must be flexible in instruction to allow space and opportunity for exploration and allow time for reflection and extended learning opportunities to facilitate further inquiry.

Incorporating Problem-Solving into Instruction

Providing opportunities for creative problem solving within instruction effectively creates an engaging and successful learning experience. Students become more **intellectually involved** when encouraged to actively participate in learning and utilize **critical thinking skills** to test hypotheses, analyze results, and devise creative solutions to problems. This hands-on, **student-directed** approach promotes success in learning by allowing students to interact with learning materials as they seek answers to complex ideas and problems in an engaging environment. Problem-solving enables students to make deeper connections to their learning to enhance understanding, as this strategy prompts them to employ and develop background knowledge. In addition, problem-solving activities allow for collaborative learning in which students can actively engage with peers to build on one another's knowledge and experience, thus enhancing successful learning.

Intellectual Involvement, Active Student Engagement, and Success in Learning

A productive learning environment is composed intellectually involved students that are actively engaged in successful learning. A strong correlation exists between **intellectual involvement**, **active student engagement**, and **success in learning**, and each component is necessary for effective instruction. Effective instruction consists of challenging students based on their abilities and teaching them to think deeply about new ideas and concepts. This ultimately encourages students' intellectual involvement, as it prompts them to utilize their critical thinking skills to build on their background knowledge, consider alternative perspectives, and synthesize their learning to devise creative solutions. When students are intellectually involved in instruction, they become more personally invested and engaged, as learning becomes relevant, interesting, and challenging. Engaged students are active participants in their learning, thus enhancing their overall productivity and academic success.

Effectively Structuring Lessons

When developing instruction, it is imperative that the teacher is knowledgeable on how to effectively structure lessons to maximize student engagement and success. Each lesson must include a clear **objective** and explicitly state the process for achieving it. To initiate engagement, effective lessons begin with an **opening**, or "warm-up," activity to introduce a new topic, diagnose student understanding, and activate prior knowledge. Instruction of new material must be delivered through a variety of teaching strategies that are consciously tailored to students' individual learning needs to enhance participation and ensure comprehension. Direct instruction should be followed by **active learning** activities with clear directions and procedures to allow students to practice new concepts and skills. Throughout a successful lesson, the teacher checks frequently for understanding and comprehension by conducting a variety of **formative assessments** and adjusts instruction as necessary. Including **closure** activities is essential to successful learning, as it gives students the opportunity to reflect, process information, make connections, and demonstrate comprehension. In structuring lessons effectively according to students' learning needs, the teacher establishes a focused and engaging learning environment that promotes academic success.

Example of a Daily Lesson Plan Structure

Flexible Instructional Groupings

Flexible instructional groupings provide the teacher and students with a versatile, engaging environment for successful learning. Skillfully grouping students allows for productive, cooperative learning opportunities in which individual strengths are enhanced and necessary support is provided, thus enhancing motivation and engagement. When working in groups, students' understanding of instruction is strengthened, as they are able to learn and build upon one another's background knowledge, perspectives, and abilities. Instructional groups can include students of the **same** or **varied abilities** depending on the learning objective and task to increase productivity and provide scaffolding as necessary for support. This strategy is effective in enabling the teacher to **differentiate** instruction and adjust groups as needed to accommodate varying learning styles, abilities, and interests to maximize engagement and success in learning.

Effective Pacing of Lessons and Importance of Flexibility to Students' Needs

Effective pacing is imperative to focused and engaging instruction. Teachers must be conscientious of the pace of their instruction and ensure that it is reflective of their students' learning needs and sustains their attention. Instruction that is delivered too quickly results in confusion and discouragement, whereas if instruction is too slow, students will lose interest and become disengaged. A well-paced lesson states clear learning goals and objectives while clearly outlining the means to achieve them to elicit student motivation. The teacher must consider the most **efficient** and **engaging** instructional strategies for presenting new material to establish a steady pace and maintain it by incorporating smooth **transitions** from one activity to the next. It is important that teachers are conscious of the rate of instruction throughout all stages of learning while maintaining **flexibility** in pacing in order to be responsive to their students. As individual students have different learning needs and processing times, they may require a faster or slower rate of instruction to understand new concepts and remain engaged in learning. Frequent checks for understanding and reflection activities are essential strategies in determining if the pace of instruction must be adjusted to accommodate students' needs.

Connecting Content to Students' Prior Knowledge and Experiences

Implementing effective instructional strategies for connecting content to students' prior knowledge and experiences enhances the relevancy of learning and fosters deeper connections that strengthen understanding. To achieve this, teachers must educate themselves on students' backgrounds, experiences, communities, and interests to determine what is important and interesting to them. With this knowledge in mind, teachers can successfully locate and implement **authentic materials** into instruction to enhance relevancy. Additionally, encouraging students to bring materials to class that reflect their backgrounds and including these materials in instruction makes learning relevant by allowing students to make **personal connections** to content. Instructional strategies such as brainstorming, KWL charts, prereading, and anticipation guides allow the teacher to determine what students know prior to learning a new concept, thus enabling them to connect content to students' background knowledge in a relevant way. Incorporating digital resources further enhances relevancy in learning. Teachers can locate videos or audio clips that relate to instruction and reflect students' background experiences and interests. Using digital resources to introduce a new concept is a valuable strategy in developing students' **schema** on a topic to build prior knowledge and make learning meaningful by fostering connections.

Making Learning Relevant and Meaningful

For learning to be relevant and meaningful, it is essential that teachers present content in a way that connects with students' **prior knowledge** and experiences. When students are able to apply new ideas and information to what they already know through effective instructional techniques, it facilitates strong **personal connections** that make learning relevant and meaningful. In addition, personal connections and **relevancy** are strengthened when teachers consciously incorporate materials to reflect students' individual backgrounds and experiences in instruction. Linking content to students' background experiences enables them to relate instruction to real-world situations, thus establishing a sense of purpose for learning by making it applicable to their lives. Intentionally connecting content with students' prior knowledge and experiences enhances the effectiveness of the instructional process and fosters positive attitudes toward learning.

Enhancing Student Engagement and Success in Learning

Engaging instruction employs a variety of instructional strategies and materials to create a relevant, meaningful, and successful learning experience. Effective content establishes a clear and applicable purpose for instruction that increases student participation in the learning process. Presenting relevant and meaningful content enhances understanding and engagement by enabling students to create real-world, **personal connections** to learning based upon their own backgrounds and experiences. In addition, when instruction is tailored to reflect students' unique interests and preferences, content becomes more appealing and students' willingness to learn is enhanced. When students can perceive content through their own frames of reference with instructional materials that reflect their unique differences, they are able to effectively internalize and relate information to their lives, thus increasing engagement. Engaged learning ultimately facilitates academic success in that when students are motivated to learn, they demonstrate positive attitudes toward learning and are more likely to actively participate.

Adapting Instruction to Individual Needs

Evaluating Activities and Materials to Meet Learning Needs

The careful selection of instructional activities and materials is integral to accommodating students' varying characteristics and needs. When evaluating the appropriateness of activities and materials, several considerations must be made. Teachers must consider whether activities and materials align with state and district **academic standards**. Teachers must also evaluate the quality and effectiveness of the activities and materials in supporting students' unique differences as they achieve learning goals and objectives. All materials and activities must be **developmentally appropriate** across domains yet adaptable to individual students' learning needs. In addition, they must be challenging yet feasible for student achievement relative to students' grade levels and abilities to promote engagement and the development of critical and **higher-order thinking** skills. Teachers must evaluate activities and materials for versatility to allow for student choice and differentiation in order to address varying characteristics and needs. Teachers must also ensure that activities and materials are accurate, **culturally sensitive**, and reflective of students' diversities to foster an inclusive learning environment that promotes engagement.

Instructional Resources and Technologies

The implementation of varied instructional resources and technologies is highly valuable in supporting student engagement and achievement. Effective use of resources and technologies requires teachers to evaluate their appropriateness in addressing students' individual characteristics and learning needs for academic success. Teachers must be attuned to students' unique differences in order to seek high quality technologies and resources that address their students' needs and support the achievement of learning goals and objectives. Technologies and resources must be **accurate**, **comprehensible**, easily **accessible** to students, and **relevant** to the curriculum and the development of particular skills. Teachers must also consider the grade-level and **developmental appropriateness** of technologies and resources as well as their adaptability to allow for differentiation. Effective technologies and resources are interactive, engaging, and multifaceted to allow for varying levels of complexity based on students' abilities. This allows teachers to provide appropriate challenges while diversifying instruction to appeal to varied characteristics and learning needs, thus fostering an engaging environment that supports success in learning for all students.

Adapting Activities and Materials to Meet Individual Characteristics and Needs

In effective instruction, activities and materials are adapted to accommodate students' individual characteristics and needs. Teachers must be attuned to students' unique differences and understand how to adjust activities and materials accordingly to facilitate academic success and growth. To achieve this, teachers must incorporate a **variety** of activities and materials that appeal to all styles of learners. Activities and materials should provide **student choice** for engagement in learning and demonstration of understanding. By differentiating instruction, teachers can effectively scaffold activities and materials to provide supports as necessary as well as include extensions or alternate activities for enrichment. **Chunking** instruction, allowing extra time as necessary, and accompanying activities and materials with aids such as graphic organizers, visual representations, and anticipation guides further differentiates learning to accommodate students' learning characteristics and needs. Conducting **formative assessments** provides teachers with valuable feedback regarding student understanding and engagement, thus allowing them to modify and adjust the complexity of activities and materials as necessary to adapt to varied characteristics and learning differences.

INSTRUCTIONAL RESOURCES AND TECHNOLOGIES

When teachers understand students' individual characteristics and needs, they can adapt instructional resources and technologies accordingly to maximize learning. To do so effectively, the teacher must incorporate a diverse array of **multifaceted** resources and technologies that support and enhance learning through a variety of methods. This ensures that varying learning needs are met, as students of all learning styles are provided with several avenues for building and strengthening understanding. Additionally, the teacher can adapt resources and technologies to accommodate individual students by **varying the complexity** to provide challenges, support, and opportunities for enrichment based on ability level. Supplementing technologies and resources with **scaffolds**, such as extra time, visual representations, or opportunities for collaborative learning, further enables the teacher to adapt to individual learning needs. When effectively implemented and adapted to students' characteristics and needs, instructional technologies and resources serve as valuable tools for differentiating curriculum to enhance the learning experience.

Flexible and Responsive Instructional Practices

EVALUATION OF INSTRUCTION

Evaluating the appropriateness of instructional materials, activities, resources, and technologies is integral to establishing a successful learning environment. Doing so provides students with high-quality and inclusive instruction by ensuring **clarity**, **accuracy**, **relevancy**, and **reflection** of student diversities. By determining whether these components of instruction meet varying characteristics and learning needs, the teacher can deliver **student-centered** instruction that is challenging based on individual ability and promote development and academic success. This process also allows the teacher to effectively **differentiate** instruction to provide necessary personalized support for success in achieving learning targets as well as create engaging learning opportunities tailored to students' unique differences and interests. Effectively determining the appropriateness of activities, materials, resources, and technologies in meeting students' learning needs ultimately maximizes academic achievement and fosters positive attitudes toward learning that establish a foundation for future success.

CONTINUOUS MONITORING OF INSTRUCTIONAL EFFECTIVENESS

Successful instruction must be flexible and adaptable to meet students' dynamic learning needs. To achieve this, teachers must continuously monitor the effectiveness of their instruction to determine if their teaching strategies, activities, and communication are effective. Frequent evaluation of instructional effectiveness is necessary to ensure that students understand **foundational concepts** before moving on to more advanced concepts. **Adaptations** to instruction, communication, or assessment may be necessary to ensure students are able to comprehend and retain concepts before moving on to more advanced topics. **Remediation** of missed concepts is often much more challenging and less successful than checking for comprehension within context and providing more detailed instruction. This ultimately fosters long-term achievement, as the teacher can identify and address student needs as they arise and prevent compounding issues. Continuous monitoring enables the teacher to ensure that learning opportunities are engaging, relevant, and challenging based on students' ability levels, as it provides immediate feedback on the effectiveness of instruction, which allows the teacher to make necessary changes. This ultimately enhances instruction by establishing a student-centered learning environment that is tailored to individual needs, interests, and abilities.

Pre-Instructional, Peri-Instructional, and Post-Instructional Strategies

Instructional effectiveness must be monitored on a whole-class and individual level throughout all stages of teaching. Prior to instruction, administering **pre-tests** provides teachers with insight regarding whole-class and individual understanding. This enables teachers to select effective and appropriate instructional strategies that can be differentiated to meet individual needs. Pre-tests allow teachers to identify and clarify misunderstandings before instruction to ensure effectiveness. During instruction, **observation** of students' participation in instruction during independent and group activities enables the teacher to evaluate overall and individual understanding and engagement. Frequent checks for understanding and **formative assessments** throughout instruction provide feedback on whole-group and individual learning, as the teacher can assess understanding and participation to adapt teaching strategies or individualize instruction. Leading student discussions allows the teacher to identify areas of misunderstanding among the class or individuals who may need reteaching through a different approach. Closure and reflection activities after instruction are valuable in monitoring effectiveness, as they indicate both whole-class and individual comprehension and retainment of new concepts. Likewise, incorporating **summative assessments** and analyzing the results provides teachers with information regarding the overall effectiveness of their teaching process as well as students' individual strengths and weaknesses to consider for future instruction.

Applying Feedback to Make Necessary Changes to Instruction

Continuous monitoring of instruction indicates the instruction's effectiveness on a **whole-class** and **individual** level, as it provides the teacher with immediate insight into student understanding, progress, and areas for improvement. Monitoring instructional effectiveness enables the teacher to evaluate students' **pace** in achieving learning goals and adjust the rate of instruction as necessary. Additionally, it allows the teacher to identify whole-class and individual **misconceptions** that require correction to ensure students do not fall behind schedule in meeting academic benchmarks. If monitoring reveals misunderstanding among the whole class, the teacher must alter the overall instructional approach and teaching strategies to clarify and regain understanding. Individual misconceptions indicate the need to differentiate instruction, adjust groupings, and provide supports and remediation as necessary to ensure the student progresses at the same rate as the rest of the class. By identifying student strengths and weaknesses through consistent monitoring of instructional effectiveness, the teacher can effectively make instructional decisions that are attuned to whole-class and individual student needs to maximize learning.

Flexibility in Instruction

Situations Requiring Flexibility

The classroom environment is dynamic in nature. Teachers will inevitably encounter situations throughout instruction and assessment in which **flexibility** is integral to successful teaching and learning. As students have varying learning styles, needs, and interests, teachers may find that their instructional approaches are ineffective in maintaining engagement and may need to adjust strategies, activities, or assessments to better meet learning needs. Students may have difficulty grasping new material, which could result in a lack of engagement in instructional activities and, potentially, disruptive behavior. Teachers must consistently be attuned to students' levels of comprehension and allow flexibility in their lesson plans to modify strategies, activities, or pacing as necessary to facilitate engagement and understanding before advancing in instruction. Students may also progress more quickly than others through instructional activities or assessments. **Scaffolding** activities to include opportunities for extension and enrichment allow for flexibility within instruction and ensure that all students are adequately challenged and engaged in learning. Throughout instruction and assessments, teachers may find valuable, unexpected learning opportunities. By remaining open and flexible to these instances, teachers can enhance the learning process and strengthen student understanding by incorporating them into instruction.

Enhancing the Overall Learning Experience

Flexibility is an integral component of effective instruction, as it enables the teacher to adequately address and accommodate students' individual needs and interests for maximized success in learning. When teachers consider their lesson plans as **frameworks** while allowing for flexibility, they demonstrate an awareness of their students' individual differences and the potential for deviation from original instruction. This enables them to more effectively modify instructional and assessment strategies, activities, and approaches to create a **responsive, student-centered** environment that enhances the overall learning experience and promotes achievement. When instructional activities and assessments are adaptable to accommodate students' needs and interests, learning becomes more personalized and relevant, thus strengthening understanding and increasing motivation to engage in active learning. A flexible approach to instruction and assessment also provides students with the ability to explore content of interest on a deeper level and potentially encounter unanticipated learning opportunities that foster personal connections and enhance learning. In addition, this approach allows for **versatility** in assessment, as flexibility enables the teacher to modify assessments by providing necessary support to meet students' individual needs and supports students' choice in demonstrating learning.

Poor Student Comprehension

Throughout instruction and assessments, students may have difficulty **comprehending** new or difficult material despite being engaged in instruction. This may lead to confusion that can cause students to become discouraged and disengaged in learning as well as have continued and compounded difficulty in grasping increasingly complex concepts. Difficulties with comprehension hinders academic success, as students who struggle face challenges in building the foundation of understanding necessary for advancing through curriculum. To ensure student comprehension throughout all stages of learning, the teacher must be aware of students' individual learning styles and needs and be able to respond flexibly to obstacles they may encounter. **Formative assessments** during instruction enable the teacher to evaluate the level of student comprehension and identify areas of need for flexible **adjustment** or additional support. This includes modifying **pacing** and allowing additional time for student processing to ensure understanding. In addition, the original lesson plan may require **chunking** into smaller, more manageable parts to allow students to internalize new concepts before moving on. The teacher may also need to respond flexibly to students' needs during instruction by **differentiating** teaching strategies, activities, groupings, or assessments to ensure that material is accessible and comprehensible to all students for enhanced success.

Unanticipated Learning Opportunities

Unanticipated learning opportunities, when embraced by the teacher, are often highly valuable in establishing a classroom environment that promotes student engagement, motivation, and success. These instances often divert from the original lesson plan, but when utilized effectively, they serve to strengthen student understanding and foster **personal connections** for an enhanced learning experience. Facilitating such opportunities allows students to investigate topics that are interesting and relevant to them on a deeper level, thus increasing active engagement and promoting **self-directed** learning. This ultimately supports students in forming connections and recognizing the real-world applications of their learning, which increases the likelihood that they will internalize and **retain** new information. Responding flexibly to unanticipated learning opportunities includes acknowledging students' questions and comments as well as demonstrating an awareness of their individual differences and learning needs. This enables the teacher to maximize the effectiveness of these opportunities by facilitating student-led instruction that is attuned to their learning styles, interests, and preferences for enhanced engagement and achievement.

Conducting Ongoing Assessments and Making Adjustments

Conducting **ongoing assessments** throughout instruction provides teachers with continuous feedback regarding student comprehension, engagement, and performance. When practiced consistently, teachers are more attuned and responsive to students' individual learning needs. This enables them to effectively modify instructional strategies, activities, and assessments accordingly for a **student-centered** learning environment that provides the support necessary for enhanced engagement, comprehension, and achievement. It allows teachers to identify and address areas of **misconception** and student need to ensure understanding prior to progressing through the curriculum. Feedback from ongoing evaluation of student performance indicates areas of instruction in which adjustment is necessary to effectively support students in achieving learning goals. Teachers may need to adjust their pacing to ensure comprehension and engagement as well as differentiate instruction based on feedback regarding individual progress to ensure all students are adequately challenged and supported based on their ability levels. Student groupings may need to be adjusted to scaffold instruction and facilitate increased comprehension. When teachers effectively apply feedback from ongoing assessments of student engagement and performance, they can tailor instruction to accommodate their individual needs and interests to enhance success in learning.

PROGRESSING AHEAD OF SCHEDULE

Throughout instruction, teachers will encounter instances in which individual students or the whole class progresses **faster than anticipated**. When this arises, the teacher must be prepared to respond flexibly to ensure that all students are engaged, on task, and challenged based on their ability levels. Lesson plans should be **scaffolded** to include opportunities for enrichment and extended learning for students who finish before others. This includes incorporating materials such as increasingly complex texts, practice activities, and project opportunities. Teachers can also establish a designated area in the classroom in which individuals or small groups that finish early can participate in **extended learning** or **review** activities that reinforce learning objectives. Such activities allow students to explore instructional topics on a deeper level for strengthened understanding and ensure they are engaging productively in meaningful activities that are relevant to instruction. When the whole class progresses faster than expected, the teacher can respond flexibly by incorporating **total participation** activities to reinforce instructional material. Activities such as review games, class discussions, and digital resources for extra practice ensure that the class remains engaged in instruction when they finish a lesson early.

The Role of Assessment in Education

ROLES OF ASSESSMENT

INSTRUCTIONAL PLANNING FOR INDIVIDUALS AND GROUPS

Effective assessments provide valuable feedback to teachers on how to design and adjust instruction for individuals and groups. Both **formative** and **summative** assessments give insight into student understanding and needs before and after content material is taught. Assessment provides the information necessary to effectively design instruction based on students' individual needs. **Diagnostic** assessments provide teachers with pertinent information about students' individual background knowledge, experiences, and learning needs, thus allowing them to understand students' skills and abilities to focus and plan future instruction accordingly. Additionally, assessments provide teachers with feedback on student progress and areas of individual need that drive instructional planning in allowing teachers to more effectively plan curriculum that is tailored to students' individual needs, skills, and abilities. Assessments inform future instruction through highlighting concepts that students are not understanding for reteaching. Furthermore, it allows them to group students more effectively in future planning to provide scaffolding and ensure that all students are supported in achieving academic standards.

PROVIDING TEACHER ACCOUNTABILITY AND EVALUATING TEACHER EFFECTIVENESS

Teachers are responsible for ensuring that all students are properly supported in achieving lesson objectives, instructional goals, and state academic standards. Thus, they are responsible for effectively designing and implementing instruction, lessons, and activities that are tailored to meet individual students' needs as they work to achieve learning outcomes. Assessments provide feedback regarding student mastery of academic standards and are reflective of the effectiveness of the instructional practices and strategies implemented to support them in their achievement. Consequently, student achievement on assessments reflects and measures the effectiveness of the teacher in designing instructional materials that meet individual students' needs, foster engagement and understanding, and facilitate desired learning outcomes. When teachers are evaluated based on student assessment results, they are held accountable for developing effective instruction and identifying areas for improvement in their teaching practice.

Methods and Applications for Analyzing Students' Strengths and Needs

Instructional assessment takes many forms, and each method has different applications and provides distinct feedback for analyzing students' strengths and needs. All forms of assessment should be incorporated in order to develop comprehensive instruction that is tailored to students' individual strengths and needs. **Formative assessments** are an informal, ongoing method of measuring student understanding throughout a lesson. They are valuable in allowing the teacher to adjust and adapt instructional practices and strategies to individual student needs as necessary as they move through a lesson. **Summative assessments** generally occur at the end of a lesson or unit and are intended to measure student achievement of a particular objective or instructional goal. These assessments allow teachers to identify students' individual strengths and needs, and they influence future instruction by highlighting areas of understanding or misconception for reteaching. **Standardized assessments** reflect student mastery of state academic standards and illustrate whether students have met academic benchmarks for their grade level. The results of these assessments can be applied to identify students' strengths and needs to determine the starting point of future instruction and proper grouping of students based on skills, needs, and abilities.

Use of State Standards and Assessments

Instruction Development

Effective instruction is driven by state standards and assessment. State academic standards serve as a framework for grade-level academic benchmarks that students are expected to achieve during the school year. From these, teachers derive instructional goals and objectives and determine instruction, activities, and materials that will support students in academic achievement. Additionally, teachers use state standards as assessment criteria to monitor student progress and evaluate how successfully students are reaching them. These assessments provide feedback to teachers that influences future instruction by helping teachers identify areas of misconception that require reteaching or individual student needs. State standardized assessments influence the development of instruction in that student achievement on these assessments indicates their level of success in meeting academic targets. They highlight areas of strength and need among students, providing teachers with a framework for effectively designing instruction to address these needs and support students in meeting academic goals.

Evaluating Student Progress, Strengths, and Needs

State and classroom assessments provide data that allow the teacher to effectively analyze whole-class and individual student performance in meeting learning targets to determine further instructional planning. Whole-class achievement on assessments is indicative of the effectiveness of learning objectives, instructional strategies, and lesson activities in supporting students' achievement of academic standards. Whole-class assessments also provide insight on areas for improvement and reteaching. Individually, in analyzing where students fall on a bell curve for assessment, teachers can effectively identify specific strengths and needs of students to determine instructional planning. This information indicates student progress and where they may need additional support, which allows teachers to better meet students' individual needs in planning future instruction by implementing strategies which are tailored to their skills and abilities.

Chapter Quiz

Ready to see how well you retained what you just read? Scan the QR code to go directly to the chapter quiz interface for this study guide. If you're using a computer, simply visit the online resources page at **mometrix.com/resources719/osatspeechdd116** and click the Chapter Quizzes link.

OSAT Practice Test

Want to take this practice test in an online interactive format?
Check out the online resources page, which includes interactive practice questions and much more: **mometrix.com/resources719/osatspeechdd116**

1. Which of the following is not an effective listening technique?

a. Interrupt to ask questions; paraphrase
b. Focus; don't form opinions too soon
c. Lean forward; tap on the table
d. Make eye contact; avoid being defensive
e. Nod and mirror the body language of the speaker

2. Which of the following series lists the elements of effective communication?

a. Sender, receiver, message, channel, feedback
b. Sender, receiver, message, direction, response
c. Speaker, listener, point, medium, reaction
d. Speaker, respondent, purpose, route, organization
e. To, from, directionality, reason, accomplishment

3. Broadly speaking, in our culture personal space is typically ____, while social space is ____. Of these types of spaces, ____ is more likely to affect how communication is shaped.

a. 0-3 feet; 4-12 feet; social space
b. 1 ½-4 feet; 4-12 feet; personal space
c. 1 ½-4 feet; 4-12 feet; social space
d. 0-3 feet; 4-12 feet; personal space
e. 1 ½-4 feet; 3-7 feet; personal space

4. Which type of nonverbal message deals with belonging, control, respect, or disapproval?

a. Emotive messages
b. Relational messages
c. Relationship messages
d. Interpersonal messages
e. Intrapersonal messages

5. What is involved in language comprehension?

a. Hearing sounds, processing words and organizing them
b. Hearing sounds and understanding their meanings
c. Speaking the same language as the sender
d. Identifying word units, knowing their meanings, understanding their syntactical use, processing abstractions, interpreting meaning
e. Understanding complex ideas, interpreting meaning

6. To what degree is effective listening natural to all people?

a. An innate ability to listen effectively is inborn.
b. An innate ability to listen effectively is inborn for some people.
c. An innate ability to listen effectively is inborn, but is quickly lost if not nurtured.
d. An innate ability to listen effectively is inborn for some people, but will be lost if not nurtured by age three.
e. An innate ability to listen effectively is not a natural skill.

7. Expressive language competency requires all of the following except:

a. Oral language
b. Gesture
c. Tone
d. Context
e. Written language

8. The best way to emphasize an important point in a public presentation is:

a. Prepare the audience by telling them you are about to reveal a key point.
b. Speak more quickly to attract the audience's attention.
c. Speak more slowly to give the audience time to consider what is being said.
d. Pause for a long moment before delivering the point.
e. Speak loudly to alert those whose minds are drifting.

9. Within a classroom setting, the reason for a debate is:

a. To determine which side has the most correct answers
b. To teach students to research, collaborate, argue, and listen
c. To demonstrate to students that there is no ultimate truth
d. To cast doubt on the other side's position
e. To convince students to change opinions

10. The earliest known writing on dramatic theory was:

a. Plato's poetics
b. Aristotle's poetics
c. Virgil's poetics
d. Virgil's dramatica
e. Plato's allegories

11. Another word for "tragic flaw" is

a. Hamartia
b. Peripeteia
c. Catharsis
d. Character fault
e. The unraveling

12. The study of aesthetics in literature and drama is concerned with which of the following?

a. Practical concerns
b. Moral concerns
c. Political concerns
d. Ethical concerns
e. Appreciation of ugliness

13. A good storyteller relates a story using:

a. Sensory images
b. A moral
c. A thesis statement
d. Rhyme
e. Song

14. A teacher with an inattentive class can use which of the following dramatic techniques to gain their attention?

a. Raise her voice above theirs.
b. Make her voice commanding by speaking loudly at a low register.
c. Drop a book or slam a drawer, lean forward on her desk, and speak slowly and deliberately in a low voice.
d. Drop a book or slam a drawer, march forward, and speak in a loud, angry voice.
e. Mumble so that students have to pay extra attention to what she is saying.

15. A detective and a therapist are working with a young child who was kidnapped to determine what occurred and in what order. They have provided stuffed animals, a toy car, some puppets, and various daily objects such as kitchen utensils, books, clothing, some toy buildings, etc. Following the child's lead, the detective "plays" with the child as she dramatically enacts her version of what happened. What theatrical element is being used?

a. A puppet show
b. Jungian psychology
c. Creative dramatics
d. Symbolism
e. A musical

16. Which of the following is a principle actors follow?

a. Allow skill and training to show in your acting.
b. Speak your lines to someone rather than to yourself.
c. The bigger the emotion, the more dramatically it must be expressed.
d. Be fully aware of your performance and control.
e. Always have the next line of dialogue in the front of your mind.

17. Compared to recorded history, is oral history more or less accurate?

a. More accurate; it was first told by someone who was there.
b. Equally accurate in its own way
c. Less accurate; each generation forgets details and adds some that aren't original.
d. Less accurate; the people passing down oral history are often not educated.
e. More accurate; the people passing down oral history can stick with the truth rather than with a political agenda.

18. The history club has decided to do a reader's theater of an obscure 18th century British play they have come across. Which of the following best describes their production?

a. Period costumes; full historically accurate staging; lighting done with candles for authenticity
b. Period costumes; full historically accurate staging; lighting is dim to suggest authenticity
c. Period costumes; minimal but historically accurate staging; low lighting for mood; actors improvise
d. Minimal or no costumes; minimal or no staging; actors read from scripts
e. Period costumes; no staging; actors read from scripts

19. The exercise called repetition used by Meisner in his acting training involves:

a. Two actors repeating the same phrase back and forth repeatedly
b. One actor repeating the same phrase over and over
c. One actor speaking and another acting as a chorus
d. Two actors speaking chorally
e. Two actors speaking in unison

20. Which of the following does an actor not use to develop a character?

a. Read the play to understand how the character relates to others.
b. Learn lines quickly to internalize them.
c. Find commonality with the character.
d. Use stereotypical responses.
e. Research the character's setting and other personal details.

21. Effectively speaking extemporaneously involves:

a. Memorizing the speech so you don't need to read it
b. Speaking energetically and quickly without knowing yourself what you'll say next
c. Letting the audience see that you are not prepared so they will relate sympathetically
d. Pausing to gather thoughts before speaking
e. Researching the topic you will be covering thoroughly

22. Making a strong argument in a speech, conversation, or debate requires:

a. Forceful delivery
b. Acknowledging the opposing point of view with respect
c. Demonstrating the weakness of the opposing view with mockery
d. Seizing the floor when the opponent's point is strong
e. Seizing the floor when the opponent's point is weak

23. Lincoln-Douglas debate format emphasizes:

a. Logical thought, ethics, and philosophical point of view
b. Logical thought, ethics, and passion
c. Passion, control, and ethics
d. Virtue, kindness, and compassion
e. Strength, control, and determination

24. Among the types of debate formats used in high school and college debates are:

a. Classical, extemporaneous, impromptu, moot court, and mock trial
b. Classical, policy, simulated legislature, and spontaneous
c. Extemporaneous, Montreal style, Australian universities, and online
d. Mock and rhetorical
e. Timed and topical

25. The three main purposes of oratory are to:

a. Influence, convince, persuade
b. Inform, entertain, influence
c. Inform, control, delight
d. Delight, entertain, amuse
e. Control, entertain, convince

26. Metaphor, a rhetorical device, is used in oratory to:

a. Compare two distinct things using "like" or "as"
b. Surprise listeners
c. Introduce a new idea via a familiar one
d. Make the speech poetic and beautiful
e. Cause listeners to think philosophically

27. Which of the following is true of a debate coach?

I. A debate coach is highly trained in logic.
II. A debate coach teaches a body of knowledge to team members.
III. A debate coach nurtures and develops mental skills.
IV. A debate coach questions and responds instead of leading and ordering.
V. Debate coaches deserve respect; team members must never disagree with them.
VI. A debate coach wears many hats; she raises money, reads arguments, and does administrative paperwork.

a. I, II, III, IV, V, and VI
b. I, II, and III
c. I, II, III, and V
d. I, II, V, and VI
e. III, IV, and VI

28. Synecdoche is:

a. A city in New York State
b. Comparing two unlike things using like or as
c. Two events that happen simultaneously in the act of public speaking, often a verbal event juxtaposed with a nonverbal one
d. Substituting the part for the whole
e. A term for the pregnant pause before the main point is delivered

29. The week-long National Speech and Debate Tournament offers Supplemental Events in which of the following categories?

a. Extemporaneous Commentary, Expository Speaking, Prose Interpretation, Dramatic Irony
b. Extemporaneous Speaking, Expository Commentary, Prose Interpretation, Dramatic Irony
c. Impromptu Speaking, Expository Speaking, Prose Interpretation, Poetic Interpretation
d. Extemporaneous Commentary, Expository Speaking, Prose Interpretation, Poetic Interpretation
e. Impromptu Speaking, Expository Speaking, Prose Interpretation

30. Interpersonal communications can be unclear due to all of the following except:

a. Misinterpretation
b. Assumptions
c. Environmental context
d. Relational context
e. Similar backgrounds of communicators

31. In what way is a lucid dream intrapersonal communication?

a. Every object in the dream is symbolic of the dreamer.
b. The dreamer, in the midst of dreaming, is signaling herself that she is asleep and dreaming.
c. In no way; dreams have nothing to do with communication.
d. By speaking in her sleep, the dreamer is attempting to communicate.
e. Dreams are subliminal messages from the people the dreamer interacted with the previous day.

32. One form of interpersonal communication common to businesses is gossip. The negative aspects of gossip are widely recognized. It causes hurt feelings, destroys self-confidence, and can be cruel. In what way might gossip be considered a useful form of interpersonal business communication from a manager's perspective?

a. It offers a way of passing the buck.
b. It clarifies status.
c. It can be used to share unofficial information quickly.
d. It strengthens social connections.
e. In no way; gossip is always destructive.

33. How many meaningful facial expressions have been catalogued?

a. 76
b. 154
c. 10,000
d. 136,549
e. Over a million, but many are variations within a category

34. Understood cultural "rules" regarding acceptable modes of expression that men and women share, those that are appropriate for men only, and those that are appropriate for women only are called:

a. Gender display rules
b. Gender distinction rules
c. Gender distinction conventions
d. Sexual characteristics
e. Sexual display

35. Sub vocalization is:

a. Tone of voice that shades meaning
b. Groaning, moaning, whimpering, or other nonverbal vocal expressions
c. Mentally "spoken" words when reading
d. Talking without awareness, such as in one's sleep
e. Poor enunciation

36. What do microexpressions communicate?

a. Nothing; they are transitional muscular contractions as one facial expression changes to another.
b. Fleeting, minor emotion
c. Emotions that are being suppressed
d. Passing thoughts
e. Reactions to what is being heard

37. Which of the following behavior clusters are found in people with a high degree of interpersonal competence?

a. Developed vocabulary, maintains relationships for many years, avoids conflict
b. Prioritizes others' feelings, finds value in serving others, highly empathetic
c. Self-disciplined, excellent language skills, interested in human nature
d. Self-aware, maintains healthy relationships, uses positivity to resolve disagreements
e. Strong communication skills, good listener, concerned with opinions of others

38. How would intrapersonal communication not enhance interpersonal communication?

a. Daydreaming is a type of personal rehearsal for a potential intercommunication.
b. Reflecting upon a conversation can lead to deeper understanding of the communication's meaning.
c. Keeping a journal creates self-awareness.
d. Gesturing, a type of self-talk, adds to a message's meaning.
e. Self-reflection ensures that sent messages are understood by the recipient

39. Within an office or organization, interpersonal communication can be seen as vertical or horizontal. The term vertical communication refers to communication that involves:

a. A speaker and a listener
b. Messages that descend from upper echelon to lower level employees, becoming less reliable with each drop
c. A sender and a recipient
d. Messages that move from the top down and from the bottom up
e. A series of communications, each of which depends upon the previous communication for its meaning to become clear

40. Which of the following situations might affect someone's self-concept?

a. Expecting someone to accept an invitation and being turned down
b. Successfully teaching someone a skill you know well
c. Failing an exam after studying hard
d. Being the subject of gossip
e. Constructive criticism from a friend

41. An identity crisis arises when:

a. The sense of a unified self through time is challenged.
b. A primary relationship dissolves.
c. An individual is the object of an attack.
d. A group or team someone wants to join rejects him.
e. A friend provides constructive criticism.

42. Identity achievement occurs when:

a. An individual is accepted into a family, team, or group.
b. An individual discovers she is fully self-enabled.
c. An individual makes a commitment to a single identity.
d. An individual rejects a person or situation that threatens her sense of self.
e. An individual accomplishes a major life goal.

43. Two people on a first date are taking turns telling one another about themselves. They are communicating their histories, their aspirations, and details about their daily lives. This is an act of:

a. Courtship
b. Self-disclosure
c. Self-assessment
d. Self-revelation
e. Self-sacrifice

44. Which of the following acts of self-disclosure is most revealing?

a. Sharing details about long past events that were emotionally laden
b. Sharing details about current events that are emotionally laden
c. Offering a comprehensive timeline of one's personal history
d. Holding back information you know will hurt the other
e. Sharing details about an emotionally laden current event experienced by a close friend

45. How can a teacher best assess whether her lesson has been fully understood by students?

a. Give them a 360-degree assessment.
b. Ask them to complete a self-assessment.
c. Ask them to write about the lesson in their journals.
d. Ask them to explain the lesson back to her.
e. Ask them to create a practice quiz for the lesson they just learned.

46. Which three components does the Spitzberg & Cupach component model of communication competence include?

a. Knowledge, skill, motivation
b. Sender, receiver, message
c. Desire, plan, achievement
d. Concept, organization, delivery
e. Creation, sharing, interpretation

47. A study group facilitator has one member who dominates the conversation and one member who is unwilling to participate at all. What is the best course of action?

a. Open a group conversation in which members confront the domineering individual.
b. Privately ask the domineering member to allow others to speak.
c. Privately ask the reticent member to participate more.
d. Nonverbally communicate to both members.
e. Call on the reticent member more often in the group setting.

48. Which of the following statements about discussions held to resolve an issue is/are true?

I. Each member of the group should get an equal amount of time to speak.
II. All ideas are equally important, regardless of what they are or who said them.
III. Individuals with greater knowledge should contribute more.
IV. Individuals with greater knowledge should not be resented.
V. The floor should be held by each speaker in turn, and no interruptions should be allowed.

a. I and II
b. III and IV
c. I, II, and V
d. III, IV, and V
e. I, II, IV, and V

49. Which of the following strategies for managing conflict within a group is a win/win?

a. Compromise
b. Accommodate
c. Collaborate
d. Compete
e. Avoid

50. What are the drawbacks of compromise?

a. Essential principles and goals can get lost.
b. There is no clear winner.
c. As a strategy, it is very time-consuming.
d. It is often the result of bullying.
e. No one gets what they want.

51. When is avoidance an appropriate strategy for a leader or member of a business team?

a. Never; problems must be dealt with head-on.
b. When the individual has lots of influence and wants to be delicate
c. When more important things must be dealt with
d. When the issue occurred in the past
e. When the situation has become uncomfortable

52. What is the first step in the reflective thinking or standard agenda approach to group decision making?

a. Selecting group members
b. Clarifying the issue or problem
c. Brainstorming
d. Writing the questions the facilitator will ask
e. Deciding upon whether the group will be open, closed, or open by invitation only

53. A marketing group has assigned a team to a new ad campaign. The team is having their initial meeting. Someone suggests that everyone throw out as many ideas as possible without editing or suppressing any that may seem off the mark. Chaos erupts, yet by the end of the meeting the team has a clear idea of the direction they would like to go. This is called:

a. Chaos theory
b. Multiple minds
c. Thunder thinking
d. Brainstorming
e. Groupthink

54. A group of very close church members are interviewing ministers. They share the same values and ideals, and are certain the community trusts them absolutely and believes they would never make a bad decision. The group's leader is very strong-willed and capable. This group:

a. Has a healthy self-concept
b. Lives their principles
c. Is vulnerable to groupthink
d. Is vulnerable to attacks from people of lesser values
e. Is invincible and can handle any problems

55. Which of the following are not outcomes associated with a group that has fallen under the influence of groupthink?

a. Seeking only information that supports pre-existing positions
b. Failure to consider a number of alternatives
c. Failure to examine one another's ideas thoroughly
d. Failure to have a contingency plan to fall back on
e. Greater unity and chances of success

56. Research and experience have proven that abdicratic groups typically:

a. Are difficult to penetrate and nearly impossible to challenge
b. Are composed of group members who are happy with their relative positions
c. Are able to accomplish more in less time than other types of groups
d. Disintegrate quickly
e. Are authoritarian

57. Four common leadership styles are:

a. Autocratic, democratic, laissez-faire, abdicratic
b. Autocratic, abdicratic, abracadabracatic, disincratic
c. Autocratic, community-based, familial, abdicratic
d. Autocratic, one-man-one-vote, cooperative, dissociative
e. Autocratic, cooperative, collaborative, abdicratic

58. Initiator contributor, information seeker, opinion seeker, elaborator, coordinator, evaluator-critic, energizer, and procedural-technician are all examples of:

a. Self-identifications
b. Task oriented group roles
c. Social group roles
d. Anti-social group roles
e. Individualistic group roles

59. Harrison Whitlock is writing a speech. He has researched the topic thoroughly and has a number of facts and statistics to include. He has completed an opening, outlined the purpose, and is in the process of collecting points to support his position. He will finish with a strong conclusion. This type of speech is a(n) ____ speech.

a. Persuasive
b. Introductory
c. Demonstration
d. Informational
e. Toast

60. Which of the following is true about an informational speech?

I. It should be no longer than 45 minutes.
II. The speaker's position should be supported with sophisticated visual aids.
III. Non-verbal communication should be incorporated.
IV. The speech should be written in highly charged, emotionally strong language.
V. It is acceptable to read the speech from a text, especially when a lot of visual aids are being used.

a. I, II, III, IV, V
b. II, III, V
c. I, IV, V
d. III
e. IV

61. Esteban has been asked to speak to a group of music students about his work as a professional musician. He wants to talk about his instrument, the bass, and how he must make adjustments for the various sound systems and acoustics he must deal with. What type of speech should he present?

a. Informational
b. Persuasive
c. Demonstration
d. How-to
e. Personal narrative

62. Before writing a speech, the writer needs to do an audience analysis, which considers all of these factors except:

a. Age, gender, culture
b. Nationality, religious affiliation
c. Skills and experiences with the topic
d. Audience needs and interests
e. Speech setting

63. Yi's grandmother turns 90 this year. Yi has been asked to give a speech in her grandmother's honor. The grandmother's 9 living children, 32 grandchildren, and 57 great-grandchildren will be present, as well as family friends, neighbors, and members of the press. What should Yi include in her toast?

a. Visual aids showing the family tree
b. A timeline scroll that marks all the important events in her grandmother's life
c. Funny and moving anecdotes about her grandmother and various members of the audience
d. Historically accurate information about the times when her grandmother was young
e. A detailed biography of her grandmother's life

64. Which of the following statements regarding eye contact is false?

a. It suggests confidence and presence of mind.
b. It lends a humanizing sensibility to a speech.
c. Audience members are drawn into the presentation if the speaker makes repeated eye contact that lasts long enough to suggest emotional intimacy.
d. It sparks audience interest because the occasion of the speech seems, on some level, to be a conversation in which they are engaged.

65. Extemporaneously presenting a speech might be done because:

a. It clarifies the major points in the appropriate order.
b. The digitally produced visual aids add sophistication.
c. It results in the audience adopting a can-do attitude and leads to action.
d. It heightens the sense of immediacy and originality.
e. It doesn't require control over the presentation.

66. The company Mr. Gibbons works for hopes to make connections with another company in Japan. Because Mr. Gibbons is funny, uses body language dramatically, and isn't the least bit shy, he has been chosen to introduce his company's recent work in a brief after-dinner speech in Tokyo. While delivering his speech, he is horrified to discover that many of the audience members are nodding with their eyes closed. What is going on?

a. He has offended them somehow; they are giving him the chance to save face.
b. His dramatic nonverbal style has overwhelmed them.
c. They are listening intently.
d. They are bored.
e. They've just eaten and are comfortable enough with him to drift off.

67. Successful public speaking is ultimately always about:

a. Achieving the speaker's objectives
b. Persuading the audience
c. Provoking deep thought
d. Inspiring an audience
e. Challenging pre-conceived ideas

68. Rehearsing a speech by videotaping it will help a speaker do all of the following except:

a. Recognize effective nonverbal information
b. Recognize confusing nonverbal information
c. Recognize effective speech patterns
d. Recognize where the speech loses focus
e. Recognize how her audience will receive the message

69. Public speakers want to give speeches that make their audience pay attention, but they also want to give speeches whose messages are meaningful enough to remain in audience member's minds. This can best be accomplished with:

a. Simple language and stories
b. Strict logical progression
c. Sophisticated language and ideas
d. Intense emotion and drama
e. Eye contact

70. In the event of technology failure with a computer or projector, the speaker should:

a. Make entertaining comments while trying to repair it.
b. Ask for help from technologically savvy audience members.
c. It depends upon the subject and the audience.
d. Describe the visual aids since they can't be seen.
e. Speak extemporaneously.

71. Nervousness can make inexperienced public speakers stammer, speak in a monotone, neglect gestures or overuse them, or talk too much or too little. Experienced public speakers:

a. Have conquered nervousness through practice
b. Mentally undress audience members to turn their own nervousness into amusement
c. Use skills and techniques to manage nervousness
d. Know they are in control
e. Never experience nervousness

72. How should statistics, numbers, and percentages be used in a speech?

a. The more the better; they prove points.
b. The more the better; they demonstrate to the audience that the speaker knows his subject.
c. The more the better; they will convince the audience.
d. Judiciously and carefully; too many may confuse audience members.
e. Not at all; people don't like numbers.

73. Mr. Diallo feels that his speech is going very well. Several of his audience members have closed their eyes and a number of others are scribbling notes like crazy. A few are checking the conference materials. Mr. Diallo's audience is likely:

a. Inspired by his presentation
b. In agreement with his position
c. Opposed to his position
d. Disinterested in his position
e. Partially engaged, partially disengaged

74. Which of the following methods of assessment are not useful for student presentations?

a. Dialogue with audience
b. Audience feedback with a rubric
c. Videotape
d. Self-assessment with rubrics
e. Direct, public audience feedback following the presentation

75. Cookie Baker is excited about her new job with a cookware company. She will appear at cooking shows, county fairs, exhibitions, and culinary schools to acquaint the audience with a new line of cookware. What type of speech should she employ?

a. Informational
b. Instructional
c. Debate
d. Demonstration
e. How-to

76. Numerical data should not be:

a. Presented visually as well as orally
b. Presented in the context of an image
c. Repeated throughout the speech
d. Translated into something the audience can relate to
e. Presented as the entirety of the presentation

77. What strategies might be useful for a leader who wants to introduce a change in a company's culture?

I. Announce the change; emphasize the transition will be smooth.
II. Encourage general questions, but discourage specific ones.
III. Create a vision; ensure senior management members show enthusiasm.
IV. Have senior management members change their behaviors to align with new ideals; modify the structure of the organization to facilitate the changes.
V. Extinguish water-cooler gossip regarding the upcoming changes. Provide information regarding old behaviors no longer tolerated and new behaviors that will replace them.
VI. Remove employees who don't fit the new ideal; integrate new hires into the company's culture.

a. I, II, III, IV
b. I, III, IV, V
c. III, IV, VI
d. I, II, IV
e. I, IV, V, VI

78. According to the two-step flow of communication model, ideas initially flow from ____ to ____.

a. Speakers, listeners
b. Mass media, society
c. Opinion leaders, the public
d. Mass media, opinion leaders
e. Politicians, constituents

79. One mass communication theory holds that when an individual believes her position on a particular topic is not in alignment with that of most others, she will not speak up. This theory is called:

a. Spiral of silence
b. Don't ask, don't tell
c. Silence is golden
d. Safety in silence
e. Groupthink

80. Which of the following statements about the spiral of silence is false?

a. The spiral of silence has a temporally limited hold on public view.
b. There must be a moral or ethical factor involved for the spiral to become active.
c. Social consensus deactivates the spiral.
d. Mass media has little effect on the spiral.
e. It decreases willingness to speak out on an issue.

81. According to Marshall McLuhan, the medium is the message. This means:

a. The medium in which the message appears affects how the message is read.
b. An advertiser's message is easiest for the public to accept when it falls in the middle range of popular beliefs.
c. Effective advertising should be transparent, as though it were channeled by a medium.
d. Consumers do not like to imagine themselves at the far end of the spectrum; ads should be aimed at the average.
e. The manner in which a message arrives matters more than the message itself.

82. Some types of new media that scholars are turning their analytical eyes to include:

a. Cable, wireless computers, Internet
b. Internet, mobile phones, video games
c. Internet, video games, faxes
d. Internet, video games, semiotics
e. Internet, gang signs, semiotics

83. The culturalist theory developed in the early 1990s holds that:

a. Culture is determined by media.
b. Media is determined by culture.
c. The public uses mass media messages to interpret their own meanings.
d. Mass media messages use the public to gain ever-widening influence.
e. Influence and power feed and feed upon one another.

84. In television situation comedies, thin female actors are more often ____ by male characters, while heavy female actors are more often ____.

a. Praised; insulted
b. Protected; sacrificed
c. Rejected; pursued
d. Praised; ignored
e. Treated politely; treated competitively

85. Which of the following is <u>not</u> an effect of new media?

a. The way the public involves itself with media has changed.
b. More diversity of cultural and political opinion is being expressed and supported.
c. There is a heightened sense of personal responsibility for opinions.
d. Consumers are more educated.
e. Consumers are suffering from information overload.

86. ____ describes an individual who is focused on a medium's message. ____ describes an individual who is absorbing the message while doing something else. ____ describes an individual focused on another task while a medium is delivering a message.

a. Absorbed; considering; distracted
b. Absorbed; distracted; absent
c. Primary involvement; secondary involvement; tertiary involvement
d. First level involvement; second level involvement; disengaged involvement
e. Single involvement; dual involvement; disengaged

87. The uses and gratifications model holds that motivations for attending to media include all of the following except:

a. The audience identifies with values or roles expressed.
b. The audience seeks a sense of relationship and security.
c. The audience seeks information or knowledge.
d. The audience wants a clearer picture of their reality.
e. The audience reinforces their behaviors, beliefs, and identity.

88. The theory concerned with the effect advertising and voter campaigns have on behavior is called:

a. Effects theory
b. Causes theory
c. Considerations theory
d. Manipulations theory
e. Control theory

89. Which of the following are political actors?

a. Politicians
b. Politicians and strategists
c. Politicians, strategists, and interest groups
d. Politicians, strategists, interest groups, and the media
e. Politicians, strategists, interest groups, the media, and consumers

90. Videoconferencing, the Internet, mobile phones, and intranets and other information and communication technologies have done all of the following except:

a. Have changed the face of business
b. Have created a global marketplace
c. Have changed the face of politics
d. Have major impacts on economies
e. Have changed the fundamentals of communication

91. Formative assessment is also called:

a. Growth assessment
b. Development assessment
c. Cumulative assessment
d. Educative assessment
e. Peer assessment

92. One way in which objective assessment differs from subjective assessment is:

a. Objective assessment is summative; subjective assessment is cumulative.
b. Objective assessment is cumulative; subjective assessment is summative.
c. Objective assessment has only one right answer; subjective assessment does not.
d. Objective assessment can have numerous correct answers; subjective assessment cannot.
e. Subjective assessments are often computerized; objective assessments are not.

93. In terms of teaching, moral motivation means:

a. Recognizing and insisting upon fairness
b. Being aware of how actions affect others
c. Living one's moral convictions through action
d. Placing moral values above personal values
e. Doing the right thing, even when no one is watching

94. Performance-based assessment:

a. Evaluates a student's concert, speech, or other public performance
b. Is based upon real-life tasks
c. Is a formative assessment
d. Has been largely discredited
e. Is an instantaneous, one-time evaluation

95. A teacher is composing a test. Half of the questions involve discrete point items, which are:

a. Questions with multiple correct answers
b. Essay questions
c. Cumulative questions
d. Questions that require deductive reasoning
e. Questions that focus on one point only

96. Which of the following rubric criteria might a teacher not use to assess a student's public speaking project?

a. Chooses and fine tunes a topic for a specific audience
b. Communicates the thesis sufficiently
c. Ideas progress logically
d. Selects appropriate and quality support material
e. Spends adequate time preparing for the project

97. A teacher has an English language learner in her speech class. His English is excellent, but his accent is pronounced. When he presents his class project, a speech about folk tales from his native country, the class is confused. It is difficult to understand what he is saying. This is probably because:

a. His accent is too strong.
b. He is making a lot of grammatical mistakes.
c. He is stressing words incorrectly.
d. He didn't practice enough.
e. His cultural references are confusing.

98. When selecting a text for a public speaking course at the high school level, the teacher should look for:

a. A comprehensive text
b. A text written at a level slightly above students' abilities
c. A text written at the level of students' abilities
d. A text that employs contemporary slang
e. A classical text with traditional, if dated, concepts

99. A teacher wants to give her public speaking students exciting topics so they will get involved with their material. Which of the following is the least desirable place to find appropriate topics?

a. Online
b. From other teachers
c. From books
d. From her students
e. An old, dated textbook

100. Is it better to assign a topic that is extremely specific or one that is open to interpretation, and why?

a. Specific, so students know what is expected of them
b. Specific, to keep students on-topic
c. Open to interpretation, so students can bring their own experiences into play
d. Open to interpretation, because teenagers don't like being told what to do
e. It completely depends upon the topic, but somewhere in the middle is best.

Answer Key and Explanations

1. C: Listening effectively requires the conscious use of a number of skills. First, the listener should focus on what's being said. The listener can show the speaker she's being heard by making eye contact or leaning forward. Forming an early opinion or judgment can cause a misinterpretation of the intended message, and becoming defensive shuts down an open mind. Paraphrasing and asking questions can help clarify the speaker's intended meaning. Paying attention to tone of voice, inflection, mood, or emotion is also an effective listening technique because they contribute to the message. Mirroring also communicates engaged listening. Tapping on the table (c) is not an effective listening technique.

2. A: In both writing and speaking, effective communication involves a sender who initiates the communication and a receiver (audience) for whom it's intended. The message is the communication that is received, which may be different from what was intended. The channel is the medium by which the message travels. It might be an e-mail, a presentation, a commercial, or a verbal exchange. Feedback is how the receiver responds, and helps the sender know if the message arrived intact.

3. B: The environment in which a communication is initiated and received plays an important role in how that communication manifests, both because the environmental context contributes to meaning by offering reference, and because the environment can enhance or detract from the receiver's ability to process the message. Personal space (about 1 ½ - 4 feet) has a greater bearing on the formation or receipt of the message than does social space (about 4 – 12 feet). It's important to recognize that both social and personal space vary from culture to culture; what is acceptable in one may not be in another.

4. B: Relational messages, as opposed to content messages, are concerned with the relationship between a speaker and a recipient rather than with the overt subject of the communication. They may convey belonging, respect, or disapproval, among other things. They are frequently largely or entirely nonverbal; because of this, they may be supported with verbal feedback to confirm them. The content of the message, "Should I come over after work?" is a logistical request. If a speaker leans forward to touch a recipient who is weeping, the relational message is "Do you need my support?" The recipient might respond with a nod and a grateful look, or might clarify the speaker's offer by saying, "I won't be good company, but you can come."

5. D: Language comprehension doesn't necessarily involve sounds or speaking. For example, sign language and written language use different materials to form words. It does, however, require identifying words, knowing their meanings, recognizing how they are being used in the context of a sentence, understanding abstractions such as idioms or references, and drawing a conclusion regarding the message's meaning.

6. E: Listening is an essential communication skill. In any type of communication, participants spend a substantially greater amount of time listening than speaking. Listening is a learned skill as opposed to a natural, innate ability. Children learn to listen by modeling behaviors demonstrated by others and by practicing. They quickly learn that listening to tone, speed, and volume can offer important nonverbal clues about the overall meaning of a message.

7. E: Expressive language competency is the ability to express oneself orally, not in writing. In order to use expressive language capably, the speaker must have control over nonverbal as well as verbal aspects of language. First, he or she must obviously know how to use oral language. Body language and gestures can add to or clarify the meaning of an oral message. For instance, turning away suggests dismissal, while leaning toward the recipient suggests inclusion. The tone in which a statement is made can indicate irony, satire, or enthusiasm. It can also introduce emotional or psychological overtones. The context in which a statement is made also affects meaning.

8. D: Before delivering a central point in a speech, the speaker should stop talking for a moment. During that moment of silence, however, it's important not to disengage. Instead, the speaker should make eye contact, lean or step forward, take an audible deep breath, raise his or her eyebrows, or use other nonverbal methods to alert the audience that what follows is important.

9. B: Debate is a highly useful classroom technique in that it teaches the skills necessary for communication. Each participant must conduct research and consider what he or she knows about the subject; work collaboratively with other students to clarify beliefs and positions; present an argument that is logical, lucid, and on-point; listen to the response as well as to the other team's message; and respond when appropriate.

10. B: Aristotle's poetics, written around 335 B.C., is a philosophical text concerned with dramatic presentations and poetry. Poetic genres are categorized in terms of the vehicle of language (language, harmony, and rhythm); objects [agents (actors or symbolic objects) and actions]; and their representative modes, specifically tragedy, comedy, lyric poetry, epic poetry, and dithyramb, a hymn sung and danced by performers.

11. A: A hamartia is a flaw in a character's perception, belief, or personality which results in an action that leads to the undoing of that character or a situation. The hamartia might be an accidental error, an evil or wrong action, or a sin. While a hamartia might arise because of an evil done to another person, the action itself contains an element of innocence. It is never intended to cause the results it does.

12. E: Aesthetics is concerned with the appreciation of beauty (or ugliness) for its own sake. It examines how an object, whether a song, a dramatic monologue, a poem, a color, or another artistic element, affects the feelings and thoughts of a perceiver. Aesthetic appreciation is immediate and visceral, and is not concerned with whether an object is "good," socially acceptable, moral, ethical, politically correct, or practical. In other words, social judgments have no bearing on the value of an object with respect to its ability to move an observer.

13. A: One of the most important elements of a good story is words that create vivid images in the minds of listeners. Images are mental pictures, and are primarily created with sensory detail such as sound, aroma, texture, visual description, and sometimes taste. Vivid images can describe a detailed setting that springs to life in the listeners' minds, characters that are unique and easy to tell apart because of their individual descriptions, and action that is easy to imagine.

14. C: Creating a loud sound that isn't a verbal one will grab the students' attention because it is percussive and unexpected. Leaning forward on the desk makes the teacher appear larger and more powerful. Changing the pace of a verbal delivery alerts the listeners (or in this case, the non-listeners) that something important is being said. Deliberate pronunciation allows the teacher to place emphasis on certain syllables, which forces students to pay attention to the message. While screaming might be tempting, it causes listeners to turn away from the message rather than pay attention to it. When the teacher lowers her voice, it causes the students to lean forward in order to hear what is being said.

15. C: Creative dramatics involves an informal, usually spontaneous, acting out of a story or event. While it is theatrical in presentation, any staging is also spontaneous, and consists of objects at hand. Creative dramatics is often symbolic in nature, and the participants (as well as observers) recognize that the actors' movements, words, and choice of props all contain meaning that goes far beyond the surface. This means that not only are the actors involved in symbolic play, but the listeners must also participate creatively by determining the symbolic importance of the performance.

16. B: Lines don't become part of a theatrical conversation unless the actor directs them towards a listener. Unskilled actors may memorize their lines and speak them according to the director's instructions, but if the actor doesn't have an internal conviction that his part of the dialogue is part of a conversation that is unfolding at that moment for the first time, the audience will sense it and the illusion will fail.

17. B: One way of looking at historical records, whether written or spoken, is that all records are produced based on the perspectives of individuals. All perspectives reflect perceptions, attitudes, beliefs, mores, and values. All perspectives are shaped by some kind of agenda, even if the historian is unaware he or she even has one. It can be said that history recorded by human beings will always be incomplete and flawed. Oral history, like written history, captures a period of time within some sort of perceptual framework. As the tale is passed from generation to generation, certain details that don't resonate will be dropped or replaced by others. In this way, a piece of oral history becomes composed of multiple layers over the years, each of which reflects not only the perspectives of the tellers, but also the teller's times.

18. D: Reader's theater, or RT, is used to support the reading of literature. While the form is rather fluid and can manifest in a number of ways, reader's theater is typically minimal in terms of production elements. The narrative, not the staging, is primary in importance. If there is any staging, it is simple or even symbolic. For instance, a large drawing of a chair may be used instead of a real one. Costumes are rarely used. Any that are used are symbolic or uniform. Actors don't memorize scripts. They are held by the actors, who refer to them as needed.

19. A: Sanford Meisner, who trained with method actor Lee Strasberg, developed a set of interconnected exercises that become increasingly more complicated as they progress. These exercises teach actors to draw upon their own emotional experiences and improvise around a situation. Repetition, one of Meisner's central exercises, involves two actors repeating the same phrase back and forth, with each repetition being somehow unique in that it is spoken as a reaction to the other actor's tone of voice, behavior, or other element used to add uniqueness to the phrase.

20. D: In order to develop a character, an actor must first understand the character. A thorough understanding of a play helps the reader understand how the character responds to other characters and situations. Internalizing dialogue helps the actor "own" the character's words. Finding commonality between the character and personal life experiences helps an actor relate to the character. Playing the character without making stereotypical or obvious choices is also important. For example, an irritable person doesn't snap at everyone constantly in real life, but only sometimes.

21. D: Speaking extemporaneously requires spontaneity. Being invited to say a few words at an award ceremony, being asked to elaborate on a point during a business meeting, or being asked to speak under other circumstances in which the individual does not have a speech prepared does not mean speaking without thinking. Among the techniques that make speaking extemporaneously appear easy is pausing for a moment before beginning to make eye contact or communicate a nonverbal message, such as an amused look. In this time, the speaker can gather a couple of thoughts on the subject and start by speaking slowly and with confidence. Keeping the speech brief and concentrating on relating to the audience are other techniques.

22. B: A strong argument is not made by forcing people to pay attention, interrupting another speaker, or belittling an idea, person, or group. These behaviors simply weaken the speaker's position because they each demonstrate in a different way that the speaker is not in control of his own ideas, and must therefore try to control the situation by using emotion. The most successful arguments acknowledge the strongest points of the opposition, and then unemotionally dissect those points in order to find and demonstrate how they are flawed.

23. A: The Lincoln-Douglas debate format focuses on making a logical argument, communicating the speaker's ethical standards, and taking a philosophical position. This debate format is commonly used by debate leagues and in competitions. In this type of debate, 40-minute rounds are broken into 3-5 minutes of prep time and 13 minutes of speaking time for each debater.

24. A: Classical debate, an alternative to the more common policy debate, focuses on real-life discussions rather than abstract strategic arguments. Extemporaneous debate involves no pre-planning and very limited research. In an impromptu debate, which is less formal than other styles, each team member is given five minutes to speak. This is followed by a 10-minute discussion period and a brief rebuttal. Moot court and mock trial debates involve creating a courtroom environment and using a courtroom approach.

25. B: The reasons for public speaking are many: to teach, trade, punish, exhibit, advertise, apologize, denounce, plead, train, and reflect. These purposes, however, can be grouped into just three categories. A teacher lecturing her students or a CEO addressing shareholders at an annual meeting are both using rhetoric to inform. A public speaker might also seek to influence an audience. A politician running for office, a missionary speaking to villagers, and an attorney arguing before a judge are all using oratory in this way. Finally, oratory can entertain. Examples of individuals that use oratory in this way include stand-up comedians and storytellers.

26. C: Every school child is taught that metaphor is the direct comparison of two different things. An example of a metaphor is: "The clouds are pillows of cotton." Looking more deeply into the heart of how metaphor operates, however, it is clear that it is an effective rhetorical device. Metaphor simultaneously allows for great linguistic economy while inviting listeners to embrace new ideas by linking them to ideas with which they are already comfortable and familiar.

27. E: A debate coach nurtures and develops students' mental skills. Debate coaches guide team members to understand and embrace their own ideas and express those ideas logically, aesthetically, creatively, and fully. Rather than instructing team members on how to handle a debate, the role of the coach is to listen and respond with questions so that the debater learns to fine-tune his argument. Coaches have many responsibilities in addition to encouraging individuals to think and express their unique ideas. They are often also responsible for practical tasks such as fundraising, scheduling, paperwork, and more.

28. D: Synecdoche is a rhetorical device in which a part of something is used to represent the entirety. Conversely, it may involve referring to an entire object to represent one specific manifestation. For example, referring to a business man as a "suit" is a figure of speech in which a part (his suit) is used to signify the man himself. Alternatively, when a thief tells his partner to run because "the law" is coming, the abstract idea of law is used to represent a specific individual who manifests it.

29. D: The National Speech and Debate Tournament offers Extemporaneous Commentary, Expository Speaking, Prose Interpretation, and Poetic Interpretation as Supplemental Events. Qualifying Events include Domestic Extemporaneous Speaking, Foreign Extemporaneous Speaking, Humorous Interpretation, Duo Interpretation, Dramatic Interpretation, Lincoln-Douglas Debate, Original Oratory, Policy Debate, Public Forum Debate, and Congressional Debate. Consolation Events are Impromptu Speaking and Storytelling.

30. E: Theoretically, no message arrives intact. Words ultimately don't mean the same thing to different people, so messages can easily be misinterpreted. A sender assumes recipients will interpret the meaning of each word in the same way, which can result in interpersonal communications being unclear. Gender, culture, and age contribute greatly to how speakers formulate and interpret messages. The message's physical environment can contribute to confusion due to distractions. The relationship the sender and receiver share, as well as the relationships under discussion, all shade a message's meaning.

31. B: In the midst of a lucid dream, the dreamer "awakens" within the dream and recognizes it as such. The lucid dreamer "plays" with the dream as an artist plays with materials, exploring impossibilities and manipulating the dream in a way that is highly conscious. This is a very intimate form of intrapersonal communication. The dreamer is simultaneously utterly vulnerable and at the mercy of the dream, and also a God-like presence that can shape the dream however she desires.

32. C: Informal communications are both common and essential within an office environment. A savvy manager knows that gossip is how employees share information, rumor, and innuendo. A manager who wants to prepare his department for an upcoming change that has not yet been officially announced can simply drop a suggestive hint to the right person to make sure everyone in the department hears the news. To the gossips themselves, gossip enhances social bonding. Although it is informal, gossip is also a political communicative channel.

33. C: Just 43 muscles in the human face are responsible for roughly 10,000 distinct expressions. Some posit that expressions are culturally bound and therefore learned, while others believe they are universal, shared, and innately recognized. The most basic emotions—sadness, anger, fear, disgust, contempt, joy, and surprise—are shared with primates, who recognize their meaning not only when they appear on the faces of other primates, but also when they are observed on the faces of human beings.

34. A: Display rules is a term describing the shared, understood norms regarding acceptable modes of expression for specific groups in specific situations. Meanings assigned to emotions vary from culture to culture, from gender to gender, and across generations. Emotional expressions that are considered perfectly acceptable within a romantic relationship or between a child and parent may violate the unspoken display rules in an office, for example. As another example, women are permitted and even expected to express sorrow through crying in many cultures, while men are expected to deny such a "feminine" feeling. If it must be expressed, it must be expressed incognito, perhaps as anger or disappointment, both of which are acceptable gender display rules for men.

35. C: Subvocalization occurs during the act of reading. Although it is silent and internalized, the speaker "hears" the sounds of words, and in doing so creates a way to remember what was read. During subvocalization, some people, especially children, may move their lips as though they are speaking aloud. Some genres demand greater attention to subvocalization than others. For example, the cadences and aesthetic language choices of poetry beg the reader to "hear" the aural music in the midst of reading silently.

36. C: Microexpressions appear and vanish so quickly that up to 90% of observers don't register them at all. In fact, the owner of the face that wears them may not even be conscious of the feelings that create them. Microexpressions are the result of buried emotions. A liar is likely to briefly wear a series of microexpressions as he denies a truth. A lover breaking up with another may say one thing, but her face might reflect something else. Anger, sadness, fear, contempt, disgust, happiness, and surprise are triggered on a non- intellectual level and seize the body. A speaker who tries to suppress the associated expression is most likely condensing it into a microexpression. The speaker may be aware or unaware of its manifestation.

37. D: People with interpersonal competence are self-aware. They create and maintain healthy relationships by being honest with themselves and others. They disclose what they know and feel, offer emotional support, and are willing to risk vulnerability in order to initiate and continue relationships that are important to them. Although empathy is associated with interpersonal competence, these individuals maintain a healthy dose of self-respect. Should the words or actions of another disappoint these individuals, they will bring their feelings out in the open. They will attempt to work with the other individual to resolve the issues that have brought negative feelings to light in a positive manner.

38. E: Intrapersonal communication is a dialogue with the self; the sender and receiver embody the same being. Intrapersonal communication is how we make sense of the unknown, frightening, or confusing. It is also how we practice how we will communicate with another. Daydreaming and journal keeping are both used to clarify one's feelings and thoughts, and to practice how to shape them into words. Private reflection upon a conversation that has ended keeps that conversation alive as the individual doing the reflecting discovers greater meaning. Gestures are the body's way of underscoring or adding information to a message, and are one way the body talks to itself. Patting your belly while telling someone you're hungry, for example, is a message to both the sender and recipient. However, self-reflection does not necessarily ensure that sent messages will be understood by the recipient.

39. D: Vertical communication is passed from a higher level employer to one below him, or from a lower level employee to a supervisor or manager. Vertical communication is used to send formal messages to employees at various levels, to announce policy changes, to inspire, and to provide direction. Bottom up communication, also called upward communication, offers subordinates a formal means by which to deliver information to superiors, ask questions, or report on the status of an assignment. Both top down and bottom up modes of communication function inside a collection of understood rules that permit these communications to proceed efficiently.

40. B: Self-concept is related to self-awareness and self-esteem, but is not the same thing. Self-concept is the full collection of beliefs and perceptions an individual has about herself in all dimensions, including interpersonal, intellectual, creative, and logical skills. Self-esteem, in which the self assesses or judges the self, is a sub-category of self-concept, and self-awareness is simply a consciousness of self. Self-concept changes little through time because it is concerned with stable characteristics ("This is who I am") rather than passing conditions ("I am angry"). Self-concept is reinforced or enhanced when expectations are met. When they are not, it is not affected much, except in times of serious self-doubt. Therefore, while successfully teaching someone else a skill would reinforce someone's self-concept, being the subject of gossip, having an invitation rejected, or failing an exam would not likely drastically alter an individual's self-concept.

41. A: While the dissolution of an important relationship, being attacked, or being rejected can certainly affect one's self- esteem, an identity crisis is a radical unraveling in which an individual loses the connection with the self he knew in the past and the self he now knows himself to be. It is literally a sense of disintegration, a true loss of integrity. Such a split can result from a trauma such as war or other violence, a cultural shift, a period of soul-searching and reflection, and other transformative experiences.

42. C: Identity achievement is the result of an individual fully embracing a unified, single, integrated self-identity that integrates the totality of who she is. It follows a period of intense introspection or tremendous upheaval, and can occur at any point or at several points in an individual's life, from childhood through old age. After considering or experiencing a number of identities and finding one that is "the right fit," the individual will turn away from other identities that challenge the "true" one or subsume them if they are not contradictory to the primary identity.

43. B: Self-disclosure is communicating the things that are important to oneself with another. Some acts of self-disclosure are more telling than others. For example, telling a date that you fear spiders, love hiking, and have a favorite aunt offers a glimpse into your emotional life, but nothing of major importance is being risked. Revealing that you've undergone several surgeries to remove scarring from a fire in which your identical twin died risks tremendous vulnerability. There is a cultural expectation that information disclosed at the beginning of a relationship is less intimate than that shared as the relationship deepens.

44. B: Emotionally intense events that occurred long ago gain a kind of mythology through time. We visit those events repeatedly at different stages of life, trying to understand what they meant, why they occurred, and what effects they had. We are, in truth, reforming the original event, shaping it into a story. All stories, even histories, contain elements of fiction. Objects or actions are symbolically transformed and charged with layers of meaning. Not all acts of self-disclosure are conscious. When consciously sharing a story about an event that occurred long ago, the teller is also unconsciously sharing another, more symbolic one.

45. D: The question is not concerned with assessing the students' competency in listening or learning, but with assessing the teacher's instruction. When a sender creates a message that is delivered to a receiver, there are many points along the way in which the message might become altered or ultimately be incompletely or incorrectly understood. Feedback, or the receiver's response, can take the form of questions, repeating back key information, or furthering the conversation. Feedback lets the sender know if the message needs clarification.

46. A: The Spitzberg & Cupach model of communication competence describes knowledge as the understanding of what a specific situation calls for in terms of behavior. Skill is knowing how to demonstrate that specific behavior appropriately, and motivation is the speaker's desire to make her communication clear in an appropriate way. When these three components are present, the speaker has achieved communication competency.

47. D: The facilitator should send a strong nonverbal message to each. When the domineering participant attempts to take over, the facilitator should stand, turn her back, and pointedly invite another member to speak. If the domineering member continues to talk, the facilitator should hold up her hand in a "stop" position directly at the individual and repeat her invitation to another member. By mirroring the quiet participant's movements, the facilitator will send a message that she is recognized and welcome in the group.

48. B: The purpose of this type of group discussion is to define an issue and then work toward its resolution. The purpose must remain central, and must not be eclipsed by emotional issues. While some of the discussion participants might feel slighted if they are interrupted, if someone disagrees with them and others concur, or if the group does not hold their ideas as highly as those of others, it would be inappropriate to display those feelings. Participants who have greater experience, knowledge, or skills related to the subject under discussion should be expected and invited to contribute more to the discussion. They should not be resented for their greater knowledge.

49. C: Collaboration relies upon the premise that working together is a framework in which everyone can achieve their secondary goals when the primary goal is reached. It works best when no one wants to be personally held solely responsible, when individuals are somewhat willing to be flexible, and when everyone wants to share in the credit. In a collaborative situation, an individual will willingly give up a position for the greater good, thereby participating in the ultimate success of the group.

50. A: In a compromise, all sides agree to give up something in order to play a role in gaining something more important. When both sides bend, no one feels they've been taken advantage of or manipulated. However, in the process of negotiating what will be given up, the danger is that a central ideal or essential part of the true goal will become eroded or erased entirely.

51. C: There are many situations in which avoidance is a useful, though usually temporary, strategy within a group. If a minor disagreement arises, it may be best to overlook it and focus on the goal at hand. In other words, avoidance is appropriate if more important things need to be dealt with. If a discussion has gotten out of hand, stepping away from the issues gives everyone a chance to calm down. An individual with little clout will reasonably prefer to avoid a confrontation rather than lose face. Avoiding making a decision is appropriate if more information is required, or when an acceptable answer has not yet become clear.

52. B: Standard agenda, or reflective thinking, is a six step process that systematically looks at a problem that requires a decision to be made. The first step is to clarify the issue or problem. Secondly, the problem must be analyzed. Next, given the goals of the decision, criteria must be chosen. Fourth, a comprehensive list of possible solutions must be gathered. Following this, each potential solution must be assessed using the criteria that were previously chosen. The most appropriate solution should then be selected. Finally, the selected solution should be applied.

53. D: Brainstorming is a useful technique for getting members of a group to think outside the box, generating unexpected ideas, and making unusual connections. In a brainstorming session, an idea is offered or a question is asked. Members are encouraged to begin rapidly generating ideas, saying them aloud. Interruption is allowed, and the sessions often erupt into a playful frenzy. Because ideas aren't being judged or categorized, brainstorming creates intense mental and creative energy.

54. C: Groupthink is a psychological phenomenon that is likely to manifest when a group's primary focus is on the solidarity of its members rather than on the task or purpose for which the group has been formed. "Groupthink" causes members to disown any individual thought that might disturb the group's amity. Members may be unaware or completely aware that they aren't in full agreement with a point of view or decision, but will push their own different ideas or ideals aside because they are unwilling to be seen by the others as different.

55. E: There are many negative outcomes and no positive ones to groupthink. Groupthink's ultimate goal is to preserve the status quo. Therefore, groups under the influence of groupthink cannot tolerate people who think for themselves, opposition, or even an idea just a shade different from their own "official" positions. These groups will seek only information that supports pre-existing positions, and typically have no contingency plan to fall back on. A group under groupthink influence will neither look for information that runs counter to their own beliefs, nor consider a range of alternatives. The group will not look too carefully at ideas the group approves of because the group believes itself to be infallible. Ultimately, groupthink causes its own demise because of its inflexibility. New members to a group might not be willing to accept the party line. Because they don't yet identify strongly with the group, they will be more willing to express other ideas.

56. D: Abdicratic groups typically disintegrate quickly. An abdicratic group is one in which there is no leadership, either because none of the individuals are willing to assume responsibility, or because the group holds an ideal that presupposes leadership is not necessary or desirable. A leaderless group will either pull itself apart because its members will go off in various directions, or it will experience no movement and, through the force of inertia, simply dissolve. The group may reorganize, but this time the leadership will be autocratic.

57. A: Autocratic leaders are strong-willed and authoritative. They do not allow decisions that do not work in their favor, further their cause, or benefit them in some way. Democratic style leadership gives authority to all group members, who make decisions together. Laissez-faire style leadership involves the group making its own decisions without interference from the leader, who acts only as a guide. Abdicratic groups recognize no authority in any of the members, and give equal freedom and responsibility to all.

58. B: All groups form around some kind of task. Roles such as initiator contributor (generates ideas), information seeker (gathers necessary information), opinion seeker (gathers group values), elaborator (clarifies), coordinator (finds connections between ideas), evaluator-critic (weighs group activities against an ideal), energizer (stimulates and inspires), and procedural-technician (handles logistics) are all essential. Other important roles include information giver (offers facts), opinion giver (offers positions about group concerns), orienter (changes the direction), and recorder (keeps the records).

59. D: An informational speech generally follows a formulaic format. The opening puts the topic of the speech in front of the audience and offers a thesis. A brief preview of what will be discussed and in what order is provided. A strong hook, often a humorous remark, is used to pull the listener in. The purpose of the speech is explained in a point by point fashion in the body of the speech. The conclusion reviews the information, circles back around to something that was said in the opening, and ends the speech with a flourish. In addition, informative (also called informational) speeches often use a number of facts, quotes, or statistics to support the speaker's position.

60. D: Informative speeches should be relatively short – typically under 20 minutes – so as not to overwhelm the audience. Some visual aids can be helpful, but should only be used to clarify the verbal message, not replace it. Eye contact, deliberate gestures, standing and moving with confidence, and other types of nonverbal communication should be used to enhance the speaker's message. The purpose of this type of speech is to inform, not to persuade or enflame. Therefore, the language should be simple, direct, and logical. A few notes are fine, but the speaker should be well prepared and not read from a script.

61. C: Demonstration speeches are designed to offer directions or instructions to an audience that explain how to do something. Before presenting a demonstration speech, it's important to know the degree to which the audience is familiar with the subject. If Esteban's audience is composed of graduate students in a well-respected music department, his presentation will need to be sophisticated enough to be of interest and use to them. High school students with little experience, however, will need a presentation they can understand.

62. E: Effective speeches are not written to appeal to anyone and everyone. A speech needs to be fine-tuned for its audience, who will receive it, interpret it, and apply it in ways that are meaningful within the framework of their own experiences. While no speech writer can accurately determine every detail of the lives of her audience, the more she knows, can find out, or can make an educated guess about, the better able she will be to fine-tune her message into something of lasting interest and value to her audience. Factors that should be considered include age, gender, culture, nationality, religious affiliation, the audience's skills and experiences with the topic, and the audience's needs and interests.

63. C: A toast is a type of ceremonial speech in which an event or person is honored and celebrated. These types of speeches should move the audience and cause them to have an emotional reaction to hearing about the subject. Toasts should not be used as an opportunity to educate. While the family tree or timeline might be fascinating to some of the older audience members, the younger ones lack the perspective to fully appreciate them. A mention of a historical fact or two is fine, but dwelling on history doesn't celebrate the individual. Stories about the person being honored in the toast and family and friends who are present in the audience interest everyone. They demonstrate character, are moving, and directly involve audience members.

64. C: Effective eye contact suggests confidence, piques audience interest, makes the speaker's message seem familiar, and suggests the speaker is an expert on her subject. Excessive eye contact, however, can cause considerable discomfort for audience members. Audience members enjoy being singled out briefly and made to feel special. Holding a gaze for too long, however, removes the protective sense of anonymity, and can make someone in the audience feel embarrassed, uncertain, or even angry.

65. D: When done correctly, extemporaneous speaking has a sense of immediacy, vivacity, and originality that a canned or memorized presentation does not. Speaking extemporaneously requires a solid understanding of the material and the ability to respond to audience cues quickly. Extemporaneous speaking should also give the impression of informality. A joke, for instance, can establish a relaxed mood and create interest. It is important to note, however, that the impression of informality isn't the same as true informality. The speaker still needs to remain in control over the presentation.

66. C: Without knowing the habits and expectations of other cultures, it is easy to make a faux pas, accidentally offend someone, or misunderstand a nonverbal communication. In this case, the audience is simply concentrating. Listening with closed eyes is not only socially acceptable in Japan, but is also a sign of respect. Nodding agreement is also considered respectful. As a side note, Mr. Gibbons might want to tone down the humor in his presentation, especially humor that gently mocks himself or his country, as the Japanese find this offensive.

67. A: Ultimately, all types of public speaking come down to the speaker's objectives and how they relate to the audience's needs. Whether the speech is a toast designed to inform, persuade, or entertain, the speaker has a purpose or reason for presenting the speech, and the audience has a reason for listening to it. To be truly successful, a public speaker must meet his objectives and the audience's needs.

68. E: Rehearsing a speech is more than simply practicing it in order to learn the material. An effective speaker knows that everything she does contributes to or detracts from the overall meaning of the speech. A videotape offers both verbal and visual feedback, and can help the speaker become conscious of whether the gestures, eye contact, tone of voice, pitch, and speech patterns used are effective or ineffective. A videotape will show the degree to which visual aids are helpful or hurtful in terms of clarifying the message, and can also help the speaker recognize confusing nonverbal information and identify sections where the speech loses focus.

69. A: Audience members are most likely to retain the points of a speech or lecture if they are offered in the form of a story and the speaker uses language that is simple and direct enough to be transparent. The stories need to be simple, and must drive the speech directly toward an essential and clear point. Including anecdotes is most effective when the speaker uses storytelling techniques that will bring them alive, such as varying pace, pitch, and intensity, using body language to suggest a change in speakers, and using the stage to suggest a setting.

70. C: The approach a speaker should take in the event of equipment failure depends on the subject and the audience. For instance, a speaker who is presenting to a group of techno savvy young people might be saved by a volunteer from the audience. While the technology is being repaired, the speaker should ask for questions or carry on an informal, entertaining dialogue with the audience. On the other hand, a speaker presenting to a group of children will need to quickly switch into extemporaneous mode in order to keep the attention of the audience. A presentation being given to a group of scientists might rely heavily upon graphs, charts, and numbers. In this case, the speaker can illustrate points using a flipchart if the visuals cannot be repaired.

71. C: For most public speakers, nervousness is less of a problem when they are presenting to the type of audience with which they have considerable experience. The stakes are higher, however, when the audience or the material is new. Knowing about and using a handful of tricks, skills, and techniques that anticipate specific problems that can arise in the midst of speaking is an essential part of successful speaking and dealing with nervousness. A few notes on a card will prompt a blank mind. Anticipating difficult or even hostile questions and preparing responses allows the speaker to continue with confidence. Sometimes, re-directing a feeling is all it takes. Channeling anxiety into excitement, for instance, will charge the speech with energy.

72. D: Appropriate numbers, statistics, percentages, and other data presented to strengthen a point will clarify concepts and help the audience understand what is being said. However, it should be kept in mind that it takes more time to comprehend the meaning of a number than it does to comprehend the meaning of a word. Numbers need to be processed, and presenting too many of them in a row will only befuddle the audience. Too much data is overwhelming, and will cause audience members to shut down. Therefore, this type of information should be used judiciously and carefully.

73. D: The audience is showing signs that they have disengaged. They are neither in agreement nor disagreement. Rather, they have tuned him out entirely. When an audience member is scribbling a lot of notes, those notes probably have nothing to do with the speech. Instead, the audience member is likely doing other work. Closed eyes might mean concentration, but could also indicate boredom. Studying a conference catalogue or other materials indicates that the audience member is disconnected from the speech. Other signs that an audience is distracted are staring, touching hair or face, sighing, foot tapping, whispering, dropping items, sprawling back in seats, and glancing around the room. When a speaker notes even a few members of the audience engaging in these actions, he needs to change pace, incorporate body language, and vary voice tone to recapture their attention.

74. E: When a student gives a presentation, several methods to help him understand what worked and what didn't should be used. Audience comments are useful if they're honest and clear. For instance, a popular student who has given a mediocre speech isn't helped by commentary that only praises her. Specific critiques, however, such as a student pointing out that the speaker's fiddling with her hair is distracting, are useful. Rubrics completed by students, the teacher, and the presenter can be extremely useful, both because a rubric looks at a number of specific areas, and because the presenter can see areas that everyone agrees need to be improved upon. A videotape will give strong, accurate feedback on the student's diction, speech patterns, voice tone, and nonverbal communication skills.

75. D: A demonstration speech, which combines the speaker's words with activities and visual aids, is a complex style of public speaking. To be successful, Cookie needs to know the speech inside and out to give the impression she is speaking spontaneously. Like an informational speech, a demonstration speech is organized into an introduction, a body, and a conclusion. Because she will be demonstrating as she speaks, it's important that Cookie uses simple vocabulary and direct statements rather than poetic or dramatic language and complex sentences.

76. E: When properly used, numerical data can enhance a speech and illuminate important points, but numbers on their own are hard to grasp. Presenting numbers verbally, and then showing them in a chart or graph helps the audience see the relationship between the numbers and the points presented in the speech. Translating numbers into a concrete image that audience members can relate to can be powerful. For example, the statement "By the time I finish this speech, seven more children will be diagnosed with cancer in the United States" brings the message home. Repeating this fact or the numbers associated with the fact at key points throughout the presentation will bring the information home in a way the audience will not forget.

77. C: A change in company culture is difficult, even if it's necessary. Lower level employees need to be reassured with a true vision infused with energy and hope for the future. Senior management members will need to change their behavior to align with the company's new ideals. Seeing senior management enthusiastically embrace the changes, not just with their words but also through their actions, will further assure employees it is safe to trust the vision. Employees will have questions, and the leader must know how the organizational structure will be re-designed to facilitate upcoming changes. Employees who have displayed deviant behaviors prior to the change, such as chronic absenteeism or an unwillingness to work with others, must be purged. New hires that more closely align with the new model need to be brought in.

78. D: According to the two-step flow model developed by Lazarsfeld and Katz, mass media does not directly affect the public, but instead channels ideas through what they term opinion leaders. Opinion leaders are individuals who have the greatest ready access to a specific media, have an understanding of the ideas disseminated by mass media, and can spread those ideas by explaining or popularizing them to a more general audience.

79. A: The spiral of silence theory is concerned with both mass communication and political science. According to the theory, when people believe their position on a subject doesn't match the majority's, they remain silent rather than risk censure. It is called a "spiral" because the more confident those who hold the majority view feel, the more likely they are to voice their opinion. The more they voice their opinion, the less likely the opposition is to voice a different, opposing viewpoint.

80. D: Mass media has a very strong influence over the spiral of silence because it shapes public opinion about an issue, and also reports or suggests that the majority opinion or viewpoint is the "correct" one. Mass media can also make it seem as though a local and minor issue is a much larger social concern, which invites the public at large to develop opinions (which are usually those the media has fed them). By reporting on the opinion of the majority, that opinion becomes the status quo.

81. A: According to McLuhan, a message cannot be divorced from the manner in which it arrives, and so the medium affects how a message is read. This suggests that in order to deliver the message the sender intends, an awareness of the characteristics of the medium is necessary. For example, a comic requires the creative involvement of the reader, who not only "hears" the voices of the characters, but also fills in the missing details from box to box.

82. B: Traditional media studies have focused on print media, including newspapers, books, magazines, journals, broadsides, brochures, flyers, coupons, and the like; visual media, including photographs, movies, videos, and television; and aural media, such as radio and recordings. New media has been studied as a subset of these, but that is changing. Interactive television, online videogames, mobile devices such as phones that bring the Internet wherever the user goes, digital media, videoconferencing, Twitter, Facebook, instant messaging, and more are beginning to be seen not as mere extensions of traditional media, but as entirely separate media types.

83. C: The culturalist theory is something of a marriage between two earlier theories. The limited effect theory of the 1950s claimed that media had a limited ability to influence people who were already knowledgeable about or experienced with a particular topic, and a greater ability to influence those who were less knowledgeable. The class dominant theory held that the media is controlled by an elite minority of corporate rulers who manipulate it to their advantage. The culturalist theory states that mass media, which is controlled by a tiny portion of the population, offers raw material—images, sounds, and vocabulary—intended to relay a message. Individuals take that material and craft or fine-tune their own messages based on their experiences and prior knowledge, meaning a single message can have multiple meanings when interpreted by different people.

84. A: A 2000 study of characters in situation comedies found that male characters were more likely to be given lines praising characters portrayed by thin female actors, and were more likely to be given lines insulting characters portrayed by heavy female actors.

85. C: The Internet, mobile devices, Twitter, Facebook, and other new media have altered the way information is received. In the past, television, radio, and newspaper scheduling controlled when and how content was received, as well as the nature of the content. As the public becomes increasingly more sophisticated in using the Internet, they have taken control over when they will receive content and what type of content they will receive. Members of the public have also gained a means by which they as individuals or groups can contribute to the pool of information. However, since the Internet allows for a great degree of anonymity, participants are able to express opinions or offer what they believe to be facts without assuming responsibility for the fairness or accuracy of their contributions.

86. C: Primary involvement is the term used to describe an audience fully focused on a medium's message. Reading a book, watching a television show, or listening to a debate demonstrates this type of involvement, which has the most immediate and strongest impact upon the audience. Secondary involvement means the audience is simultaneously absorbing the message and doing something else. A parent watching the news while preparing dinner is somewhat less open to the information being channeled. Tertiary involvement means the audience is paying little attention to the medium and is focusing primarily on something else. While part of the message may be received, it is less immediate and considerably less influential.

87. D: McQuail's uses and gratifications model finds that there are multiple, and oftentimes overlapping, reasons a consumer accepts a medium's message. A message that reinforces one's beliefs enhances his or her identity. Watching or reading about relationships gives an individual the illusion that he or she is involved in those relationships, and so the media is fully embraced. Consumers turn to media to gain specific information or escape the problems of their own lives through entertainment.

88. A: Proponents of the effects theory claim that the influence of media on values, beliefs, and behaviors is profound. This theory suggests that there is little autonomy in audiences. If the message is aggressive or convincing enough, they believe and behave as they are told to and do not seek further information elsewhere. One piece of information used to support the theory is the direct correlation between rising crime and violence in media reports, movies, and games and instances of these events in real life. Critics, however, point out that most viewers do not imitate behaviors they have been exposed to, and those who do generally have extenuating psychological conditions.

89. D: All forms of communication media contribute to and influence how a political message is issued and received. The media is a source of information, and only information that is offered can be received and reflected upon by consumers. This is a political act in itself. The form the message takes, the words chosen, and the visual presentation all contribute to the message's meaning. In politics, the media serves to entrench particular beliefs in those who already hold them and to sway those who have not yet made up their minds. It is obvious that politicians, political strategists, and interest groups have a role in shaping the political field. The media also plays an important role.

90. E: Information and communication technologies such as the Internet, mobile devices, intranets, networking, videoconferencing, and the like have radically changed the pace at which information can be disseminated, accessed, and shared. Videoconferencing and the Internet have resulted in changes in the way organizations and businesses are structured, giving them greater flexibility that has resulted in a rise in virtual offices, permitted the development of a global marketplace, and relocated jobs to nations where the labor force is plentiful and cheap. While making goods and services less expensive to consumers, it has also affected economies. In some areas, job losses have been considerable; in others, new industries have emerged, creating more jobs. These technologies have also radically altered the way political campaigns are run by surrounding voters with layers of information from every corner. In order to be successful, politicians must be sensitive to the ways younger voters use the Internet.

91. D: The purpose of formative, or educative, assessment is to support learning by offering feedback over the course of the learning experience. This is a diagnostic assessment used to determine the student's current level of knowledge and skills, specifically what the student is doing capably and what the student needs to focus on improving. A formative assessment can take many forms, including a rubric completed by the instructor, other students, or the student himself; informal verbal feedback; or a response journal.

92. C: Objective assessment allows for only one correct response. Subjective assessment, on the other hand, can have multiple correct responses or a correct response that can be worded in a number of ways. Among the types of objective assessment questions are multiple choice, true or false, and matching questions. Objective evaluations are frequently found online. Subjective assessments often consist of essay questions.

93. D: Placing the importance of moral values above personal ones is moral motivation. Justifying behaviors that don't fit within one's moral code, ignoring aspects of those behaviors in order to avoid confronting oneself, or denying a misaligned behavior when confronted by another all indicate a turning away from one's moral center. Prioritizing personal values (particularly contradictory ones) above moral values results in a schism in belief and behavior. When a teacher says one thing but does another, students become confused. When a teacher justifies behavior despite her moral values, students learn that they too can live unreconciled lives in which their responsibility for doing the right thing is changeable rather than absolute.

94. B: Performance-based assessments are concerned with evaluating a student's overall performance of a particular skill, including the planning, execution, and analysis of that skill. This type of assessment is most often ongoing over a period of time. It can be informal in nature (such as conversations between teacher and student) or formal (such as assessments that follow a rubric). Performance-based assessments are concerned with real-world tasks and experiences, such as delivering a public speaking performance, writing a speech, directing a play, or writing a review.

95. E: Discrete point items require knowledge of a single piece of information, such as the definition of a word. In contrast, an integrative question is one that tests the student's ability to consider more than one point simultaneously. A question that asks a student to complete two tasks, such as identifying the correct definition of a word and using it in a sentence, is integrative. An objective question has a single answer, while a subjective question is open to interpretation.

96. E: Among the skills a good public speaker must possess is the ability to select a topic and fine tune it for a particular, specific audience; clarify the information by sufficiently communicating the thesis; transition logically from point to point throughout the presentation; and support the speech's purpose or position with appropriate statistics, graphs, charts, or other professional quality visual aids. A teacher evaluating a student's public speaking skills should also look for appropriate word choice and sentence structure; naturalness of delivery; variation in pitch, intensity, and pace; appropriate nonverbal support; and comfort with spontaneous additions as appropriate. The amount of time spent preparing is not directly related to the quality of the final product: some students work more quickly than others.

97. C: Since the student's English is excellent, it can be assumed he has a good grasp of both grammatical structures and vocabulary. A pronounced accent is noticeable, but isn't sufficient cause for misunderstanding unless he is not differentiating between phonemes such as /b/ and /d/ or /l/ and /r/. Again, since his English is excellent, it can be assumed this is not the problem. Although it isn't clear if he failed to practice, such a failure wouldn't likely contribute to the audience's inability to understand what he is saying. It is common for non-native English speakers to place the accent incorrectly on a single word or multiple words within an orally produced string. Doing so skews a listener's mental organization of sound units into words. This is most likely the problem.

98. B: The teacher needs to find a text that will challenge the students to learn. One that is written with language, structure, or ideas slightly beyond the students' current level will inspire them to grow. It's important, however, that the teacher select material that is within their grasp. If the ideas or language are far beyond what the students are currently capable of, they will not respond to it. A text that employs contemporary slang will have a limited shelf life. As the idioms go out of fashion, the book will rapidly become dated.

99. E: Potential topics for public speaking abound. As the teacher gets to know her students, she will become familiar with their interests, worries, hopes, and values. These areas offer a rich source of potential topics and material. Other teachers can make suggestions based upon what they know about students or about her students in particular. They can also make suggestions based upon their own areas of expertise. While her classroom text is sure to contain some interesting topic ideas, the teacher can broaden her search to books of every kind for inspiration. Finally, the Internet offers countless topic ideas for students at every grade level.

100. C: One mistake teachers make is assigning a public speaking topic that is far too narrow in focus to allow for personal interpretation. The ubiquitous "What I Did on My Summer Vacation" is such a topic. Because the premise lacks life, the writing and presentation will too. Selecting a topic that requires interpretation and can be interpreted in a number of ways allows each student to bring her own knowledge and experiences to the topic to make it resonate. For example, asking students to create a performance about something that has been lost permits one student to write about a lost love, another about a lost pet, another about the loss of a belief, and a fourth about being lost at sea.

Online Resources

Due to our efforts to try to keep this book to a manageable length, we've created a link that will give you access to all of your online resources:

mometrix.com/resources719/osatspeechdd116

It's Your Moment, Let's Celebrate It!

Share your story @mometrixtestpreparation